Wivelsfield

The History of a Wealden Parish

Edited by

Heather Warne

Plate 1. Wivelsfield Parish: view looking south to the South Downs across Wivelsfield, taken from the 'top' of the parish in Haywards Heath.

Wivelsfield

The History of a Wealden Parish

Researched by
Wivelsfield History Study Group

&

Edited by

Heather Warne

pier point
&
WHSG

First published in 1994 by Pier Point Publishing
and the Wivelsfield History Study Group

British Library Cataloguing in Data:
A Catalogue record for this book is available from the British Library.

ISBN O 9524577 0 9

Reprinted 1995

Typeset in Times New Roman, 11pt on 12pt
Typesetting & origination by Pier Point Publishing
21 Lynton Close, Hurstpierpoint, Hassocks BN6 9AN
Printed by Pardy & Son Ltd, Ringwood, Hants

v

CONTENTS

ACKNOWLEDGEMENTS

The Wivelsfield History Study Group would like to acknowledge their grateful thanks to all who have contributed their time, skill and knowledge to help with the background research for this book.

We thank Roger Davey, the County Archivist of East Sussex, for his permission to publish extracts from original documents at East Sussex Record Office, and we thank his staff for their time and help; Mrs P Gill, the former County Archivist of West Sussex and her staff for their help.

The editor gratefully acknowledges the help of all those who have read chapters and have offered their comments: Dr Colin Brent, Dr Richard Coates, Mark Gardiner, Dr Fred Gray, Dr Tim Hudson, Timothy McCann, Dr Brian Short and Christopher Whittick.

To publish the book required money, and we are very grateful to all those who have made donations for this purpose:-

Mrs G Baldock, Rhonda Baldock, M L Bartholomew, H J Bartholomew, Mrs & Miss Bartlett, Miss I L Bartlett, Peggy Bunning, Freda Callam (In Memory), J C & H M Charman, R P Chimley, Corbett Family, W B & B E Deadman, Muriel Deighton, Ensom Family, Joan Finzel, Marc Fitch Fund, John & Ruth Gale, Carole & Bruce Haithwaite, Mrs D E Henderson, Henderson Family, E Herbert, G & H Johnson-Poensgen, S Lacy, Law Family, Lay Family, Mr & Mrs M Long, D & N Miller, Mitchell Family, Mr & Mrs Orell-Jones, Osborne Family, Mrs Ann Phillips, D G M Roberts, Mr & Mrs D F Sheffield, R A Scott, Mr M & Mrs R Singh, Sowrey Family, Stening Family, Tanner Family, Lord Teviot, Mrs Tipper (In Memory), G Theakstone, David N Thompson, University of Sussex, Van den Bergh Foods Ltd., Miss M Weatherstone, Miss J Winchester, Winn Family, Wivelsfield Parish Council, Wivelsfield Village Fund, Mrs M M Wright.

Plate 2. An historical collage: wooded hills in the north of the parish were colonised in the medieval period by the "Inthehurst" family. Brick-making descendents rebuilt their farmhouse in the 17th century. A back-cloth of woodland was replaced in the 19th century by the siting of the "Sussex County Asylum" on high ground with a southerly aspect.

"Unless a man understands the Weald, he cannot easily write about the beginnings of England, and yet historians have not understood it."

Hilaire Belloc (1909)
The Weald in "On Everything"
(Essays in *The Morning Post*)

WIVELSFIELD HISTORY STUDY GROUP 1990-1994
A Profile

SHEILA BLAIR, although born in Birmingham, has lived in this part of Sussex since 1947. She moved to Wivelsfield in 1959. After training at Brighton Art College, she married a local poultry farmer and has carried on this profession ever since. This has led to an interest in past land use and local history. For the past 16 years she has worked in her spare time with a local handicapped-riding group.

MARGARET GOODARE, a retired architect, has lived in Wivelsfield since 1970, coming to Sussex in 1953 from Carshalton in Surrey. Her interest in the local timber-framed houses started when she attended a course of lectures given by Mrs. Margaret Holt, whose help and guidance is hereby gratefully acknowledged. Among her many interests are photography, nature study and the countryside.

BARBARA HALL, retired Senior Nursing Officer (Community) moved to Wivelsfield in 1960, and has lived on Lunces Common for 34 years. Coming from an ecumenical background her commitment to the Church is long standing and the study of its history is now an ongoing interest. A life member of the Open Spaces Society and a keen supporter of several conservation societies, her latent interest in local history was brought to life by curiosity about the history of Lunces Common. She has attended, from the first, the Adult Eucation local history classes at Wivelsfield.

OLIVE MORLEY, retired in 1975 as Senior Peripatetic Teacher of the Deaf for the I.L.E.A. Having migrated from Croydon to Wivelsfield in 1969 she feels she is still a "new-comer" to the village, although a Parish Councillor of many years standing. One of her hobbies has been committee work at all levels, from national to local clubs. For ten years she was secretary of the Fund Raising Committee involved in building Wivelsfield Village Hall.

IAN NELSON, lived in Purley, Surrey for many years. Just before he retired from a career of practising and teaching dentistry, his lifelong interest in history led him to take an Open University degree, one module concentrating on local history research techniques. He is now collaborating with Dr. Brian Short of Sussex University on the history of poor relief, combined with social and economic development, in 28 parishes in mid Sussex. He has lived in Hurstpierpoint for 38 years.

EVELYN REYNOLDS, has lived in Wivelsfield since 1970. Married with two grown sons, she was forced to leave her job with an insurance company through ill health. Apart from local history her leisure pursuits are gardening, crafts and walking. Her interest in local history was fostered by attending the local Adult Education classes.

ALAN SEYMOUR, was born in and lived in Carshalton, Surrey before moving to the Worlds End area of Burgess Hill in 1984. He worked for the Royal Mail for 13 years before being medically retired due to injuries received in a road accident in 1990. Married, with three young children, he has taken up local and family-history research in his retirement and he also enjoys bike riding and walking the local footpaths.

HEATHER WARNE, grew up and lived in Croydon, Surrey, before coming to Sussex in 1965 to work as an archivist at East Sussex Record Office in Lewes. Since raising a family she has pursued her career by working as an Adult Education tutor and free-lance archivist, her main work currently being at Arundel Castle where she is Assistant Archivist. She also works with other local historians and archaeologists in researching the landscape history of Sussex. She has lived since 1967 in Worlds End, on the borders of Wivelsfield parish, and has for many years enjoyed walking its footpaths and pondering its history.

THE BOOK : CREDITS

The aims, scope and limitations of this book, which is not a definitive history of the parish, are touched on in the foreword below. Each member pursued the areas of research in which they were particularly interested or skilled. All research was freely pooled and discussed and, as a result, each chapter has benefitted from contributions by other members of the group. Subject to editorial input, the main credits are as follows:

Figures and line drawings: Margaret Goodare.

The index: Ian Nelson

The text:-

Sheila Blair researched and wrote the history of the landed estates (Chapter 3) and the 20th-century Valebridge allotments scheme in Ch. 14; She also wrote up Reg Brinkley's reminiscencess for Ch. 14.

Margaret Goodare supplied all architectural observations throughout the book; researched and wrote Chapters 4 and 5 on farmers and craftsmen, their houses and cottages; and Chs. 10 and 11 from the Tithe, Census and Tax records.

Barbara Hall researched and wrote the history of the Parish Church, viz. Chapter 2 and parts of Chs. 8 and 11. She also, jointly with Heather Warne, researched and wrote the history of commons (Chapter 6); and completed the commons history in Ch. 14.

Olive Morley masterminded the sessions with older residents and wrote Chapter 13 from the results. She worked with Margaret Goodare on the Census material for Chs. 10 and 11 and assisted with Ch. 8. She researched and wrote Chapter 12 on education and compiled the 'Postscript', Chapter 15.

Ian Nelson researched and wrote Chapter 7 on the poor. He also wrote Chapter 9 on communications, based on his own research and that of **Alan Seymour**.

Evelyn Reynolds researched and drafted the history of Wivelsfield's two non-conformist chapels for Chapter 8.

Heather Warne researched and wrote the early history of the parish (Chapter 1); and, with Barbara Hall, researched and wrote the history of the commons (Chapter 6).

ILLUSTRATIONS

FIGURES

TABLES

PHOTOGRAPHS

PRINTS AND DRAWINGS

Page

Wivelsfield

The History of a
Wealden Parish

FOREWORD

In writing the history of Wivelsfield we have, to some extent, tried to grasp the nettle of the Weald - a place where profound changes took place in centuries so distant that the story has been forgotten. Unlike the hard chalk Downs whose early history lies scarred against the skyline for all to see, the Weald is still shy and hides her secrets in woodlands and green lanes.

Wivelsfield is an East Sussex parish and its history is intrinsically bound with the history of that county. However, following Local Government reorganisation in 1974, the expanded territory of West Sussex thrust an arm into Wivelsfield. It captured a large slice of land at Haywards Heath in the north west of the parish (see fig. 6), intruding, appropriately enough, at Cleavewater where a spring rises and flows west to the West Sussex Adur. A sliver of land on the north side of Jane's Lane had earlier been taken into Burgess Hill which was itself transferred from East to West Sussex in 1974. As a result, until the next Local Government shake-up at least, the ancient parish of which we write in this book is in two counties.

No history is absolute. Not only does the tale continue to unfold while a topic is being discussed, but the research itself contains omissions. Whether by accident or by design, the historian leaves out significant pieces of the past. Our history of Wivelsfield is, accordingly, incomplete. The chapters of this book were to some extent pre-ordained: on the one hand by the particular interests of the various members of our group; and on the other hand by the availibility of documentary sources.

Old documents were always an integral part of the research behind this book. At the outset we were simply an Adult Education class, tutored by an archivist whose mission in life was to introduce the uninitiated to the delights of first-hand evidence. This meant selecting from the bottomless vaults of the East Sussex Record Office material which both related to Wivelsfield and which, with a certain amount of effort and good will by the participants, could be read in photo-copied form in class.

For the second academic year in which the class ran it was decided that to go on must mean to go forward. We would not re-tread old ground by looking again at yet more photocopies. A small but determined band wanted to write up and eventually to publish what we had already discovered. We would continue as a writing class.

"Writing the History of Wivelsfield" was not everyone's cup of tea. However, it was duly advertised and succeeded in capturing two more class members to compensate for the several we had lost. The Centre for Continuing Education at Sussex University agreed to support it and we all bent our backs to the task ahead. Each emerging chapter made new demands - old notes to check, new research to be done, old houses to go and see, people to interview and landscapes to investigate. We worked individually and together, pursuing our own lines of interest but pooling ideas and knowledge.

If the work sometimes seemed daunting we were compensated by the sheer delight of discovery - a crown post seen by torchlight, proving a medieval house; the complex verbiage of a 16th-century will, telling how many feather beds, joined chests and petticoats were left to the children; the memories of elderly residents still living, recalling the slate club and reading room. All this, and much more, has charmed us along our way. We now unfold the story as we have learnt it so far, in order to pass our pleasure on for others to enjoy.

Heather Warne

13 Gladstone Road
World's End
Burgess Hill

September, 1994

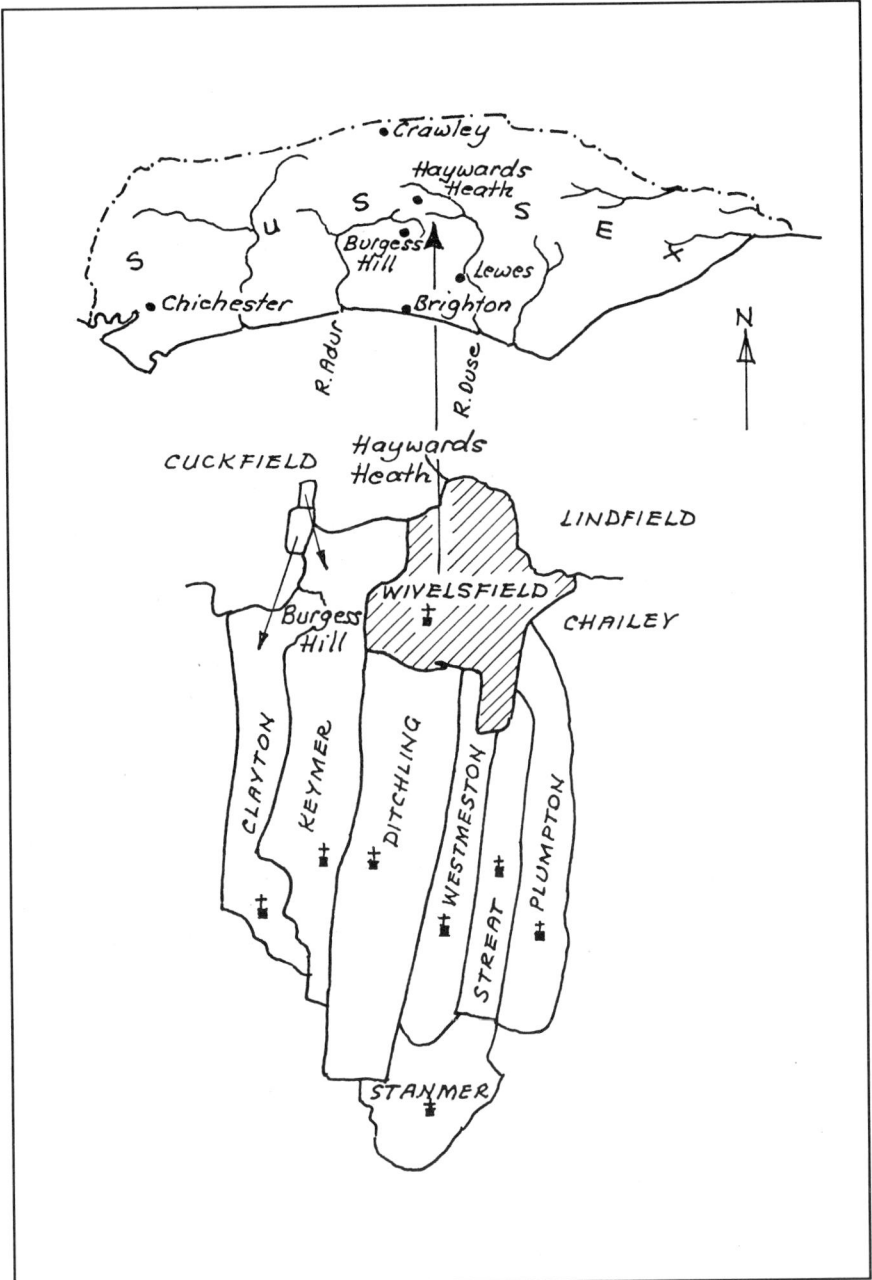

Figure 1. Wivelsfield: its location in Sussex and the adjacent Parishes.

CHAPTER 1

SHAPING THE PARISH

People first started farming in Sussex three thousand or more years before the birth of Christ. They settled on the easy soils of the South Downs and on the greensand ridges at the base of the Downs. Looking out north across the Weald they saw a great forest, stretching away to the North Downs, inhabited by wild animals, wolf and deer, boar and bear.

Today the Weald is criss-crossed with tarmac, and new housing estates consume the now-treeless fields. From Wivelsfield each morning the London commuters drive to the nearest main-line railway station; buses ply to nearby towns, children go to school and the villagers watch world events on their T.Vs.

How was this transition made, from forest to modern village? In the last 400 years there have been dramatic changes, many of which are recounted in this book. But what of the beginnings, the millenia in which man tentatively made his way into the Weald in order to farm and to settle down? How does Wivelsfield fit in with that period of history and how did that period shape the village that we see today?

i. The farmers

"This is what I prayed for; a plot of land not too large, containing a garden near the house, a fresh spring of water and a bit of forest to complete it"
Horace (1st Cent. BC)

It is likely that the first peoples who settled in the Weald of Sussex had used the high east/west ridges as access routes, or had approached along rivers and streams from the coastal areas. Temporary shelters may have been used in certain seasons of the year by early hunters or by pastoral farmers herding their animals. Natural clearings, caused by storms, fire and the browsing of wild animals, would be used as a seasonal base and might be gradually enlarged and improved. Some protection from wild animals would be necessary for those who were staying in the Weald during a summer or an autumn season, perhaps a banked and ditched enclosure. At some point a decision would have been taken to over-winter in the Weald, possibly as a result of experimenting in growing hay or corn within the enclosure; or there may have been population pressure back home. Pottery dating from the Late Bronze Age has recently been found just east of Wivelsfield.[1]

Wivelsfield is at the watershed between tributaries of the river Adur, draining westwards, and the Ouse, draining east. The two systems part at the farm called, appropriately, Cleavewater. Together they form a long east/west valley running across the parish. To their south lies a significant ridge referred to in the 8th century as 'the long ridge', a name which has survived at Longridge Farm at the eastern end of Wivelsfield Green, the farm itself now in Chailey parish (fig. 2 and 'Stanmer in Wivelsfield', below). Like the valley to its north, the ridge runs the full width of the parish, though it is disected west of the church by the main western tributary of the river Adur. It is still possible to walk the length of the ridge through the parish on what must be very ancient rights of way. (Route C, 1-4 on fig. 5) Because of its gentle contours on the south side of the ridge its presence is hardly perceptible as one walks along Green Road; but Slugwash Lane a little way to the north, having reached its summit, plunges north between steep-sided banks towards the river meadows.

Strung along the top of the ridge we find a series of dwellings: Manns, Strood farm and Shoulders, a hamlet once ranged around their own green or 'strood'; Wivelsfield Hall, on land formerly belonging to 'the Berth', and Townings at the crown of Slugwash Lane; More House further west, a moated settlement; Lunces just west of the parish church and, finally, having walked down to the River Adur from Lunces and up the other side, Antye and Theobalds, situated at the highest point of the landscape.

South of the ridge and south of what is now the built-up area of the Green is another east/west ridge occupying land now Coldharbour Farm, West Wood and St. George's Retreat. This ridge, being heavy clay, had a long history as timber woodland and furzey commons. The north part of Ditchling Common and the farm land of Little Ote Hall continue these soils west into Ditchling and Burgess Hill. Though Wivelsfield received a share in these clay lands when its boundaries were determined, nobody lived there until late medieval or early Tudor times. Interestingly, however, Roman pottery has recently been found just outside the parish on Little Ote Hall's land [2] and a Roman coin was found west of the Playing Field, south of Green Road.[3]

Let us now look at the medieval landscape of the inhabited parts of Wivelsfield. By using rentals of the various manors in the parish, together with certain early deeds, we can detect a pattern.[4] First of all we find that the dwelling sites of the two most extensive early estates in Wivelsfield, Lunces and Stanmer, were on the long ridge. Each of these estates had meadowland in the river valleys to the north. They each had unimproved land on the clays to the south, and further woodland north of their settlements. The Berth, Townings and More House all followed the same pattern.

How old are these settlements on the ridge? We can deduce from the Stanmer charter that some settlement had already established itself there by the mid-8th century. (See ii. below) The charter also tells us, incidentally, in the name 'Wifelesfelda' that Wifel had already given his name to the area. It is likely that *-feld*, meaning 'open area', indicates arable land and the existence of a farming community.[5] Some place names suggest that people had settled there before the Saxon period. *The berth* perhaps derives from an old English word *burh* meaning a defended place. Was it so named simply because the Plumpton people away to the south, who owned it, had put up a surrounding fence? Or had they noticed the dykes and ditches there of earlier settlers?[6]

An Iron-Age trackway of some importance runs past *the Berth*. (Route A, 1-4 on fig. 5) While it is likely that many minor routes in the Weald have their origins in the Celtic period or earlier, only a handful have been identified as long distance routes. Most are east-west ridgeway tracks but one has been singled out as a cross-wealden way, leading from the North Downs near Titsey, a Roman villa site, to the Iron-Age camp called Dry Hill. This lies in Surrey, at the confluence of the Surrey, Sussex and Kent boundaries. The track then plies south across Ashdown Forest and eventually into Wivelsfield via Scaynes Hill. It turns into Slugwash Lane at Moores cottage, skirting the land of *the Berth*. Climbing between steep banks it passes the old homestead site of *the Berth* at the crest of the hill and runs down through Wivelsfield Green as Eastern Road (route A5 on fig. 5). Ditchling was the final destination of the trackway. [7]

Near this track, in the meadowlands of Slugwash Lane, the word *pyll*, describing the confluence of streams, was used in the 8th-century charter. This originates as a Celtic, or British, word rather than English and its use here may imply an overlap between old British and new English people in this area.[8] As modern research proceeds more of these 'loan' words are being discovered in Sussex.[9] It begins to look as though, in the Weald as well as elsewhere in England, there was an intermingling of old and new peoples rather than the wholesale flight or extermination of native Celts.

Plate 3. Lunces Hall, viewed from Antye across the Adur valley. The river flows in a narrow valley among the foreground trees.

West of the church and of the river Adur we find Theobalds and Antye perched up on their hill. Theobalds became the more important house from the early 1600s onwards but Antye is the more-important place name because it describes perfectly the early topography here - 'at the high enclosure'. In true Wivelsfield pattern the dwellings on the hill were matched by meadows in the valley to their north. In between the two house sites there is a large pasture field, shown on a map of 1659 as 'The Great Ham' - the great enclosure.[10] If you stand at its eastern edge and look out across the valley to the church you find you are on a double-ditched, triple-banked defence: in my view an outstanding candidate as the original 'high enclosure'.

The remaining early estates in Wivelsfield were situated just off the long ridge. Otehall, south of Lunces of which it originally formed a part, nestled within a meander of the Adur on a sand-with-clay outcrop. The flinty clays on its southern perimeter were bordered by deeper clays and thick woodland. Cleavewater to the north of the long ridge utilised entirely the river valley but also enjoyed some woodlands to the north. Fanners, an important freehold of Ditchling manor had a house just south of the ridge but had land that straddled northwards up and over the ridge and on to the meadows in the valley and the wooded hills beyond.

This pattern of medieval and Tudor land holding in Wivelsfield is therefore the key to our understanding the pattern of settlement in the parish. It singles out the long ridge as the area selected for their homesteads by the early settlers. It was both accessible from east and west. Having established their base on the ridge, the early farmers staked their claim to a share of the woods and water meadows around them. As, in the course of time, kings and overlords came and went, land was allocated to this or that lord or manor, a tale told in the next section of this chapter. But the earliest patterns of settlement still left their indelible mark on the landscape and have not been entirely overwritten.

ii. Stanmer in Wivelsfield

One of the biggest estates in Wivelsfield that belonged to a community outside the area was that of Stanmer. The estate had been given away in the mid-8th century by King Aldwulf, presumably out of the Ditchling matrix (see iii below). His Earl, Hunlabe, had asked for land in which to build a monastery, or minster, and in consequence he was granted 16 hides "...in the place which is called Stanmere [and] in Lindefeldia and Burhlea." [11] As with so many early estates, we can work out where its land lay by looking at the manorial records of more recent years. This particular estate was split after the Dissolution of the Monasteries and one part descended as the manor of Stanmer, comprising most of the parish of Stanmer near Brighton.[12] All the wealden parts descended under the name of the manor of "South Malling Lindfield" [13] It is likely that the 8th-century 'minster' itself, if built, was a simple affair, possibly an earlier building on the site of Lindfield church, later to be superseded by the College of South Malling near Lewes.[14]

Fig. 2 shows where the Stanmer estate lay in Wivelsfield. The shaded area represents the estate as shown in a survey of 1830. [15] The details shown in 1830 accord very well with those found in the earlier court records of the manor of South Malling Lindfield dating back to the 1500s and earlier. Agricultural and population development had undoubtedly taken place within the estate and part of the western boundary has been blurred by additions to the Fanners estate. It is unlikely, none the less, that its overall extent had changed in 1500, or in 1830, from its 8th-century origins. I have therefore used the map of 1830 as a guide to interpreting the Wivelsfield information in the 8th-century charter.

The 8th century charter gives some names and details of the land involved. After describing the bounds of what later became Stanmer parish[16] and before going on to mention briefly by name various settlements further north, the text runs as follows:

1   *Hec sunt territoria silvarum to wifelesfelda:*
2   *Aerest on haempeles pyll and on frigedaegs east*

3   *swa to langan beccen be tweox twegen wifelesfeldes*
4   *west thannan to hennesfeldes burnen.*
5   *This is east maerc to stanmere: inn sinbl swa to*
6   *humahamme east weard to 'semmaenne'* [error for
7   gemaennes] *and langahricge maebe belandes into stanmere*
8   *thonne to fischyrstes eastward; swa north to*
9   *heanfelde to wulfpytte.*
10   *Hec sunt nomina pastus porcorum qui pertinent ad*
11   *Stanmere: fischyrste, aescincuinc, healdeswyrth,*
12   *walcanstede, lendenfelda ....*

Some of the words in the text are slightly corrupt and would not make perfect sense in an Anglo-Saxon grammar. This is because the only surviving copies of the charter date from several hundreds of years after it was written, and the copyists have made a few mistakes.[17] However, taking the Wivelsfield topography into account, an interpretation might run as follows:

> "These are the areas of woodland [that belong] to Wifelesfelda: first to Haempeles shallow pool and to Friday's [? land] and so east to the long ? valley between the two Wifelesfeldes; then west to Hennesfelde's stream.
>
> This is the east boundary of Stanmer's land: continue all along to the east of the meadows to the common and to the long ridge ?by the lands allocated to Stanmer; then to the east of the fish wood and north towards the high field and to the wolf pit.
>
> These are the names of the swine pastures that belong to Stanmer: fish wood, ash-tree nook, Heald's curtilage, Wealeca's place, the open land with lime-trees..."

The next challenge is to try to correlate the details of the 8th century charter with the modern landscape.[18] The 1810 map and the manorial records show us that the Stanmer estate in Wivelsfield was composed of several distinct areas until comparatively recent times. Between A, B, J and K (fig. 2) there were meadows and woodland, both of which appear to have been once held in common by the residents of this 'hamlet'. Their existence as late as 1879 is shown by the names "Ham Wood", Wilderness Wood", and "Common Brook Wood" on the first Ordnance Survey map.[19] The farmsteads and the arable land of the hamlet lay on top of and just south of the long ridge , between B, C, H, and J. South of this again lay 'the green', between C, D, G and H, a narrowish strip with the road running east/west through its centre. Green Park Farm, Coldharbour and Hundred Acre Farm occupy the rest of the Stanmer Estate, between D, E, F and G. This area had been a mixture of open heathland and rough woodland, but it was enclosed and turned into fields in 1626 (Chapter 6).

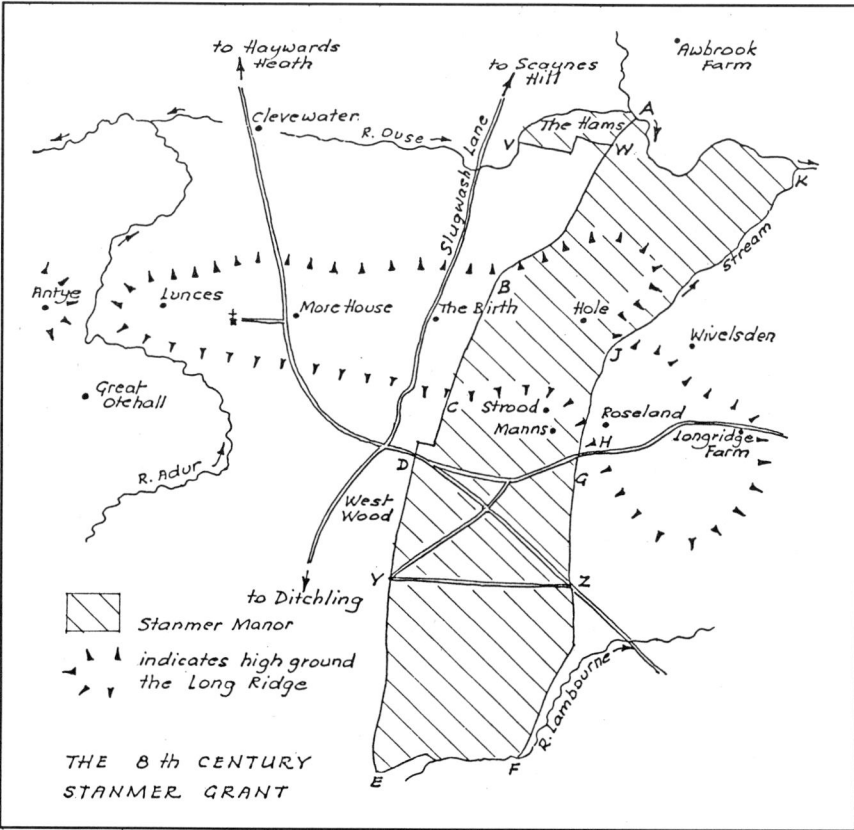

Figure 2. Stanmer in Wivelsfield: later part of the Manor of South Malling, Lindfield

The charter does three things in relation to Wivelsfield: first it describes the woodlands that the hamlet enjoyed as its own (lines 1 - 4). Their bounds began at the *pyll* or 'shallow pool'; they ran along *Frigedaeges* - possibly a personal name and meaning Friday's land; they then turned east (see plate 6) until a boundary 'between the two Wivelsfields' was reached. They went along it [north] and then turned west to rejoin the starting point at the place where a stream from 'Hennesfeld' came in. The area thus delimited contained the woods that the hamlet used as its own in the 8th century. These limits adequately encompass the 'tenantry' woodlands that the same hamlet used in 1830, the area between A,B, J and K. Today the 'shallow pool' is a rushy area at the junction of streams. The eastward section (B to J) is marked by a track (plate 6), the northward by a narrow-sided depression in the landscape with a tiny rivulet at the bottom (parish boundary). It makes sense topographically if 'hennesfeld' denotes the same place or area as 'heanfelde' (line 9), or Scaynes Hill as it is now called.[20]

The charter then specifies some details of one side of the estate (lines 5-9). Here, I believe, a copyist's error has been made. It would make more sense if it were the west side rather than the east that is being set out. The east side, or at least the north-east bounds have already been delimited and they consisted of streams. By contrast the north west side of the estate was an area of meadows owned or used by various persons - Wifel, Haempel and Friday are three who have already been mentioned. The grantor was presumably the lord of Ditchling and owned the land immediately west of this new estate. It would therefore be important to make clear at the outset precisely what was to be included in the new grant.

To go back to the same starting place, A on fig. 2, the first item on the bounds was the *humahamme*: *-hamme* means enclosures or, as the topgraphy suggests here, meadows. Meadows were indeed endemic here - it was a key meadowland area of Wivelsfield and several different manors from within and outside the parish had a stake in them (Chapter 6). *Huma-* suggests no obvious meaning and may be a personal name. Fig. 2 shows the circuit of the bounds between A, V and W and it may be that the charter takes us around them before coming to the 'common'. The charter itself has already told us that this northern section of the Stanmer land at Wivelsfield was the "territoria silvarum" for use by the local people in Saxon times. This was their common, not the lands south of Green Road as in later centuries. From W the boundary uses the Iron-Age track until it reaches the next landscape feature of note, the long ridge. Here it leaves the track and climbs the ridge to point B. The phrase 'belandes maebe into stanmere' is not readily translatable but must have meant something important when written, because words, and expensive parchment, were not wasted. Could it perhaps have meant 'along the side of the lands marked as Stanmer's'. The medieval records of this manor, though sparse, shows that the top of the ridge and the dip slope to the south contained the arable lands of the hamlet, also once held in common.[21] The charter may also be telling us, incidentally, as other clauses have already implied, that this territory already existed and its bounds were already on the ground. They were spelt out in the charter because of a change in lordship.

After the long ridge the details are sparse, simply 'then to fish wood'. This, I believe, takes us right down to point E, after which, in the briefest fashion, we are hurried back up to point K and to Scaynes Hill and Lindfield beyond. There is a clear logic to the lack of detail south of the long ridge. The land was uninhabited clay woodland. Prior to the time of the charter it was perhaps freely intercommoned over a wide area by the various communities who lived to the south. Banks and ditches may have existed to separate one community's portion from the next but if so, the charter chose to ignore them. Instead it simply gave the names by which these areas , or 'swine pastures' were called (lines

10 and 11 of text). The names are given in a clear south to north order, the fish hurst, the ash tree nook, Heald's enclosure and on to Walsted, Lindfield and further north in the Weald. Land deals such as this were marking the end of intercommoning and the beginning of allocated waste land, one manor's portion being marked out from that of the next.[22]

Plate 4. The long ridge. The long ridge (skyline) is flanked by former common meadows, the Moor and the Breach (foreground and middleground), with Slugwash Lane winding between.

Walsted and Lindfield were over the Scaynes Hill ridge and down into the next valley. Heald's enclosure was probably the 100 acres that has developed into Awbrook Farm. It lay due north of A and K on fig. 2, continuing the Stanmer estate as a solid block right up to Scaynes Hill. This would leave fish wood and ash tree nook as candidates for the area between D, E, F and G. Fish wood had already been mentioned in the earlier bounds and logically it was the southern part of the estate, bounded by a stream which would perhaps have provided fishing. When the common was finally enclosed in 1626 the southern portion of this block became the Hundred Acre Farm and it was the lord of the manor's allocation of the former common. Remembering that fishing rights usually remained with lords of manors, perhaps his predecessors' association with this area was age old and indicated in the name. This leaves ash tree nook also to be fitted in, perhaps somewhere between D, Y, Z and G where the criss-crossing of paths and tracks might have created an odd corner of land.

The roads and tracks shown in this area on fig. 2 are those which, logically, would have existed just before enclosure in 1626. (Chapter 6, 'The Bishoprick'.) Some roads must have evolved by the 8th century, for access to the swine pastures at least, but we cannot be certain as to which they were. On fig. 5 route K, 1-5 shows the main access in to the estate, coming from Stanmer to the south, reaching the Green at K2. Between K3 and K4 there have been too many changes for the old routes to survive and the modern access to the 'hamlet' is a little further east. K4 to K5 again takes up the old tenants' way into the *territoria silvarum*, a route which is still visible on the ground but is not public and is impassable.

Whoever Wifel was, he had clearly arrived by the mid 8th century. Moreover he appears to have given his name to the area at large, so that even the Stanmer woodlands at the beginning of this extract were known as "at Wivelsfield". The *langan beccen* was said in the charter to lie "between the two Wifelsfeldes". Wivelsfield today means the cluster of houses in Church Lane to one person and "the Green", along Green Road, to another. Though the Saxon charter does not record exactly this modern duality, it does nevertheless record an aspect of it. The Stanmer land formed a solid block which left an outlier of the Manor of Lunces isolated on the east side of this valley boundary. Later known as 'Roseland' because it was held by a rose rent, this land is now in Plumpton parish. [23] A neighbouring farm, Wivelsden, now in Chailey parish, echoes, in its name, the former existence of Wifel's outlying woodland in this vicinity. Lunces was, without doubt, the largest early estate in the area, though it later declined in importance (Chapter 3). It is possible, therefore, that the Saxon charter, in giving us the name of Wivelsfield's chief landowner, has also told us that it was Lunces that was, or had been, Wifel's seat and homeland.

iii. A hotch-potch of manors

In rural areas today the unit of local administration with which we are most familiar is the parish. Indeed, the very word parish brings to mind a feeling of community and place, character and identity. Wivelsfield exists as such a place today, but this was not always so.

Stanmer may not have been the first estate to have been given land in Wivelsfield but it was the earliest grant for which any details survive. It was a typical Wivelsfield estate in that its grantor lived outside the area. From the evidence of Domesday Book, from surviving deeds, tax records and manorial documents we find that in the early medieval period all of Wivelsfield belonged to somebody else: a host of places outside Wivelsfield were laying claim to bits of its land. From where had they received their rights to Wivelsfield's soil?

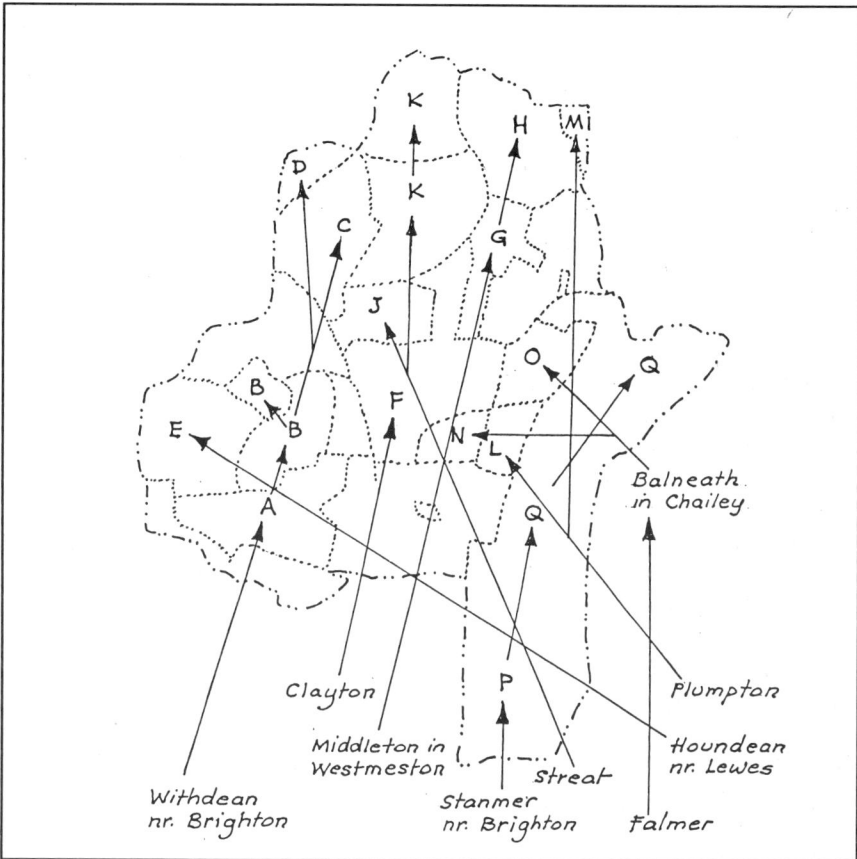

Figure 3. Estates in Wivelsfield belonging to outside Manors,

Figure 3: Explanation

Settlement	Manor	Settlement	Manor
A Otehall	Withdean Cayliffye	L The Berth, Gibbs and Strisshes	Plumpton
B Lunces, inc. Tile Barn and Griggs	" "	M Merryfields	"
C Hurst House or Asylum Farm	" "	N Townings inc. Southwish	Balneath
D Part of Hay--wards Heath	" "	O Moores Cottage	"
E Antye and Theobalds	Houndean	P Stanmer Common (later Park farm, Coldharbour and Green Park farms)	Stanmer (later South Malling Lindfield)
F More House	Clayton		
G Sth. Colwell	Middleton		
H Nth. Colwel	"	Q Manns, Strood, Shoulders, Botches farms, etc.	"
J Cleavewater	Streat		
K Franklands (both parts)	"		

The earliest areas of Saxon administration of which we know were fairly large regions based on a king's town as its administrative centre. All the villages, hamlets and farmsteads in that region (from Latin *regio* meaning 'area under a king's jurisdiction') held their land directly from the king. In the later Saxon period these large areas were broken down into smaller estates each owned by a lord who himself owed allegiance to the King - and so the manorial system began to evolve. The former *regio* usually descended as a manor which held land over a very wide area and which is recorded as having held by one or more of the Saxon kings.

Ditchling was the important Royal manor of the mid-Sussex region in Saxon times whose land stretched from the South Downs to the Surrey border and from the Adur estuary to that of the Ouse. Wivelsfield itself remained part of Ditchling parish until after the Reformation. It is therefore logical to suppose that it was Ditchling who owned Wivelsfield's land in the first place, before giving it away to the lesser owners. This bold assumption is not so much based on Saxon as on medieval and later evidence; for, by using the extant manorial records in order to discover the location of the estates in Wivelsfield, we find that Ditchling is the matrix out of which the other estates have been carved.

The kitchen might illustrate the point if we imagine a piece of rolled-out pastry about to be made into mince pies. Ditchling is the housewife, applying her circular cutter. Successive lords thus allowed dollops of their land in Wivelsfield to be signed away to a lesser lord. The odd shapes and triangles of land that were left in between, and at the sides, together with certain pieces of land that were too important to give away, remained as part of the original piece, that is, as part of Ditchling manor (fig. 4).

Ditchling was replaced by Lewes in the late-Saxon period as the principal town of the region. It is likely, therefore, that many of the new estates in Ditchling's vicinity were created in that period of change. Though a charming village, it has been a rural backwater ever since, never more than a market town and with no role in county or distrct administration. It is only by studying the origins of estates that these lost 'capitals' can be rediscovered.   Unravelling the network of intermingled lordships in Wivelsfield has therefore helped to throw light on Ditchling's former importance.[24]

In general in mid Sussex, the villages below the Downs - Clayton, Westmeston and Streat for example - received a continuous south to north strip of territory as their 'manor'. This allowed them each a slice of all the local soils, which run east to west in bands. In addition, and this is where Wivelsfield comes in, they were given outlying territories further north in the Weald. Some villages situated further into the

Downs, such as Stanmer and Falmer were also given a wealden block of land, presumably to provide them with a balanced agricultural resource. (See fig. 1)

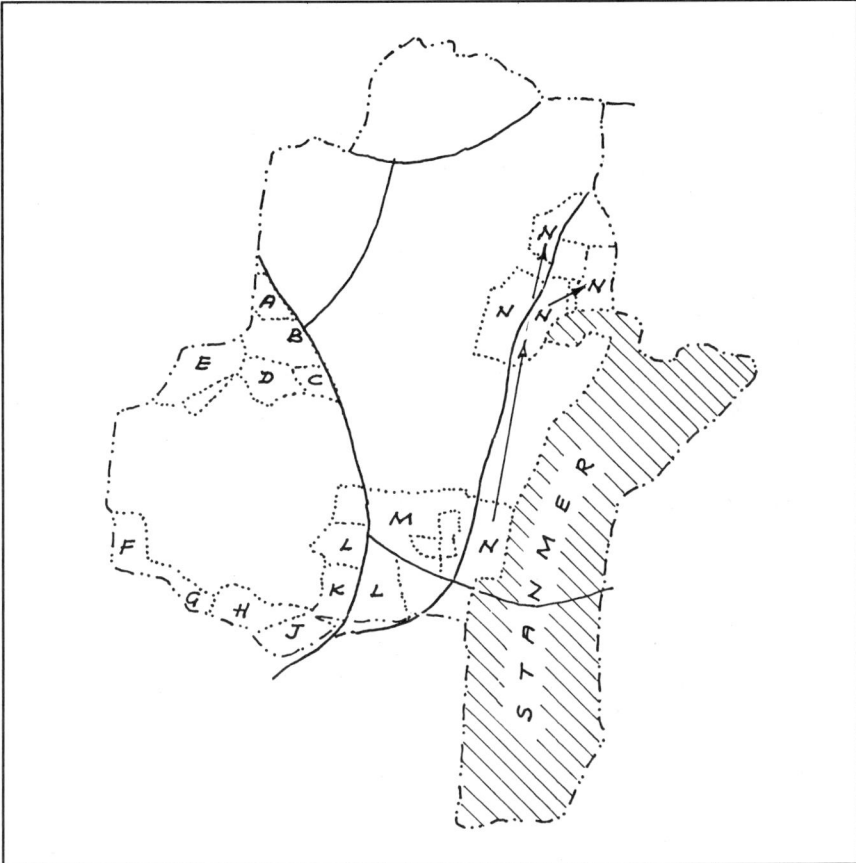

Figure 4. Settlements in Wivelsfield of Ditchling Manor.

Explanation

A Scrases Farm, Fox Hill (? Webbs Inholmes)	J Inholmes, later Bankside Farm
B Cottages at Jefferys Green	K Godman's Inholmes
C Lunces Common	L Lockstrood; Smiths' later Blackmores
D Rogers farm	
E Clearwaters farm	M Peppers
F Dartfords	N Fanners: with outlying land further north in Slugwash Lane,- Furners, Home Farm, Slugwash etc.
G Cross Inholmes	
H Folders and ? Otehall Inholmes (Little Otehall)	

The outlying wealden land was often due north from the home village. In Wivelsfield this holds good for the outliers not only of Ditchling itself, but also of Stanmer, Middleton, Streat and Plumpton (fig. 3). The system was probably based on the ancient custom of droving animals up into the Weald for extra food - spring shoots, grasses, leaves and autumn nuts. This system of using up-wealden land is much older than the manors themselves. Because the system had a sound economic purpose, maximising the overall land resource, the outlying territories were generally included with the home base when a new lordship was created. The result was the elongated north/south 'manors' so common in the Weald of Sussex. In return for their land the new lords gave allegiance and service to their king or overlord.

The manors of Withdean (Lunces and Otehall) and Houndean (Theobalds and Antye) do not follow a south/north pattern. Their land is a hotch-potch of bits and pieces flung around the Downs, the Ouse valley and the Weald.[25] Their origin as composite estates may have been a century or two later than the south/north manors, perhaps based on the need for loyalty of service just before the Norman Conquest. This is not to say, however, that the land concerned was virgin unoccupied territory. It was almost certainly the reverse, for all those particular estates occupied very favourable locations within the parish. More House which was held of the Manor of Clayton by military service and by payment of five broad arrows was perhaps attached to that manor for similar reasons.

All manors had two types of land, the demesne and the tenants' land. The demesne was the land that the lord kept in hand, lived upon, visited from time to time or leased out for profit. From his demesne he drew various other benefits such as the profits from timber, mineral and fishing rights and the pleasures of the chase. The agricultural farmland of Ditchling's demesne lay near Ditchling village and is now Court Farm. Other parts of Ditchling's demesne plunged northwards into the Weald, and were chases, or hunting grounds, called Frekebergh and Shortfrith. Wivelsfield now contains part of the latter. The chase started at what is now the Ditchling Industrial Estate on the common and ran up through all the grounds of St. George's Retreat and into Wivelsfield to 'Kydds Gate' (vicinity of Stream Cottage, Green Road), where it ended.[26] Further north the river between Clearwaters Farm and Lunces Common in Wivelsfield was all part of the fishery of 'Stottesforde and Wivelsfield'. This comprised all the river westwards from Lunces as far as Fairplace Hill on the north of Burgess Hill. Although first recorded in the 13th century as belonging to the Barony of Lewes, the fishery lay within Ditchling's demesne.[27]

These important parts of its demesne were not given away by Ditchling in the Saxon period but remained with the manor until the modern period (fig. 4). They, along with a considerable amount of land near the river, were generally not granted out of the demesne until the medieval period, However, there were two tenanted farms that were certainly older. The first was Fanners. This sits at the northern end of the demesne hunting ground and its tenant held the land by military service. We do not know, for most early documents of the manor are now lost to us, but it is likely that the tenancy depended upon the performance of some duties pertaining to the hunt (Chapter 3: Fanners)

The fishery may have had its origins in the Roman period. It lies along the stretch of the river Adur that is crossed by the Roman road from Hassocks to London. It is a stream remarkable in recent years for the amount of fresh water mussels, a possible indicator of Roman use.[28] Beside the stream of the fishery was a holding so clearly attached to Ditchling that the manor of Keymer's boundaries circumvent it in a pronounced manner. This was the farm now called Clearwaters, formerly ' Clevewater'. Along with seven other Ditchling tenants, all of whom lived in Ditchling, the tenant of Clearwaters had to perform the duty of reeve of the manor when his turn came round. This involved submitting the annual accounts of the whole manor for audit. It was both a privilege and a burden, and no mean task for its farmer who, without the benefit of reading skills, would have had to rely upon tally sticks, trust, the fear of God and a good memory. It indicates that Clearwaters was an integral part of the economy of Ditchling Manor. Though it was never more than a humble copyhold farm its origins were pre-Norman and may even once have been linked with the day-to-day running of the demesne fishery.

To sum up, therefore, Wivelsfield became a hotch-potch of other people's estates. Whether they belonged to the original parent, Ditchling, or to lesser lords, the farmers of Wivelsfield owed allegiance and paid taxes outside their immediate neighbourhood. Though Wivelsfield is not mentioned by name in Domesday Book in 1086, most of the manors which had land there (figs. 3 and 4) were mentioned by name. In 1086 Withdean would still have been reckoned under Patcham (or possibly Ditchling), Balneath under Falmer and Houndean probably under Ditchling. The statistics given for all these manors would, in part, have been made up by contributions from Wivelsfield's soil and Wivelsfield's people. Gifts of tithes to Lewes Priory in the early 12th century (Chapter 2) suggest that arable farming was well established in Wivelsfield by that date. However, it has been wrongly assumed that one holding in Wivelsfield *was* named in 1086. This was 'the Berth', which was taken to be the Domesday manor of 'Berts'. It is a clear error, for the Berth was merely a peasant holding in Plumpton manor. The mistake was noted as long ago as 1934 by Gordon Ward.[29]

to Ardingly

to Cuckfield

to Lindfield

Haywards
Heath

H4

D1
to
Scaynes Hill

D2

L3

B1

H3

J4

to
Scaynes Hill
A1

G5

to Valebridge

F4

F6

F3

F5

to
Valebridge
Common

H2

J3

G4

F2

L2

K5

F1

H1

A2

C2 G3 C3

C4 A3

K4

C5 — to
N. Chailey

to
St. Johns
Common

C1

G2

B2

K3

E4 — to
S. Chailey

to E1

G1

J2

L1

The Green

E3

B4

K2

E2

A5

B3

Ditchling
Common

J1

B5

A4

to Ditchling

to
Westmeston

to Lewes

K1

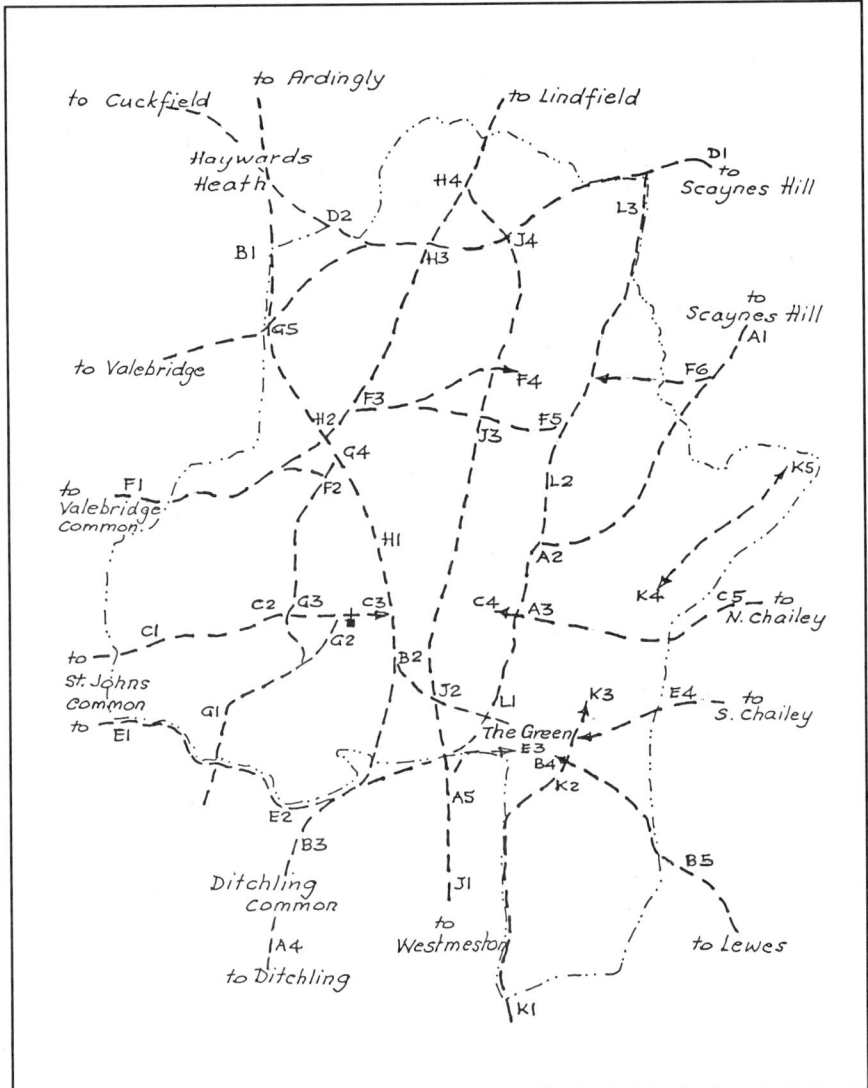

Figure 5. Roads, tracks & droves

ROADS, TRACKS AND DROVES

Explanation

Iron-Age, or earlier*

Route A: a track NE to SW from Awbrook farm in Lindfield towards Ditchling, entering Slugwash Lane at Moores Cot. (A2); past 'The Berth', along Eastern Road and out of the parish at either A4 or A5.

Route C: an EW ridge way passing all the settlements of the 'long ridge'; ? diverted between C2 and C3; forming a cross roads with route A at the Berth; now mainly a footpath.

Route D: an EW ridgeway, now the main A 272 between D1 and D2; a branch continuing to Valebridge Common by Rocky Lane, a deeply sunken road, is probably as old

Drove-roads

Route B: B3 to B1 via B2 (Otehall Chapel area) was Ditchling's main drove road north, now a main road, to Ardingly, Turners Hill and Crawley Down.

Route C: Wifel's drove road from Lunces (C2) to Wivelsden (C5); Antye's drove to outpastures at N. Chailey. Saxon use as a drove, probably lapsing in early medieval period.

Route F: F1 to F2: drove from Clearwaters to Lunces common.

Route G: superseded C above in medieval period, giving access between Otehall (G1), the church (G2), Lunces (G3) and outpastures N.(G4, G5), and to Ditchling S.

Route H: Clevewater/Franklyns (H1) route via Jefferyes Green (H2) to their outpastures at Franklyns (H3) and Franklands wood (H4, now Franklands village).

Route J: Middleton manor's drove from Westmeston to South Colwell (J1--3) and on to North Colwell (J4). Now a path at W. edge of the playing field but lost (hedgeline only) between J2 and J3.

Route K: Stanmer's drove via Hundred Acre Lane to the Green (K1-2). Medieval and later developments have interfered with the ongoing route but the hamlet's access to commons picks up again from K4-5 (no right of way; track visible but overgrown).

Route L: Slugwash lane: access for several manors converging from different areas from the South at L1; onwards to the meadows at L2; onwards for Plumpton and Streat to hill pastures at L3 and so on further north into the Weald.

Medieval routes

Route B: the 'King's Highway' from Cuckfield to Lewes, diverging from the Ditchling drove at Otehall chapel (Green Road); NW to SE course diverted at B4 after 17th cent. (round new enclosures at the Green) but Lewes road later takes up old alignment (B5).

Route E: St. John's Common to Wivelsfield Green and on to Chailey Common; now Janes Lane E1-2, tracks on Ditchling common and at Lockstrood E2-3, and Green road etc. to E4.

Route F: drove F1-2 above connects on eastwards to Colwell Lane, itself perhaps an earlier track (F3-4) and by footpath F3-F5; line lost near Abbots Leigh but continues E. out of parish towards Scaynes Hill.

The ages of all tracks is unproven but based on field work, manorial evidence, estate maps and deeds and Ordnance Surveys.

In common with other Wealden parishes whose origins had been similar, as for instance, Cuckfield or Lindfield, the early-medieval period saw significant developments. The bonding of a society around its church and the natural interdependence of neighbours were forces that served to weaken and diminish the old ties to a distant manor. The Wealden community in the far north of Ditchling established itself under its own name, Wivelsfield.

iv. The community evolves: Wivelsfield 1100-1500

Wivelsfield had its own church from the Anglo-Norman period onwards and this must have been an important focal point for the developing community. Though officially a chapel, or daughter to Ditchling church, it would have drawn the local population to its doors each week and provided their regular meeting place. Its place in their hearts is shown by the care they lavished upon its fabric, a story told in the next chapter. Though the Canons of South Malling, at some time in the medieval period, endowed a chapel at Scaynes Hill for their tenants in the locality it is by no means clear how much it was used by the people from the 'Stanmer' hamlet (see also St. Peter's Chapel, chapter 2). Indeed, the clerk to that manor was careful to refer to the 'parish' of Wivelsfield in the year 1379.[30]

The larger landowners were busily expanding their land base in the medieval period as we shall see in Chapter 3. Often this brought opportunities for new families to come in and take the tenancy of newly-won land. Lunces, for example, had a tenant called John In-the-hurst in c. 1296, indicating that the wooded hill lands at the north of the parish were starting to give way to agriculture. The family were still in the parish in 1397.[31] Indeed 'Hurst House farm' (plate 2) still had a Hurst family living there in the 17th century.

Ditchling Manor itself shed more of its demesne land in the medieval period, giving rise to Little Otehall, Dartfords Barn, Rogers and Scrases farms (see Chapters 3, 4). 'Smythes land', so called in 1462, was perhaps the home of Simon Smyth who witnessed a deed at Wivelsfield in 1404. This, and other nearby land sold out of Ditchling's demesne woods in 1462 brought new population to the area between Baldocks Garage and Eastern Road.[32] In the Stanmer hamlet people began dividing up their large holdings, 50 acres and more, into smaller ones, no doubt to accommodate a natural population growth. Houses on the Green, such as Jenners and Verandah cottage, can be dated to around the year 1600. But they have their origins as new house plots in this period of medieval expansion.[33]

Plate 5. The Green, 1994. Site of the 'fairplace', this area was expanded into in the medieval period. Botches, the house on the right, was the dwelling site of 'a tenement called Boccys' in 1493. (Ref B.L. Add. ms. 33182).

Wivelsfield's great asset, its meadowland, began to be sold off in the medieval period. Some was Ditchling's demesne, other parts were in copyhold tenure. Much of the latter remained unenclosed and, to some extent, managed communally, until the 17th century (Chapter 6). Sales of freehold meadowland however gave rise to several new farms. Lands, for example, later called Griggs and Breakspear's, south of Fox Hill, can be associated with 14th-century freeholders Richard Grygg and Richard Brekespere.[34] 'Strisshes' in Slugwash Lane probably belonged to poll-tax payer William Trisse in 1397. [35] Meadow was valuable and there was money to be made from it. Thomas Pyper (Pepper), living perhaps at what became Pepper Hall, sold a six-acre piece in 1322, carefully noting *"...as it is set out with metes and bounds"*.[36]

There must have been much work for local craftsmen as the community expanded. Chapters 3-5 will look at a wealth of medieval and Tudor house-building, which would have employed sawyers, carpenters, plasterers, blacksmiths and a host of others. The local tanning trade, reasonably documented from the 16th century (Chapter 5) may have established itself earlier in the parish. The Pilbeam family who lived for centuries in the area of Strood farm were represented from 1460-1495 by Thomas Peltebem/ Pyltebeme. This is surely a surname associated with the tanning trade, perhaps the person who supplied the wood for, or made the fleshing beam or the stretching frame for the pelts or skins. The pelt 'beam' played a central role in the tannery and often had its own 'beam house'.[37]

Manorial ties began to break down. The old drove-den roads flourished where they linked people within the parish to places they wanted to go, such as routes G and H in fig. 5. Others faded away, such as route J, serving Middleton Manor. As the ties of South and North Colwell with their parent manor weakened so the people living there lost the need for their own route out. Only a long straight hedgeline exists today to indicate the path of the old drove.

Medieval Wivelsfield was clearly a place of opportunity for the upwardly-mobile rural peasant. Even those whose tied tenure in the manor of Stanmer might have induced a subservient attitude were clearly not so inclined. The ecclesiastical lords of Stanmer/South Malling called in vain throughout the 14th century for their wealden tenants to come to Stanmer to perform the duties of their tenure.[38] In 1393 for instance, Richard Holmere (of Hole farm, now a deserted site north of Strood farm) acknowledged that he was liable to go to Stanmer with one extra hand, and that they should do three days reaping there, the lord of the manor providing their food.

Plate 6. Old road to Hole Farm. Hole Farm, a medieval or earlier dwelling site, was served by this track, itself now disused. The track grew up along a boundary route used in the Anglo-Saxon Charter (between 'B' and 'Hole' on figure 2).

The tenants of Strood and Manns farms (plates 14, 27) and of Shoulders and Botches were also expected to perform such tasks but it is doubtful whether any of them did. Secular lords had long since ceased demanding such service and had commuted the liability into a money payment but the Church tended to cling to old-fashioned concepts of Lordship far longer.

In 1333 Wivelsfield had in fact carried out a major *coup* in a war of independence. The problem revolved around a common pasture called Stammeryngferth (part of the Stanmer charter lands; later known as The Bishoprick, see Chapter 6). People from Wivelsfield were putting their animals out to graze there, up to their allowed maximum. But 'foreigners' cattle were also being put out there, all year round, at the whim, it appeared, of people from Stanmer. Moreover, the Stanmer people were being paid by these 'foreigners' for the grazing.

Clearly there was not enough pasture for both groups to rub along in a friendly manner. Matters had to be brought to a head and Wivelsfield took the initiative. They went to court at South Malling as 'plaintiffs' and the case came before a panel of four canons. Stanmer appeared as defendants. They claimed most emphatically that Stammeryngfergth was *their* 'pasture and heath' and not Wivelsfield's and it was up to them whether they leased out pasture there or not.

An enquiry was held. As was usual in manorial inquiries it was left to all the other tenants of the manor to look into the problem and to come up with a verdict. The dice were weighted in Wivelsfield's favour because the wealden tenants of the manor clearly outnumbered those from Stanmer, and no wealdener in his right mind was going to aid a judgement in favour of a downland parish. It might open up all sorts of awkward enquiries about the commons they themselves were using. The votes from Walsted, Lindfield, Ardingly, Turners Hill and Crawley Down were all duly cast in Wivelsfield's favour.

Right, in one sense, had been on Stanmer's side. *Stammeryngferth* does mean - 'the bushy ground belonging to Stanmer people', their 'swine pastures' of the Anglo-saxon charter, south of Wivelsfield Green. (fig. 2) Wivelsfield's own common was to the north. Yet, in Wivelsfield's favour, Stanmer's custom of using the heath for its own animals had clearly been dropped, while Wivelsfield's had not. The final verdict was that the pasture belonged to Wivelsfield but that Stanmer should be allowed to put their sheep on it to feed on the heath in winter and to use the heather for other needs, but not to sell it. The matter ended with Stanmer, having lost the case, paying the costs. [39]

This was a symbolic victory for Wivelsfield. It shows the wealden peasant as a forceful element in his own community. Our plaintiffs, Richard Holmere, William atte Nellone, John of Sonde, John Maye, William Shereve, Walter of Apebroke and Robert atte Nellene were acting in their own selfish interests. They were contributing to the long slide into poverty of the downland peasants, cut off from their wealden resources and destined ultimately to become labourers in 'closed' parishes. Yet selfish or not, our plaintiffs, and many others like them throughout the Weald, were forging a good future for their children. They were helping to shape the future of their parish.

CHAPTER 2

THE PARISH CHURCH BEFORE 1672

"Come all to church good people"

A.E.Housman, *A Shropshire Lad*, 1896.

i. In early years

The Parish Church today, the result of building and rebuilding over the centuries, remains simple and unpretentious. Set snugly in, yet somewhat apart from the village, it is surrounded by a churchyard probably older than itself. Built on high ground at the western end of the 'long ridge' it lies close by Lunces which, as we have seen in Chapter 1, was undoubtedly a Saxon estate and possibly the oldest and largest in the area.

i. Ancient yew tree in the churchyard.

Even earlier settlers are perhaps hinted at by the ancient yew tree in the churchyard. During his recent studies Allen Meredith has come to believe that yew trees grow at a far slower rate than previously thought and that the placement of yew trees in a churchyard gives a clue to the age of the site. He is of the opinion that an ancient yew growing on the north side of a church indicates the site of a Neolithic graveyard.[1]

Since Wivelsfield's most ancient yew grows on the north side of the Church does this mean that here, as in so many places elsewhere, the early Christian Church was built on pagan hallowed ground? If the Celts before the Saxons had also settled on the 'long ridge', as seems likely, had they also gathered here to worship?. The dedication of the church to St. John the Baptist may also indicate an early religious association with this spot. Midsummer's or

St. John the Baptist's day was the second most important festival of the Celts, Christmas day being the first. All this must remain conjecture until archeologists discover the history beneath the soil.

Early churches are known to have been given by individuals, perhaps, in this case, by Wifel or one of his successors as a lord of 'Lunces'.[2] Built on his land conveniently nearby to serve his household yet not too far from his neighbours, the earliest structure was perhaps made entirely of wood. When, in the Anglo-Norman period it was decided to use stone, the builders were, in all probability, local workmen who copied and did their best to follow, the fashions of the century in which they worked, making the most of the few materials which they had near at hand.[3] This was sandstone, rubble and ashlar, which some believe was dug from the quarry on Lunces Common.

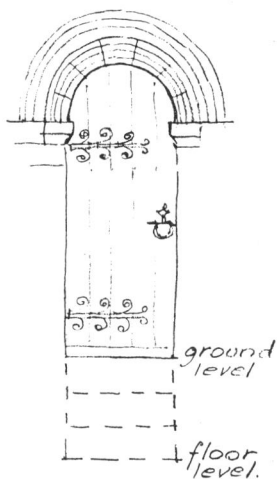

ii. Church, north doorway.

By looking at the architecture that remains today it is apparent that the church at Wivelsfield in the early Norman period had only a chancel and a twenty-seven foot long nave, without seating but possibly with wall paintings. In the chancel there is likely to have been an altar and a crucifix in accordance with the Roman form of Christianity, brought by St. Wilfrid to Sussex around the year 680 AD. All that now remains is the north doorway, so Saxon in its simplicity and narrow construction but just possibly Norman in date.

ii. Medieval growth

About the year 1095 this little Church was gifted to the Prior and monks of St.Pancras Priory in Lewes by William, 2nd earl de Warenne. The 2nd earl had founded this great Cluniac monastry, the first of its kind in England, in 1077. It must be said that such a gift was really appropriation, for churches were viewed not only as spearheads of pastoral activity but also as a steady source of income. The early monastic cartularies tell us that Wivelsfield was one of a large network of churches throughout the Weald contributing its tithes, that is, one tenth of the local farming profits, to Lewes Priory. From this it seems clear that by about the year 1100 Wivelsfield had both cultivation, an attendant population and an emerging parochial organisation.[4]

Though a 'church' was mentioned at Wivelsfield in A.D. 1095, it seems that Wivelsfield was a 'chapelry' to the Church of Ditchling in

1121.[5] In that year Ralph, Bishop of Chichester (1091-1125) confirmed that various churches belonged to Lewes Priory. The list included "...Dichenings with the Chapell of Wivelsfield".[6] With the consent of the Bishop, a chapel (daughter church) served a remote place which was too far from the mother church for people to walk there regularly for services. We do not know whether Wivelsfield had evolved in that way as a true 'daughter' or whether it had been made subordinate to Ditchling for financial reasons.[7] Be that as it may, the early medieval period was one of growth for the Wivelsfield area and the term 'parish' of Wivelsfield begins to be recorded.[8] For the local farmers the Church was their parish Church and into it they lavished their care and their wealth. No documents survive to tell us this, but the building speaks for itself.

The fact that not only the congregation but the wealth of the community was growing, is indicated by the extensive rebuilding of the Church in the 13th century.[9] A larger chancel was built with a triple-lancet east window and in the north wall an arched recess was made, possibly to receive an effigy. The small oblong window was added at a later date and may have been a "squint" to enable someone standing in the churchyard to see the service celebrated at the altar. Another explanation is that, as an unglazed opening, a small bell was rung from it at the sanctus and at the consecration of the Elements, so that the Real Presence might be known outside. The position of the altar can be judged by the piscina opposite in the south wall of the chancel. This also indicates where the 13th century chancel ended. The south wall of the nave was taken down, replaced by two arches supported by a massive central pillar and half pillar at each end and a flat roofed south aisle added.

About this time the Chantry Chapel was built, no doubt by a local landowner, where masses could be said or sung for his soul and for his family. Who this benefactor was we do not know. From a taxation list made in 1296 it appears that, at that time, John Atte Ree was the wealthiest landowner, followed by John of Ottehale and Walter More.[10] The east wall of the Chantry Chapel is unusual having a small lancet window high up in the gable and under it an arched recess. After the Conquest until the mid sixteenth century the undersides of nave arches were frequently decorated with lozenge shaped panels and similar patterns adorned pillars. The same ornamentation also covered wall spaces not occupied by figure designs.[11] This lozenge pattern was still evident in the chantry chapel recess as recently as Victorian times.

With a still growing and prosperous population during the 14th century the church was again enlarged. The nave and south aisle were lengthened westward by fourteen feet and a new west wall with a doorway and a two-light window over was built. The chancel was not altered although the lengthened nave put it quite out of proportion. By the common law of England, presumably existing from time immemorial, the repair and upkeep of the chancel was the responsibility of the owner of the tithes, whilst the nave, where the parishioners gathered, was the duty of the parishioners themselves.[12] The Prior of Lewes, as tithe holder, was perhaps unable or unwilling to emulate the parishioners' building programme.

Plate 7. South view of the church circa 1847 (By kind permission of Rev. A. Fallows).

It is clear that the local community themselves rejoiced in their church and were prepared to spend money on it. There is evidence that support for Wivelsfield church extended beyond the parish bounds. At the 'halmot', or court, of Keymer manor held at Ditchling on the 6th November 1343 "...Ralph the Bedel of Keymer" was ordered to pay 3s.6d. to John Hentye, who was described as "...attorney general of the church and of the parishioners of Wyvelesfelde". Though the up-wealden residents of Keymer and Clayton manors had a small chapel of ease for their occasional use at Fairplace Hill, on the north side of what is now Burgess Hill, it did not develop into a proper parish church and it was perhaps only used occasionally.[13] It would seem that the people living in the northern parts of Keymer in the 14th century used Wivelsfield Church, perhaps for baptisms, weddings and burials as well as services and because of this, were required to contribute to the church expenses. Ralph the beadle, whose duty it was to collect the contributions, lived at Bedelands farm in Keymer, a relatively short walk away from Wivelsfield church, across the fields to the west whereas his own parish church was a good three miles away in Keymer village.

Later, in 1598, Richard King was ordered to unstop the footpath from Keymer to Wivelsfield Church obviously to allow Keymer residents continued access.[14] The 17th-century registers of Wivelsfield witness the continuation of this custom when they record the baptism of a child of Thomas Ridge in 1646.[15] He lived at what is now Folly farm between Burgess Hill and Haywards Heath.

The zeal for the church building continued in the fifteenth century. About 1470 the Church was re-roofed with trussed rafters and crown posts and covered with Horsham slabs. The south aisle roof was raised and the south doorway with carved spandrels and grotesque finials built. A holy water stoup was placed on the outside to the east of the doorway. It was also during the fifteenth century that the dwarfed but sturdy tower was added to the west end of the south aisle. Considerable reinforcement had to be undertaken to bear its weight. The money to do such work came mainly from local people and from death-bed bequests. For instance, in 1474, John Sherman, living in Lewes but perhaps Wivelsfield born and bred, gave 20d. (a reasonable sum) for the fabric of the church.[16]

On the south wall of the tower, on either side of the belfry window are two 15th century carvings of an owl and a musician.[17] Stonemasons delighted in decorative carvings and these two had added significence as a double-sided image handed down from the Celtic tradition - wisdom the stationary owl enhanced by the joy of music. The concept retained its appeal to those who came long after the Celtic period as a fitting adornment for a much-loved church.

iii. Carvings of an owl and a musician on the south of the church tower.

iii. At the Reformation

Churches and chapels belonging to the monastries were frequently served by the monks. A deed executed in 1267 at Lewes Priory, was witnessed by one William, the chaplain of Wivelsfield.[18] We can imagine William, dressed in his monk's habit, coming from Lewes Priory, perhaps on horseback but more probably on foot, to celebrate mass for his growing congregation.

In 1534, however, the old order changed when Henry VIII severed ties with the Pope and, by the Act of Supremacy, made himself Supreme Head of the Church of England. Roman Catholicism, the only form of worship with which people were familiar, was suppressed. Lewes Priory was suppressed. In 1538 Thomas Cromwell, who, as Vicar General, ordered the destruction of relics and shrines in all churches, was patron of Wivelsfield. The King had granted him the former possessions of Lewes Priory. In 1551, after his fall from grace, these went to Ann of Cleves. In 1547, during the reign of Edward VI the Dissolution of the Chantries occured. This was logical as masses for the dead were deemed superstitious. Among the chantries suppressed was the 'Okehurst Chantry' in Chichester Cathedral, to which Lunces and Otehall in Wivelsfield had contributed 15s. apiece each year.[19] This money was now diverted to the Crown. Cranmer's prayer books were published in 1549 and 1552. Cromwell's mandate in 1538 for the keeping of parish registers was apparently not taken up at Wivelsfield but at the sterner Royal order of 1559, the first parish register begins.[20]

In 1542 John at More, of More House, made his will and in 1544 Richard Atre of Theobalds did the same.[21] Each committed his soul to God and to "our blessed lady St. Mary" and to all the saints in heaven and each went on to make meticulous and generous bequests for Wivelsfield church and for the form of worship they had known over the years. John at More wanted his executors to provide:

"...at my buryall day xx (20) prestes if so many may then be provided to syng diriges and masses for my sawle and all christen sawles or els if so many cannot be gotten at that day to have them the next day foloyng every prest beyng at masses to have vid. / Item I will that my executors in lykewise provide at my yeres mynd 30 masses if so many can be provided or els to have the said number fulfillid within the monthe next foloyng my said yeres mynd every prest to have as Is aforesaid at my buryall day...."

Atre had similar wishes, adding that the cost of providing five masses a year for 20 years after his death was to be paid for out of his freehold lands in Wivelsfield. In addition, each man was generous in his provision for candle wax. Wax would have been a vital requisite for the pre-reformation church. John at More directed his executors to:

"... fynd contynually for the space of vii yeres from the day of my buryall ii wex tapers every one of them to be ii pound of wex thei to be lyght and to be borne before the blessyd sacrement of the alter every sonday and holyday in the yere at masse...."

Atre insisted:

"... I wyll have a taper of soo myche wax made as may be bowght for vs. [five shillings] to berne before the holy sacrement / Item I will therbe bowght a torche and gyvyn to the church of Wevilsfeld aforesaid."

From the tenor of these two persons' wills, both substantial local worthies, it would seem that Thomas Dicson, incumbent from 1541, had introduced no sweeping changes at Wivelsfield and indeed, the King himself still claimed to be Catholic at this date. However, the impact of Thomas Cromwell may have been felt before 1547 for in that year Richard Adeane alias Warren bequeathed his 'soul to almighty god and to all the Saincts in hevyn' and made no mention of priests or masses.[22]

In 1551 the local priest was recorded as 'Romanus amans' which, literally translated, means 'Roman-loving'.[23] We should suppose, therefore that even if he had adapted happily to the novel idea of marrying and raising a family, he baulked at celebrating the protestant communion in an unadorned church; and in 1553 with the accession to the throne of Roman Catholic Mary Tudor he would have welcomed the new law obliging him to use the Latin Mass. His successor, Thomas Hopkyns was appointed during Mary's reign in 1554 and was undoubtedly a Romanist. All Protestant legislation and prayer books were abolished in 1555 and the Marian persecutions of Protestant "heretics" began. Bishops Cranmer, Latimer and Ridley were burnt at the stake and any committed Protestants in Wivelsfield must have felt their blood run cold when they heard of the martyrs burnt at Lewes.

Agnes Adeane alias Warren of Wivelsfield made her Will in 1557.[24] Living in a country which was once again formally Roman Catholic, was it compromise which caused her to:

" ...have dystributed and bestowd of my burying xxs. at my month in mynde xxvis. viiid. and at yeres mynde xxvis. viiid."

Jane Gyfford also in 1557 was more assured. *"...I will that William Arshefould see me honystly beryd with dirige and masse and refressyng to the poer..."* [25]

Mary died in 1558 and Elizabeth I came to the throne. England became a Protestant nation once more, having endured two violent changes of religious direction in less than 10 years. The Anglican church was established in 1559 and in that year the Book of Common Prayer came into use as the only legal form of public worship. The majority of the clergy and populace accepted, without openly questioning, the successive alterations in doctrine and services which were now imposed with all the authority of both Church and State and enforced by the punishment of protesters. Clergy were now allowed to marry although popular prejudice was against it at first. What with hardly knowing from one reign to the next whether they were legally married or not and having to put up with disparaging remarks from old fashioned parishioners, the pioneering generation of vicarage ladies must have led a precarious and harassing existence. Perhaps Anne Hamlen was one such for she came to Wivelsfield with her husband, Amphiable Hamlen when he became curate in 1573.[26]

Though in their hearts and minds the local people may have clung to the past for a while, there was no long-standing bid for Roman Catholicism in Wivelsfield and by 1676 the parish was firmly protestant if not firmly Church of England. The pulpit began to occupy a prominent place in the church and in its worship. This is illustrated in the will of Alice Warren who in 1640 bequeathed:

"...unto the Parson of the parrishe to preach at my Funerall Thirteene shillings foure pence."[27]

Many pagan ideas and symbols had been incorporated into Christian worship and continued to circulate throughout the Middle Ages and later. The hawthorn or may tree was thought to have supernatural powers against witches, fairies and lightning. After the Reformation, however, such superstitions were preached against. In 1634 one Elizabeth Godman was indicted at a church court:

"for pulling down the May boughs, in a rude scornfull manner, which were brought to the churche to adorn it." [28]

Mistress Godman presumably felt that her actions had been in good faith, against the works of the Devil, but the church and her local community did not support her.

iv. St Peter's Chapel

In the east of Wivelsfield parish (Manns and Strood Farms, Shoulders, Botches, etc.) where loyalties had been officially tied to the Canons of South Malling, support for the parish church in the medieval period may have been dilute. There was a chapel near Scaynes Hill, which, like Keymer's, fell at the Dissolution. Referred to as the Chapel of St. Peter, it was finally demolished in the period 1611-1630 while

William Newton was Lord of the Manor of South Malling.[29]   It would originally have been provided by the College of South Malling to serve their people living in the vicinity of Scaynes Hill, that is, in Wivelsfield to the south and at Walsted to the north. The annual fair in this part of Wivelsfield had reputedly been on the feast of St. Peter and St. Paul. The ties of 'Wivelsfield hamlet' to their own churches is made clear in 1394. In that year Richard atte Holmere, heir to Agnes atte Holemere (Hole Farm) claimed he was not liable to a heriot of one cow. However his claim was refused and the Beadle ordered to seize the cow and give it, not to the Lord of the Manor as was usual, but to the Rector of Lindfield.[30]

It took the Reformation to bring this area of Wivelsfield - 'Wivelsfield Hamblett' as it was still called in 1730 into the full parochial net;[31] and even then the Deanery of South Malling retained a nominal probate jurisdiction over the people who lived there. Their Wills were sometimes still proved in the Deanery court and not in the Archdeacon's court at Lewes.

One Nicholas Hurst of Wivelsfield, in his will dated 13th August 1547 expressed the desire to be buried in the Church "...of St.Peter of Wivelsfield." [32] The word "yarde" was added, but later deleted, making it evident that he wished to be buried within the building. Did he wish his last resting place to be the wealden chapel of St. Peter - perhaps a favourite hallowed place, in which the Reformation now inexplicably denied his worship. Alternatively, there may have been an attempt by the 'South Malling' residents of the parish to have their chapel remembered in the dedication of the Parish church. Be that as it may, St. Peter's Chapel was eventually forgotten but a connection with St. Peter was reinstated in this century in the dedication of the parish Church to both saints, St. Peter and St. John the Baptist.

v. Still the focal point

On a personal level nobody could fail to have been affected by the Reformation, and among those whose conscience brought them into conflict, permanent or temporary, with the official views of the day, there were no doubt many heartaches. In other respects, however, things tended to go on much as they always had. The church continued to look after the community in its midst and in return, the community looked after its church.

Outside the church itself, the church yard was the most important focus for community life. The term 'yard' comes from an Old English word meaning 'an enclosure' and churchyards were originally church gardens where the protected yew trees grew. Its exceptional life span

Plate 9. More House circa 1900.

vii. The seeds of dissent

The Advowson, or patronage, that is the right of appointing a priest to Wivelsfield, was vested in William, 2nd Earl de Warenne and as patron he presented his chosen priest to the Bishop for institution and induction. This right, together with the Church, he gifted to Lewes Priory in 1095. It may be assumed that the Priory supplied a chaplain until the Dissolution of the Monasteries 1536-39. In 1558 the living, still not an independent parish, became a perpetual curacy in the Archdeaconry of Lewes. It was not until the 19th century that a vicarage was built in Wivelsfield. Appointed in perpetuity and licensed by a bishop, a perpetual curate could not be dismissed or removed by the patron, although it seems that the patron had to finance him.[47] At the Reformation, as we have seen, the proprietor of More House was receiving the profits not only of the Chapelry of Wivelsfield but of Ditchling Rectory as well. In 1600 the family consolidated their position of authority in Wivelsfield when Francis More purchased the advowson, or patronage of the church. This right remained with the More House estate for several generations.[48]

It has been said that at the beginning of Elizabeth's reign the clergy were poorly educated but Wivelsfield seems to have received a fair share of scholarly men. After the death of Amphiable Hamlen in 1577 the succession of pastors included, in 1620 one Hugh Williams, M.A., kinsman to the bishop of Oxford and in 1623 John Lichfield, B.A., who married the daughter of Thomas Godman of Otehall. Although the educational status of Rowland Prigg 1639 is not known he came as one 'commended by the Seirgent of the house of Comons.' It was during this period that a fine three-decker Jacobean pulpit was installed in the Church and many erudite sermons must have been preached from it by these learned men.

With the outbreak of Civil War in 1642 political and religious principles once again divided the country. Parliament and Puritanism triumphed against Charles I and Anglicanism and England became a Commonwealth. These divisions were surely reflected at Wivelsfield . Though located in a strongly parliamentarian area, in which protestant dissent was gaining an ever louder voice, the patron was a Royalist and was clearly an old-style churchman. One wonders where the sympathies of minister Edmund Luke lay when, in 1642, he signed the Parish Registers in the outmoded Latin as "presbyterum" (priest).

In 1650 Thomas More gent. was paying a curate £10 yearly and his board out of the £100 or so profit he received from the impropriated tithes. The parishioners, however, had their own preference in ministers. James Nicholls, described as a 'jackmaker', was surely their choice and not that of the patron. Matters came to a head over John Oliver, a 'maultman'. In 1660, as soon as the Commonwealth had ended and the monarchy had been restored More had him ejected from the living for non-conformity.

The parishioners were clearly furious. They must surely have resented the enormous sum, around £100 a year that Thomas More now gained from the parish tithes, making him twice as wealthy as the Godmans at Otehall. It is no surprise that the Godmans were among those lined up against the patron. The Bishop was called upon to mediate between parish and patron. [49] He pointed out to the patron that:

"*a petition has been delivered against you to his Majesty, by the inhabitants of the parish of Wivelsfield, that showeth the want of a minister among them for the space of three years last past; that though raised in their tythes by you their impropriator, no allowance for a minister hath been made them, which was not omitted by yourself or your ancestors for above forty years before these unsettled times; through which neglect, their children and servants, wanting instruction in the grounds and principles of religion, and nursed in ignorance, have been forced to wander into other parishes*"

When the Bishop then requested that the parish be provided with "*...an orthodox minister with a competent mayntenance...*", Thomas More replied :

"*...I confesse myself not a little surprised at the unneighbourly attempts of some of the inhabitants of Wivelsfield, whereby they endeavour to devolve the whole burden on my shoulders ..... My lord,* *my grandfather before me, and myselfe, out of the natural addiction we had to a scholar's company, and the respect we bore to a divine function, did uninteruptedly entertayne some student as a companion, to whom we did not only show the civility of a gentleman, but in consideration of his office in the parish, we allowed some salary, not out of necessity, but as we always hoped, out of charity, till the late sad times, when the sword was supreme arbiter in all cases, both eccliastical and civil ..."*

"Many of my good neighbours were such good friends to the Church of England as not only to suffer but to introduce an unlearned and unordayned maultman to be their minister, who endeavoured to compel me to mayntayne him, by giving him over all the tithes, whom I judged worthy of none."

The bishop, finding More's reply unsatisfactory, summoned him to his lodgings in London, and directed him to bring his grant (proving the right to the advowson and tithes) but More found himself "confined to my chamber by sickness" and sent his son instead. The patron clearly felt ruffled and misunderstood :

"My lord, I thought my unconstrained concessions might have proved satisfactory to the parish ..... but my parishioners not accepting them, and your lordship, as I suppose, acquiescing in them, I have in obedience to your lordship sent up my grant ..... I could acquaint your lordship of the violent breaking open of the church doors on the 30th of March last, to make way for an unordayned, illiterate, schismatical, fanatical fellow, to preach as any the country yields...... On my son's demanding by what authority he came with a hundred fanatics to preach, he answered, 'Upon the desire of the parish' and when he asked him of whom of the parish? Thomas Hunt, who had formerly brought in the maltman to supply the place, (where he continued too long) answered 'I desired him.' Thomas Godman, also stepped up, and sayd his father desired him, saying he had more to do there than anyone else, his father being churchwarden bidding him go on against all opposition; and when my son told him your lordship would give them little thanks for this action, Thomas Godman answered that he had acquainted the bishop, who bid them get whom they would, which put an end to the dispute..."

He signed himself, perhaps with tongue in cheek:

"... your lordship's solicitiousness for the good of the church as well as your dignitye constrains me to subscribe myselfe your lordship's most humble servant."

In a further letter the Bishop decreed that More should find an "...able and orthodox minister" and pay him £30 a year, and that the parishioners should also be involved by making an additional contribution. To this Thomas More replied: "*...if I should condescend*

to give £20 per annum, I presume it will give satisfaction to his
majesty and to your lordship; and this I am contented to doe upon my
parishioners giving £30 a year, and that I may have my tithes duly
and quietly, without molestation or suits of law." And, to be on the
safe side, he added a postscript extolling:

"... the exquisite composure of the Common Prayer Book, a jewel I
have ever held of that high esteeme and price, that I have constantly
caused it to be read in my house and family, in the greatest heat of
these distractions, and in the worst of times."

v. More coat of arms.

In June 1661 Walter More reported back to
his father by letter in which he writes that he
was cordially received by the Bishop who was
"...sensible that you had been much injured
and also received much prejudice by the late
troublesome times." The Bishop kept the
letter in order *"...to acquaint His Majesty, Sir*
Ralph Freeman and the Parishioners with
it." However, on going again to the Bishop,
Walter More was advised *"Mr More, let it*
rest." These words finally ended this dispute as to who should occupy
the pulpit at Wivelsfield which had involved not only the parishioners
and the patron but the Bishop of the Diocese and the King himself.

Wivelsfield had thus shown its strength; the strength of an
independently-minded Wealden community insistent that their tithe
money should at least provide a minister of their own choosing. More,
the patron, a Royalist outnumbered by Parliamentarian neighbours, had
lost the battle but remained the wealthiest person in the parish and thus
had, to some extent, won the war. Some supporters of 'the maultman'
turned their back altogether on the establishment and went off to join
their own religious groups; groups which, after the Toleration Act of
1689 still play a vital part in the religious life of the parish, as we shall
learn in Chapter 8.

vi. Otehall deed, dated "Monday after the feast of the Holy Trinity," 1348. The deed is witnessed by Wivelsfield land owners Walter ate More, John Fraunckelayn, John Lons, Richard of Ottehale and Richard Grigge. Ref. ESRO SAS/HB 470.

CHAPTER 3

THE LANDED ESTATES 1240-1840

"Generations come and generations go,
but the earth goes on for ever."
Ecclesiastes, Ch. 1, v.4

i. Yeomen and gentlemen

Wivelsfield had no resident great lord or squire because of the way
that its landholdings were distributed among several different manors.
This helped breed a spirit of independence in politics and religion.
Rather than one overall authority to shelter the villagers and to
command their patronage there were instead a number of small estates;
some just a house and adjoining farm with a few scattered parcels of
land in this and neighbouring parishes, others owning several farms
besides the home farm. Through the centuries these estates waxed and
waned: families grew rich and expanded or, falling on hard times or
failing to produce a male heir, handed their property over to others.[1]

The owners of these estates in the 16th and 17th centuries were on the
border between the upper yeomanry and lower gentry: a
jealously-guarded divide in earlier times when the gentry held the
middle ground between peasants and the peerage. The gentry were then
mainly country landowners, interlinked by bonds of marriage and
indebtedness. In feudal times the four ranks of the gentry had been
strictly controlled: baronets, knights, esquires and gentlemen - the
lowest estate, originally supposed to be limited to the younger sons and
brothers of esquires and their heirs.[2] Through time the strict medieval
qualifications were relaxed but it continued to be true that fewer than
one in ten of the gentry bore any sort of title: their importance came
from their ownership of land. The agricultural groups below the rank of
gentry were: yeomen, husbandmen and labourers. It was the village
families with the ancient and respected estate of yeoman who had
enough land to enable them to move into the ranks of the gentry.

In the medieval period the substantial freeholders were allowed to
pursue their civil litigation at Westminster and in the Barony Court at

Lewes. John of Otehall and William at Re   (of Great Otehall and possibly also Little Otehall) used the Barony court in 1265-66.[3]   In return the monarchy came to rely on their class as an unpaid workforce to meet the demands of an expanding bureaucracy.   In the tax collection of 1296 it was John of Otehale (Great Otehall) and Walter of the More (More House) who met the visiting officials and gave them the necessary information; while in 1327 John ate More performed this function.[4]   There was perhaps prestige involved and the chance of making money. John At Ree, Lord of Otehall, was a juror of the Rape of Bramber in 1470 and a Collector of a subsidy for Sussex in 1488, as was Walter at More, of More House, in 1570. Service was a long tradition in the More family . William atte More had been at Agincourt in 1415 where he served as an esquire or lance under John Arundell, Lord Maltravers. [5] But support was not always unerringly given to the authorities of the day. In 1450 'yeomen' of Wivelsfield, John atte Ree (of Otehall) and Thomas Esthamfeld (perhaps of Fanners) took part in Jack Cade's rebellion.[6]

Prestigious manorial posts were well paid. In 1594 Thomas More received 30s. as his accountancy fee as bailiff of the manors of Ditchling and Highley and for his "labour and diligence" in measuring all the Earl of Abergavenny's land in Sussex.[7] However, most administrative jobs of the district were carried out as an unpaid duty by lesser land holders. For instance the Attrees at Theobalds and the Hentyes at Antye would each have taken their due turn, one year in seven, in serving as reeve or 'accountant' for the manor of Houndean.[8] In the 17th century, when manorial service had lapsed and the parish had risen as the centre of local administration, their successors served as churchwardens and overseers.

Gentlemen were set apart from the yeomanry by breeding, education, greater wealth, more leisure and sometimes military rank, as for instance, the Mores of More House. Sussex gentry in the 17th century became preoccupied with genealogy and those in Wivelsfield craved, and ultimately achieved, the respectability and recognition conferred by a coat of arms. There was a great demand for this as a visible sign of gentlemanly status. The Godmans of Otehall obtained a grant of arms in 1579 and the Mores achieved their arms in the early seventeenth century. John Attree had his armorial shield on his will of 1665.

While the yeomen of the parish made their money from farming, the gentry either farmed in hand or rented out to tenants, as agricultural prosperity dictated, while also raising money by other means. Wivelsfield's woodlands were a useful resource, providing income both from coppice and from felled wood.[9]   In 1698 when owner Thomas Godman of Lambeth leased Great Otehall to a tenant he was careful to retain his own right to enter "the Great Coppice" with teams, carts and waggons, in order to cut timber or convert to coal (charcoal).[10]   The gentry often preferred business to be conducted well away from their front door. In 1744 Richard Webb of Fanners allowed 150 oak trees to be felled on his land in Clayton parish, (at West End Farm, Burgess Hill) he taking his profit from the felling.[11] Meticulous measurements of coppices and woods were included in the new estate maps that decorated a landowner's study. Otehall, Theobalds and More House, for example, each produced fine examples of such maps in the 17th and 18th centuries, a boon to present-day scholarship.[12]

Plate 10. Oak tree in Charlwood Road, Burgess Hill. The timber resources in the far west of Wivelsfield parish brought profit in the Tudor period to the Attree and Godman families who expanded their estates into uncolonised woodland.

In 1580 wealden woods were brought to the aid of the Downland which was, even then, a relatively treeless area. John A Deane at Lunces directed in his will in 1580 that *"...ther shalbe vii Tonne of Tymber cutt downe in my land called Lunces land and carried to Weghdeane in the parish of Patcham imeadiately after my decease for the repayring of houses there."* In addition his youngest son and heir William, a minor, was to receive one ton of timber at age 21 years, followed by three loads of wood a year for three years - all from the Lunces estate.[13]

Two ancient customs affected local inheritance. The first, called 'borough English', whereby succession passed to the youngest son, was followed by Wivelsfield gentry on their copyhold lands until the 17th century. The Attrees of Theobalds, for instance, settled their newly-acquired or outlying land upon the elder sons, leaving the youngest son and heir with the main estate.[14] With freeholds, such as Great Otehall, the old custom was generally abandoned earlier, though it was still used for their peripheral copyhold land. Lunces, a freehold, still practised the custom in 1580 as we have just seen.

The second important custom, the right of 'widow's bench' , entitled the heir's mother, or grandmother, to remain in the house until she died, even if she had re-married.[15] In 1659 when John Attree of Theobalds was preparing to purchase Antye and add it to his estate he first had to agree to build a new house for the vendor's mother. The vendor, Thomas Dumbrell, for his part had to agree "...*to clear the house of his mother whereby the said John may have quiet and peaceable possession by Michaelmas next...*".[16] Freeholders had a freer hand. The will of John at More of More House provided his widow Benet in 1542 with "...*the best chamber over the parlour*", a common stipulation in gentry wills when only the very richest had a dower house for the widow. But if she should happen to marry again "...*she shall clear, avoid, quit of this house and no longer to meddle with any part*".[17]

Travel to London may not have been easy but the Attrees, Godmans and Mores all did business there at various times and married their daughters to London gentlemen and merchants; for instance Abigail More, 14th child of Captain Thomas More, married John Richbell, a gentleman of London.[18] Edward, the eldest son of Thomas and Mary Godman, was described as a Gentleman and merchant of London when he took the lordship of Otehall in 1624, although his main home was still at Wivelsfield. His son Thomas was baptised in the parish and Edward was buried there. The son himself was a 'Gentleman of Kennington' in 1697.[19] Thomas, dying without heirs, passed the estate to his brother, John Godman, of London, Gent., Citizen and Cutler. He, in common with other contemporary gentry families in Wivelsfield, lacked a male heir. On his death Otehall passed through the female line to William Shirley, whose father, also William, had married John's only daughter and heiress, Elizabeth.

The prosperous rural middle class of Tudor and Stuart times was profit conscious and land hungry. The Mores of More House were prime examples. Their neighbours' acquisitions in Wivelsfield had left them little land in which to expand locally although they received some here and elsewhere through marriage. However, their judicious purchase in 1600 of the patronage of the church, and the tithe income that went with it, gave them wealth enough to buy and lease land in other places. Once acquired this was rarely separated from the main estate and most inheriting sons added more, enabling them to provide for younger sons and to give their daughters rich dowries. By 1616 Elizabeth More had married a knight, Sir Ferdinando Heybourne, Groom Porter to the Privy Chamber.[20]

THE LARGER HOUSES
A   Great Otehall
B   Lunces
C   Clevewater
D   More House
E   Theobalds
F   Fanners

FARM HOUSES
1   Antye
2   Pepperhall
3   South Colwell
4   Clearwaters
5   South Slugwash
6   Lockstrood
7   Manns
8   Shoulders
9   Strood

10   Hursthouse

11   Birth
12   Blackmores
13   Franklands
14   Hole
15   North Hole
16   Scrases

17   Bankside
18   Botches
19   Coldharbour
20   Little Otehall
21   North Colwell
22   North Slugwash
23   Rogers
24   Townings
25   Whitebreads

↗   East & West Sussex
    Boundary from 1974

Timber-framed houses

No longer there

Later or altered house

LOCATIONS OF HOUSES
pre 1600 - 1840.

0   ½   1 mile

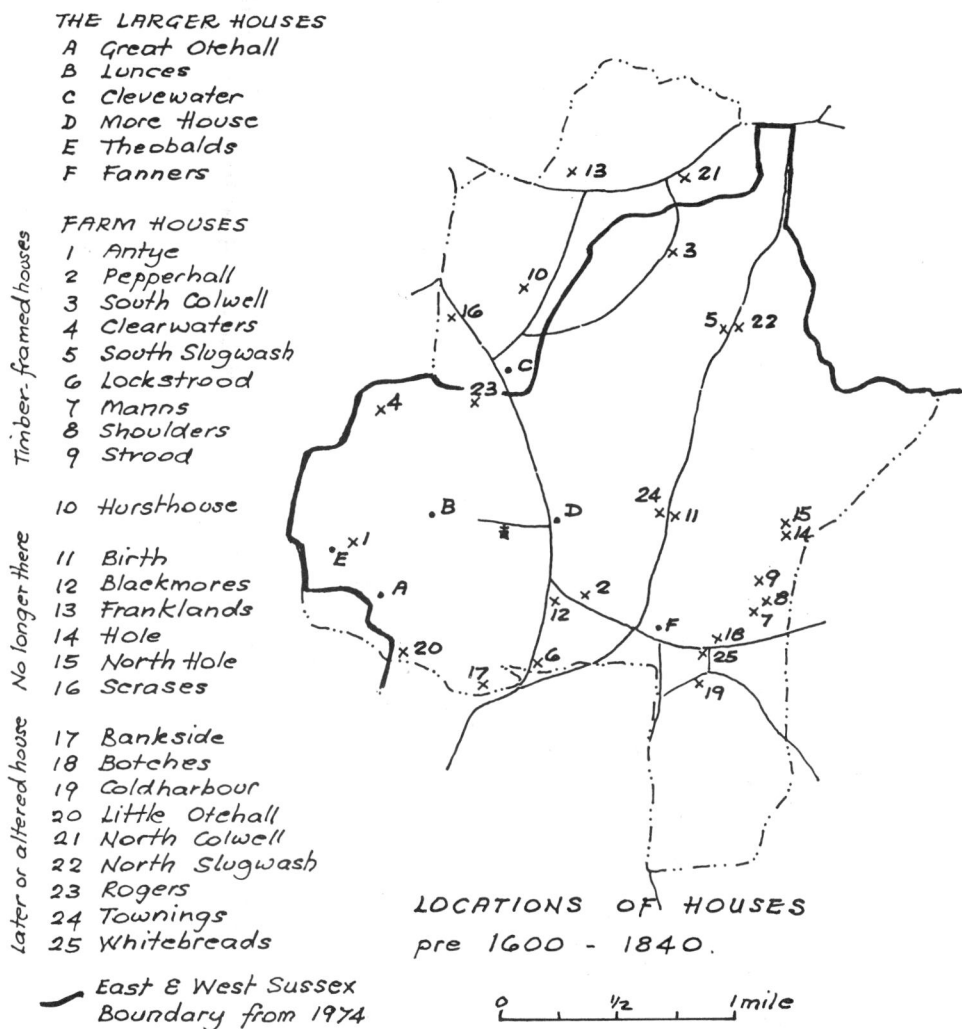

Figure 6. Locations of houses pre-1600 to 1840. Note: A-F relate ro Chapter 3, some of the farmhouses are discussed in Chapter 4.

The rural gentry might work to acquire extra land which could be settled on an agriculturally inclined son; or they were ambitious in other directions and invested in apprenticeships for elder sons, who could then become wealthy guildsmen and citizens of London. Yet, however the particular aspiratons differed from one family to the next, the life they enjoyed in Wivelsfield in the 17th and 18th centuries was based on a centuries of hard work laid down by their predecessors in the parish.

ii. Laying their foundations

Although the Wivelsfield gentry made additions and alterations to their homes over the centuries, it is fortunate that many early timber-framed houses still survive.   Some we know were built as early as the fourteenth century and, even then, on the site of a previous building. Other houses have left little or no trace of their early structure and we can do no more than sketch in a few crumbs of detail afforded from documentary sources.

The houses of the rural gentry were founded on their wealth, the main source of which was usually the immediate locality. Local landowners embellished their parish church, as we saw in Chapter 2, but not before they had lain the foundations of their own home estates. As they prospered or declined so their houses prospered, declined or were taken over by new people. The houses we shall look at were owned by families engaged not only in agriculture but in tanning and the cloth trade, in milling and iron working. All of this has contributed its measure to the architectural heritage we enjoy today.

Lunces Hall   stands to the west of Wivelsfield church, sharing the same ridge (see Plate 3). As surmised in Chapter 1, it was probably the earliest settlement site in the swathe of land that the manor of Withdean Cayliffe held in Wivelsfield. Both Lunces and Otehall (below) were sub-infeudations of this manor. Their land lay wholly within the parish of Wivelsfield apart from an outlier near 'Wivelsden' in Chailey.[21] Lunces was held of its parent manor by a 15s. annual rent.

There is no trace of the original house but from Warren family wills it can be surmised that it was a north/south timber-framed building with a central open hall and upper rooms at either end. In 1580 the hall and kitchen are mentioned, a chamber over the hall and a 'lofte' chamber at the north end of the house. [22]

In an interesting charter written towards the end of the 13th century, Alice, daughter and heiress of Osbert Le Luns, of Wivelsfield, widow, made a grant to John de Ottehale and his heirs and assigns, of people whom she describes as her serfs, together with their chattels and all lands which they formerly held of her in villeinage in Wivelsfield,

Clevewater, Wysshe and a common pasture and heath called Hothlaghe, near Hayworthe in Wivelsfield. These lay north of Lunces, in the Adur/Ouse valley and up the hill towards Haywards Heath. Thus the Otehall estate gained the "serfs", or tied tenants, and all their lands, at Lunces' loss.[23]

John Lonys is mentioned in 1332 and 1348, but by 1478 the 'manor' seems to have belonged to the family of Att Dene as the lands of Richard Att Dene, called 'Lonceslond', were mentioned in a charter of lands in Wivelsfield.   The name Adeane may indicate the family's origins in Withdean. Several generations owned houses and lived in Patcham where they used the surname Warren, which became their sole surname by the seventeenth century. By the middle of the sixteenth century they owned, not only Lunces and their houses in Withdean, but two thirds of the manor of Dymocks in Ditchling and land in other neighbouring parishes. Richard Adeane and his son, another Richard, who died in 1550 and 1567 respectively, each had sufficient wealth and status to be buried within the church at Wivelsfield.[24]

Edmund Warren writes poignantly in his will of 1634 *"...to the childe my wife now goeth with, all my landes in Wivelsfield.....If it bee a man childe"*.[25] But the pregnancy did not provide the desired male heir and an elder daughter, Catherine, eventually inherited. Catherine married John Rowe, grandson of the celebrated Sussex antiquary. When she and John found it necessary to borrow £200 against the property in 1657, it was described as the "Mannor of Lunces". There was a messuage, barn and orchard, together with   50 acres land, 20 acres meadow, 40 acres pasture, 10 acres wood and 4s. rent with the appurtenances in Wivelsfield.   Although their son John does not mention Lunces in his will of 1705 his name appears under the Church 'marks' for 1697 as "Mr. Rose [Rowe's] Mark for Lunces".

By 1706 Lunces was occupied by 'widow Rowe' and her son, neither of them as owners. The estate had been purchased by Joseph Farncombe of Patcham whose will, proved in 1706, provided for the rent of Lunces to be paid to his wife Ann. His son Joseph, then aged one year, inherited by accepting his father's challenge that he remained a member of the Church of England (Chapter 8). In 1728 he purchased some adjacent land known as Boyners or Tile Barn.[26] He died in 1753.[27] The church Marks for 1759 show *"Mr. Farncombe's [mark] for Lunces"*.

In 1833 Lunces was described as: *"...a compact and most desirable Freehold Farm, called Lunces, comprising a recently built and genteel Farm House, delightfully situated near Wivelsfield Church, with Garden, Orchard and Pleasure ground, a good three bay Barn, Stable, 2 Cart Lodges, 2 Hovels, 3 Farm Yards and several Inclosures of Arable, Meadow and Woodland, containing altogether 83 acres... lying within a Ring fence, bounded in great part by a Trout*

Stream...". [28] The estate had gradually been broken up after 1753 with land around the stream eventually being added to the Theobalds estate. The house had been rebuilt and had come into the hands of the Tanner family of More House, of whom we shall learn more later.

Great Otehall   formerly 'Otehale', lies on the south-west side of the parish. The estate nestles in a crook of the river **Adur** and was once 'Ota's, or 'Wat's' nook of land, from Old English *halh* meaning nook of land. Its owners in the early medieval period took their surname from the location - a common practise among Wivelsfield landholders at that time - and they were accordingly known as 'of Otehale' until they were suceeded in the 15th century, probably through marriage, by newcomers the At Rees.[29] A dispute dragged on for 63 years until 1502 in which there were claimants who possibly related back to one Walter of Otehale. Thomas Attree, lord of the manor in 1523, was succeeded by his daughter and heir who married Walter Godman, and their son Thomas Godman was in 1547 asserting his right to hold court as lord of the manor of Otehall.[30]

Otehall and Lunces had continued to exchange and consolidate their holdings in Wivelsfield in the 300 years following the original grant of serfs and land from Alice le Luns to John of Ottehale in 1296, but by and large Otehall gained land at Lunces expense. The Warrens perhaps allowed this to happen because, although they were at Lunces for about 200 years, their ties were with Patcham. The owners of Great Otehall by contrast were firmly based in Wivelsfield.

By 1344 it is clear that the Otehale family had extended their holding southwards from the house itself into the Manor of Ditchling for in that year John of Otehall was repeatedly summoned to attend Ditchling manor court as a landholder in that manor.[31] South of Great Otehall had previously been virgin woodland and its colonisation and conversion to agriculture must have incurred much capital expense. The new land gained lay on both sides of Janes Lane and was known as Woodwards and Folders.[32] The latter was probably the core of the estate later known as Little Otehall, the house itself being in Wivelsfield but the land mostly in Ditchling.[33] It is also of interest that when Thomas, only son and heir of Thomas Godman, married Mary Porter in 1594, the older Thomas gave his son the fulling mills in Keymer.[34] By 1594 the fulling mill was probably defunct but the medieval cloth industry could have previously been a source of family wealth.

vii. Great Otehall (late 19th century). Reprinted by kind permission of V. R. Law.

In building up their estate into an important local 'manor' the Otehale family used their house as a manor court as witnessed by a deed of 1279 and by later deeds up to the 16th century.[35] There would have been a great central hall for business and social occasions. However, nothing remains of the Otehale or the Attree family home. The oldest part of the present timber-framed house dates from about 1550 and was built east-west by the first Godman owners. It represents a hall and an original kitchen. The latter has a wide fireplace with salt cupboard and bread oven and two wide, splay-moulded and recessed beams with decorative stops. The room over has one similar beam with a Tudor rose added to each end, said to commemorate a visit to Sussex by Queen Elizabeth 1st. A very fine timber staircase round an open well, with elaborately carved newel posts, rises from the Hall up three storeys. The attic rooms on the third floor have sloping ceilings and are lighted by gabled windows.[36]

Thomas seems to have pushed the bounds of his estate out even further before his death in 1559, colonising more land in the Janes Lane area - known as Godmans Inholmes (40a.) and Crosse Inholmes (12a.). James, his five year old youngest son and his customary heir, was admitted to all these premises and his upbringing was entrusted to the widow Margaret Turner.[37] James grew into a thrusting and energetic man in trouble with the manor court for improving his land by clearing it of trees.[38] However by 1606 he was granted permission, together with his wife Joan, daughter Agnes, and son-in-law Ralph Dyne, to make the land arable.[39] Otehall passed to Thomas Godman's elder sons, first

Richard and then Thomas who married Elizabeth, daughter of Walter More of More House.

With the joint resources of two local families, as well as profits from their agricultual expansion, the Godmans were able to fund the building of the east wing of Great Otehall, of three bays. Their date stone of 1600 and initials TGM [Thomas and Mary Godman] can be seen in the gable over the entrance porch. Between the two wings an enormous, roughly-squared post, carved from the trunk of a substantial tree, rises almost to the roof and was once part of the external wall. It supports a tie beam, the central portion of which was cut out to allow access and a dropped tie beam inserted to support the attic floor. The roof throughout is constructed of heavy side purlins, necessary to support the Horsham stone covering. The purlins in the east wing are stop-chamfered, which indicates that the upper rooms in this area were designed from the outset, rather than being added later.

Externally the high quality of the construction is shown by the close-studded walls with the many projecting windows surmounted by moulded gables and pendants (see Plate 23, Chapter 8, oriel window). The three large brick and stone chimneys have three, four and five diagonally set shafts with wind vents between them and projecting brick caps. In the south bedroom the recess beside the fireplace had, at a later date, been converted into a 'privy' with a seat, to empty down a brick shaft. This would have been cleared from the outside through a rough arch. Later embellishments indoors were marked by an inscription 'ANNO TGM [Thomas and Mary Godman] 1609'.

In 1698 owner Thomas Godman was in London and Great Otehall was leased out to William Bennett of Westmeston, possibly a relative. It was "...*a mansion or dwelling house called Oat Hall with one great barn and hovel, one little barn, one brewhouse, one milkhouse, one stable and hay house and other outhouses with the orchard garden and lanes and fields*".[40] Perhaps this was the first time in its history that the house echoed to the tread of masters who were not its owners. However, the days of Otehall as an important focus of parish life were far from over.

Antye   from the Saxon *hean teag* - 'at the high enclosure' - developed as part of a small hamlet on the hill to the west of Wivelsfield church. The hamlet, which originally also included Theobalds, is separated from the rest of the parish by the river Adur which, near its source, is no more than a meandering stream. One of the fields there, known in 1659 as The Great Ham, has a double bank, suggesting ancient beginnings; perhaps as the original 'high enclosure'. A hollow way winds past, leading north to Lunces Common and Haywards Heath. The intertwined nature of the Antye holding and that of neighbouring Theobalds in 1659 (fig. 7) suggest an earlier communal system of land use and mutual self-sufficiency within the boundary bank of the hamlet.[41] Together the two holdings formed an eastern outlier of the downland manor of Houndean (Chapter 1) but their origin as a Wealden settlement perhaps predates the creation of that manor. Members of the Hentye family, taking their surname from their land, are recorded in Wivelsfield from the 14th to the 16th centuries.[42] After this the family scattered, some moving to Littlehampton and West Tarring from where they took their Merino sheep to Australia in the 18th century.[43]

The house itself, built just before 1400, was a two-bay open-hall structure with a two-storey bay on either side of the hall. The building was aligned lengthways north to south, enabling the windows to be on the east and west sides. It was thought at that time that 'evil humours', or germs, entered from the south, windows were rarely found on that side. The hall has a crown-post roof construction with a collar-purlin and collar to every pair of rafters. The central crown-post, octagonal in section, has a slightly moulded base and large curved head-braces, where traces of sooting show there had been a central open hearth. An enormous cambered tie beam supports the crown post, the decorative appearance and workmanship of which indicates a house of quality. The original construction of the south wall, where it joins the bay consists of a tall crown post, square in section, with long braces, over a flat tie beam; the in-filling between all the timbers being a wattle and daub partition. Evidence of this may be seen in what is now the attic. In this same wall, now at first floor level, is a moulded dais beam. Below and in front of this the master of the house would have sat at table, his servants sitting at the other end of the hall.

Early in the seventeenth century, when bricks became readily available, chimneys were often inserted in one bay of the hall in order to free the living area from smoke. This was done at Antye, and, there then being no reason for an open hall, a first floor was inserted making the whole a two storey house. The original north bay was built as the service area of the house and contained several rooms which would have been used as the buttery/pantry/store etc. The very wide and heavy first-floor joists still exist in what is now the ceiling of a reception room. Linen-fold panelling taken from an old house, demolished around 1930, gives an

viii. Antye, inside the open hall *circa* 1400.

attractive period decoration to the walls. Over the years a fifth bay, now a dining room, has been added at the south end of the house, an outshot on the west side, and in the 1930s yet another wing.

Outside, the timber framing is generally no longer visible, having been replaced by bricks on the ground floor. Some of this work may have been in progress in 1659 when the house was sold to John Attree of Theobalds, for the draft deed of sale specified that all the "...*morter, tyles, brickes, laths, new collumes, stools and heads for windows which are now in or about the house...*" were to be included in the sale.[44] The upper storey, except for a small portion of the north wall where the original box-framing shows, is now tile-hung.

Members of the Dumbrell family held Antye from the early 16th century until its sale in 1659.[45] Before that date it had stood on an equal footing with Theobalds and may even have had the economic edge, for, in the north-west corner of the holding, (sited east of the 'eight-arches' railway viaduct) stood a watermill and millpond to provide extra profits. However, in 1545 the mill and $2\frac{1}{2}$ acres of meadowland was sold by William Dumbrell to Ralph Rikward. In 1566, on the death of Ralph's widow, Katherine, their son Richard inherited, but by 1604 the property had come into the hands of the Attrees of Theobalds and the mill was defunct.[46]

The farming economy of the holding was firm and diverse, with good meadow land, timber and coppice to draw upon. There were orchards and fields of hops, hemp and flax and more land was added to the estate in the early seventeenth century. However, in 1659, Thomas Dumbrell sold Antye to John Attree, his neighbour at Theobalds. By December, Thomas had moved away to Horsted Keynes but the transaction was not completed until April 1661 when, having been meticulously measured and surveyed, the two properties of Antye and Theobalds were amalgamated.[47] While Theobalds then ascended as a gentlemanly residence Antye slipped down the social scale until renovated and enlarged by the Gell-Woolleys in the 1920s.

Theobalds   Excavations near the house in the last century, revealed that the massive stones of which the foundations are built extend some distance beyond the site of the present house, which seems to indicate that a larger house once stood there. There are also traces of a moat or ditch partially surrounding it but it is not known to what period this relates. It is likely to be at least medieval, perhaps earlier.

A Thomas Tebald was witness to a charter of lands in Wivelsfield in 1441 but the earliest record of 'Tebaldes' as a house was in the period 1526-1547 when Richard At Ree had inherited it from his father.[48] Being copyhold of the Manor of Houndean, the descent was 'customary' and Richard was the youngest son. He had paid a cow worth 6s. 8d. for his inheritance tax or 'heriot'. For two and a half centuries this was the residence or estate of the Attree family, who were descended from lords of Otehall. As well as Theobalds they owned various pieces of 'assart' land in the parish which had probably been newly colonised by their forebears at Great Otehall - Webbs Inholmes, Lock Crofts, Lock Inholmes, the Inholmes at Otehall, and the Inholmes at Woodwards Hill.[49]

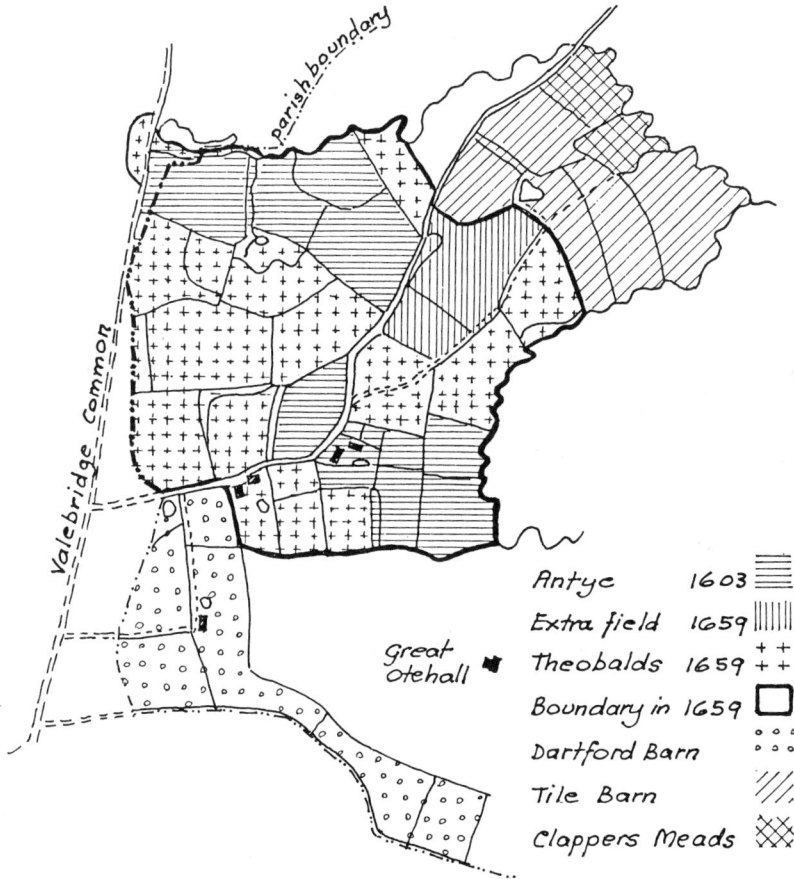

Figure 7. Theobalds Estate (with Antye) in 1659, and later additions.

One consequence of the custom of the 'borough English' was that the heir could be very young. When Richard's son, John, died in 1583, his heir, Edmund, the youngest of 17 children, was only two years old. His mother, Elizabeth, held Theobalds for him until she died in 1604.[50]

He also inherited from his father the substantial properties of
Brooklands Farm, and Birchetts Farm in Keymer parish, a continuous
swathe of land stretching from Theobalds in Wivelsfield to Heaselands
near Haywards Heath. He then consolidated his local standing by
purchasing a share of the lordship of Keymer manor and married a
coheiress, Elizabeth, daughter of George Porter, Esq.[51]

Plate 11. Theobalds from the east, 1982. Three wings, brick & tile clad with
substantial chimney stacks and outbuildings demonstrate the wealth of the Attree
and their successors.

Land was now an important source of increased wealth; land
revenues had been moving up since the second quarter of the sixteenth
century, some more than doubling between 1560-1590, with a threefold
increase between 1530 and 1620. Edmund Attree used some of this
money to diversify. The defunct watermill, which he had inherited as
part of the Antye holding, was abandoned as a business concern. In
1606, no doubt using his influence as a lord of Keymer manor, he
obtained a grant of land on Valebridge Common, on which to build a
new watermill. This would have been an expensive undertaking needing
imported stones and their dressing, special timbers (no doubt from his
estates) and much skilled engineering of dykes and sluices to cope with
the six acres of waste that he was allowed to flood. Yet in 1612 he was
granted permission for a windmill "...a little way from his watermill".
Again, whilst he had plenty of timber, this would nevertheless have
required a further substantial outlay. These two mills were just across
the parish boundary, in Keymer.[52] The tenants of that manor were not

at all pleased, having lost six acres of their common pasture and they complained bitterly that the mills were a danger to their animals.[53] The windmill was depicted in 1659 as a post mill.[54]

In 1645 Attree expanded into a nearby piece of land called Dartfords (now the Charlwood Gardens area in Burgess Hill) and by 1649 he had also acquired Godmans Inholmes and the Crosse Inholmes, both formerly held by the Otehall estate, together with adjacent cottage plots called Knobbes or Knowes, Sparrows and Knaves Crooke.[55] These were strung around the west side of Theobalds and the south side of Otehall in Wivelsfield and Ditchling. His efforts enabled him to hand on a sizable estate to his son John, whom he had educated at Magdelen Hall, Oxford and Lincoln's Inn. John continued to consolidate the estate by buying Antye in 1659;[56] and thus, with minor additons and subtractions, the estate continued into the present century.

The Attrees' expansionist policies in the period 1500-1660 are reflected in the house as it stands today, a substantial structure containing two adjoining parallel wings, a west-facing wing at right angles to the others (Plate 11) and several chimneys. The oldest part was said in 1887 by historian Captain Attree to be the pantry, the dairy, rooms over the kitchen and the small hall.[57] On the north-facing front door the date 1627 is studded in nails. In the late eighteenth century the West front was "modernised" with enlarged windows and mathematical tiles.

Cleavewater was held of Franklyns, a sub-manor of Streat, and was presumably connected with 'Dyrild' Frankeleyn, who was taxed for lands in the area in 1332. The manor house was situated on the B2112 south of the Fox and Hounds public house, between springs draining west and east respectively to the rivers Adur and Ouse. Its 177 acres of land stretched northwards, 95 acres being north of the A272, now Franklands Village in Haywards Heath. The land was presumably held by one Agnes de Cleavewater at the subsidy of 1327.[58] The manor of Streat was itself held of the de Pierpoints of Hurst and in 1397 the Manor of Hurst distrained for rent arrears on the holding late of John Franklyn as well as a holding of John Lons in the chapelry of Wivelsfield.[59]

In 1418 James Homwode, a wealthy Bolney landowner, acquired the Manor. His son James and wife Joan owned it in 1475 and around this time the west wing of the present house was built north/south as a two-bay hall. There was a northern bay of which nothing remains and a two-storey bay at the south end. Their wealth had enabled them to build a prestigious house on a par with Otehall. The south bay has heavy flat floor-joists, framed into a central beam, with the top of a moulded post just visible in the external wall. A close studded partition cuts off one side of the room, with close studding showing in the original external wall adjacent. In the hall there is a very fine 14-inch deep dais beam with the groove under for close panelling, the style of the moulding dating it to about 1475. Across the centre of the hall a 12-inch wide x 24-inch deep cambered tie beam supports the moulded base of the crown post the top of which has been cut off.

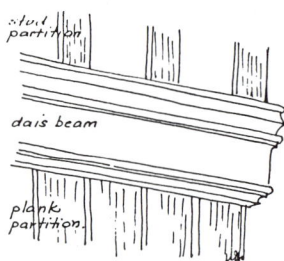

ix. Dais beam at Cleavewater Farmhouse, *circa* 1475.

In 1492 the Manor was purchased by John Michelborne alias Mascall, his wife Agnes and son Richard Mascall. The Michelborne family came to prominence about this time, making money from land improvement, but the links of the Wivelsfield branch are unclear.[60] They seem to have dropped the name Michelborne and continued as plain Mascall. The son, Richard, was the tanner of Wivelsfield around the year 1532 (Chapter 5). Extra land in the Cleavewater area had been purchased from the Attrees in 1504, perhaps including the tanyard site which lay nearby.[61]

It was probably the Mascalls who enlarged the house by adding the two-storey east wing of two bays, with its large brick chimney stack. The first floor was later divided into two rooms, both open to the roof. The roof covering of Horsham stone appears to have proved too heavy for the original timber framework of a crown purlin supported by slender crown posts and thus the present side-purlins had to be inserted. There are three original windows in the north wall, that downstairs being of six lights wide with four diamond shaped vertical bars and central mullion with ovolo moulding, which is carried all round the frame.

In 1540, after Richard's death, the manor was sold to Edmund Pope and his wife Elizabeth, in whose family it remained for 86 years. The Popes were ironmasters who at one time owned the Hendall furnace (near Buxted), which they leased or sold the the Hogges, also ironmasters. This was perhaps the time when the central chimney stack was built and the open hall was floored over with elaborate joists. On one of these is a Tudor rose medallion. In the late sixteenth or early seventeenth century, for some reason the west wing was re-roofed, with rafters supported on heavy side-purlins and the crown post and central purlin removed.

The Popes did not live in Cleavewater. At the beginning of the 17th century its tenant was George Luxford, the same who appeared before the Archdeacon for neglect of churchyard duty (Chapter 2). All his eight children were baptised in Wivelsfield. The Popes later sold part of the manor of Cleavewater, including the house, to William Mongre, gent. of London. William Bowyer was the tenant.[62] The Popes retained 'Franklands', the northern 95 acres of the estate, later selling these to John Attree. Cleavewater soon changed hands again, to George Luxford's nephew Thomas, who was made overseer of the poor in 1644. He kept it for only 20 years, selling on in 1655, to Thomas Woodyer, gent. of Lindfield, at the time of his marriage. All Woodyer's eight children were baptized in Wivelsfield and one of them, Mary, married Isaac Attree of Theobalds in 1694.

Plate 12. Cleavewater Farmhouse.

The outshot on the north side of the east wing, containing a fireplace, was built before the 1662 Hearth Tax, when Thomas Woodyer was taxed for seven hearths, the same number as today.[63] Thomas died in 1710 and his son Thomas, on inheriting, improved the look of the house by adding the stone frontage facing the road, by tile hanging the other external walls above new stone or brick built bases and by building the decorative chimney stack with a date stone TW-1712. After Thomas the younger's death, his only living child, a daughter, eventually sold Cleavewater in 1752 to Francis Warden. It thus became part of the Sergison Estate and was let out to tenant farmers.[64]

Fanners   was called the Ferns after it was rebuilt in the mid-19th century, but it has now re-assumed its older name. Ditchling Manor, had once owned all the land in Wivelsfield but had given most of it away (Chapter 1). Fanners was the only substantial freehold it retained. Of its 100 acres of land, some lay on the north side of the Green and the rest lay over the hill, some distance to the north in Slugwash Lane. South of the Green was a stretch of land which, until the early medieval period, was used as a free chase or hunting ground by the Lords of Ditchling Manor, now St. George's Retreat in Ditchling and its attendant farmland and woods.

Fanners was said in the 17th century to be held by 'military service' which means that the tenancy had carried a duty of service fitting for a 'squire' to perform. Keeping the Lord's wood in good order, fostering the game, protecting falcons' nests or providing food and drink for visiting sportsmen, were the sort of duties that might be required. The location of Fanners at the head of the wood makes it possible, though there is no direct evidence, that its medieval occupant may have had some responsibility for the wood to its south. Osbert le Furnere paid tax in Wivelsfield in 1296, an occupational surname which implies supply of provisions.[65]

By the Tudor period hunting had long ceased in the chase of Shortfrith and it was rented out for profit by the lords of Ditchling manor.[66] The northern end (between Lockstrood, the Playing Field and Otehall Chapel) was sold off altogether in 1481.[67] The original 'Fanners' seems to have been split up into three parts. One became a virgate called Furners alias Fanners, held at 2s. 11$\frac{1}{2}$d. rent; one became a virgate called 'Fanns' (perhaps a misreading for 'Fanners') held at 10s. 9d. rent; and the third was a five-acre holding called Furners, held at rent of 2s. 11$\frac{1}{2}$ d. These smaller rents were 'apportioned', meaning that they related to properties that had been split off from something larger. In 1634 the first property had title deeds going back to 1467-8. The second can be associated with a grant of 'Fanners' by the Earl of Abergavenny in 1484 to Richard and Joan Esterfield.[68] The title deed of 1484 gave Fanners a lowly copyhold status, but it nevertheless had to pay 'scutage'. This was a rent imposed on properties to excuse their tenants from any knightly duties. In 1624 the three properties were freehold and the largest of them was still said to be held by military service.

How should we interpret this complex early history on the ground? It seems certain, at least, from the 15th-century deeds, that after Shortfrith had been converted to agriculture Fanners' tenancy was redefined. It remained with the manor of Ditchling but its former duties of service were abolished. There is documentary evidence for three houses, Peppers, 'Cage Lott' and 'Bulls of Fanns' all lying on the north side of Shortfrith and all therefore possible candidates as a medieval dwelling attached to the hunt. Peppers, still standing, is perhaps less likely as it seems to have been an early independent freehold with title deeds dating back to c. 1250.[69] 'Cage Lott' was a house known to have stood there in 1585-6, while 'Bulls of Fanns', in the same vicinity, evolved later as one of the smaller Fanners holdings at an apportioned rent and is therefore the strongest candidate.

The owner of the largest holding perhaps built himself a brand new house on the site where Fanners stands today. This would not contradict local tradition which in 1887 remembered Fanners as 'an Elizabethan house'.[70] Five acres of the outlying land was tenanted by another individual, later to become the core of 'Furners' or Home Farm in Slugwash Lane (Chapter 4). The old 'village tradition' relating the name Fanners to 'fanion', a flag used in the Civil War period, is impossible because the name was in use at least three centuries before the Civil War.[71]

Plate 13. Fanners in its setting, 1994. Sited amid former common meadows, this was probably first chosen as a house site in the Tudor period, superseding an earlier 'Fanners' dwelling in the vicinity.

The ' Elizabethan house' was pulled down and rebuilt in the 1850s. Its hall was, according to Captain Attree, large enough for a horse and cart to drive into and turn round. An inscribed stone, rescued from the original house and now incorporated in the cellars of the present one, is dated 1604 TLW - presumably for Thomas and Walter Lucas, the then owner and heir apparent. Thomas Lucas, styled 'gentleman' in 1600, died in 1612 having settled Fanners and its 100 acres on his youngest son Walter during his lifetime.[72] In 1642, Walter left it to his son and heir, another Walter, who died and was buried in Wivelsfield in 1657, although his will describes him as of Cuckfield, where his main house lay. In this will he left his freehold lands in Wivelsfield to be sold to pay debts. The outlying lands were apparently sold and the house itself, now with only 30 acres, was leased to a Ditchling gentleman, John Honey.[73]

About 1672, Fanners was sold to Walter More who was described as 'of Fanners' in 1682. He sold on in 1694 to John Middleton, a London haberdasher and the future husband of his niece Elyatt. In 1695 Middleton leased Fanners to Nathaniel Coppard for seven years, describing the property as *"...his Messuage, Barn, Malthouse, Stable, Gardens, Orchards, Farm and Lands"* of 35 acres. In the lease John Middleton reserved for himself *"...the great Parlour, and the great Parlour Chamber, The Hall and Liberty of Baking in the Oven, And Brewing and Washing in the Washouse And also to sett Beere in the Roome under the Stairs together with free liberty to go come and return unto and from the said Messuage And the several Roomes Oven and Washouse"*.[74]

The medieval tenants of the house and 100 acres called Fanners had enjoyed the privilege of high-ranking service to their overlords and it is therefore no surprise to find their successors in the 17th century styled as 'gentlemen'. Outlying land was gradually sold off and in 1695 even the remaining core of 35 acres was leased out with part of the house. Medieval tenants of Fanners may have supervised the baking of bread and the brewing of drink for their visiting lords; but John Middleton, in insisting on the liberty to *"...sett Beere in the Roome under the stairs"*, simply had his own home comforts in mind.

Morehouse

was the estate of Walter of the More, a tax assessor for Wivelsfield in 1296 [75] and before that perhaps of Henry atte Moreland.[76]. The remains of a moat on the south and west sides of the house, now dried up and partly filled in, probably date from his period. Morehouse was a freehold of the Manor of Clayton, paying a rent of five broad, or barbed, arrows, later compounded to 5d. a year. In 1542 John At More had a house, barn and 100 acres called "the Morelonds", worth £4.[77]   The family's wealth increased steadily and in 1588 the two rooms that Walter at More's wife Elizabeth was to occupy, by right of her widow's bench, were amply furnished with colourful coverings and cushions, plentiful linen and bedclothes, as well as pewter and other utensils.[78]

Walter's son Francis was educated at Cambridge and greatly increased the size of the estate by buying land at Billingshurst and Pulborough. He also rented part of Keymer and Clayton sheepdown which, together with his house and lands at Standeane, gave him a sizable run of downland to complement his wealden holdings.[79] Secure income was, and is, a universal goal, and to this end, in 1600, he purchased the advowson and tithes of Wivelsfield, to which he added those of Standeane in Pyecombe. This tithe income raised the More family head and shoulders above the other land owners in the parish. (Table 1). Increased wealth and status allowed Francis to marry his sons and daughters higher up the social ladder. In his Will of 1616 Francis reflects this increase in wealth with mention of silver plate, glass, wainscot, books and armour.[80]

x. More House. Part of a print used by Captain Attree in SAC 35, showing the south side of More House in the mid-19th century. The older part of the house would have lain well away from the road on the right of this print. Compare Plate 9.

The fortune that the family enjoyed in the late 16th and early 17th centuries enabled them to rebuild their home and there are now no visible remains of a what must once have been a prestigious medieval house. A date stone of 1595, perhaps signifying a rebuild, was found in 1887 in the cellar and has since been lost. A local myth concerning the cellar says it connects underground with a cellar in Church Lane, perhaps that of Tapestry Cottage. Its conjectured use was in connection with smuggling or the Civil War. Morehouse was a lone Royalist house in a pro-Parliamentarian area.

The Mores played a strong, though frustrated hand in parish affairs as we have seen in Chapter 2. They were also prominent in the militia. Thomas More, son of Francis (d.1617), was appointed captain in the militia in 1626, a year when renewed fears about attacks on the South Coast led to an increase in muster practices. Ditchling Common was a muster ground for Lewes rape. [81] Training arrangements were the responsibility of the individual militia band captains. In 1626 three regular army sergeants were sent to Sussex from the Low Countries. The intent was to provide a short burst of intensive training for the national militia. Captains were expected to provide board and lodging as well as a horse for these sergeants. After this boost to potential military efficiency, pressure was maintained for the captains to continue to drill their bands. This they did for little reward other than the honour. The military demands upon the Mores in the Civil War, entrenched Royalists amid unsympathetic neighbours, were presumably met with determination. [82]

Captain More's eldest son, Elliot, had five children, four of whom died unmarried. Therefore, although More House passed to Major Thomas More who carried on the family's military tradition and also inherited the coat of arms, the property passed, through the female line via Elliot's youngest child, a daughter named Ellyatt, who married John Middleton in 1705. Their son, Thomas Middleton, inherited More House on the death of his uncle and, when Thomas died unmarried, it passed to his sister, Frances. She married her father's bailiff, Robert Day, late in her life. Unfortunately her three children died in infancy therefore she left More House to her "...great friend" John Fuller who owned the tanyard. [83] John Fuller had two sisters. Mary married Anthony Tanner, a Ditchling fellmonger, and Jane married his brother William, a carpenter. Both were quite well-to-do. Mary and Anthony's son, William, inherited the tanyard, and Jane and William's son, another William, became the owner of the More House estate, thus beginning the Tanner dynasty which by c.1840 held about 40% of the land and property in Wivelsfield. (Chapter 10.)

It is known that the west wing of More House was built by John Fuller for the Land Tax of 1780 mentions the "...new part of More House". Here his widow remained until her death over 30 years later. An attractive gazebo in one corner of the moat and extensive gardens enclosed by old brick walls were shown on the 1792 survey drawn for William Tanner, soon after he inherited the estate from his uncle. [84]

The More family still keeps a watchful eye open in Wivelsfield. A wooden head of one Mr More, now securely fixed to a wall, gazes out upon all who have presumed to succeed him.

xi. Carved head at More House.

iii. New opportunities

ESRO Ref. & Date	Otehall	Lunces	Theob. /Antye	Fanners	Cleve-water	More House	Hurst House	Manns	Colwell/ Slugwash
QR/E38 f.136 1637	45	?	?	78	48.5	106	56	(Several farms in this area of about £20)	
AMS/1767 Date 1728	74	42	46	43	57	253 (£100 tithes)	58	31.5 (Thos. Jenner)	
(Tithe values only are given in 1766. Multiply by a factor of 10)									
SHI 2028/ 17. 1766	8	6	5	6	7.5	16.5	7.5	(About £4 for farms in this area)	
Land Tax 1785	72	27.5	55	36.5	55	222 (£122 tithes)	50	37.5	?
Land Tax 1788	80.5	27.5	55	36.5	58	291 (£100 tithes)	50	37.5	
Land Tax 1798									60.5 Entry of J Cripps
Land Tax 1808	[73]*	27	56.5	24.5	54	Tanner Estates 408	49.5	37.5	60.5
Land Tax 1828	[66]	[32.5]	54.5	28	55	456.5	[54.5]	31	67.5
* Estates in square brackets have been purchased by the Tanner family and contribute to their total									

Table 1. Comparitive values of the main estates, 1637-1828. Annual land values expressed in pounds.

Wivelsfield provided its share of new opportunities over the years for old and new families to make their stand. The Hursts of Hurst House Farm, still living in the same place as their medieval forebears called 'Inthahurst', expanded into brickmaking in the 17th century and from then on took their stand among the wealthy of the parish (Table 1).

Richard Webb was described as a yeoman in 1702 when he bought Fanners whereas in 1685 he had been a 'husbandman'.[85] Taking their status from their property he, his son and his grandson after him were all styled 'gentleman'.[86] Richard had married Mary Martin, daughter of Richard Martin of Franklands in Keymer, a local non-conformist land owner. Their son, Martin Richard Webb, died in 1748, passing the property to his elder daughter Mary, who married Joseph Mercer of Isfield, gent. The success of such families in establishing a land base in the Weald in turn meant stablilty and a firm foundation for local non-conformist worship (Chapter 8).

Travel horizons had widened in the 18th and 19th centuries and families such as the Shirleys of Great Otehall had found a new sense of mission and opportunity in the rapidly growing colonial service. William Shirley succeeded to his mother's estate in 1718 when his grandfather John Godman died without a male heir. Shirley lived at Otehall where six of his eight children were born. Mr. Shirley was well liked, *"...a man charitably disposed, and of great hospitality, on which account he was much respected by his neighbours, with whom he lived on the most friendly terms"*.[87] On leaving Otehall to take up office in America, although he set out at midnight, his neighbours *"... testified their regard for him, as well as their regret at his departure, by accompanying him in a body to the boundary of the parish and there taking their leave of him"*.

William had been educated at Cambridge and destined for the Bar, in common with many gentry sons of this period. Sir Robert Walpole spotted his potential and appointed him Captain and Governor-in-Chief of the Province of Massachusets Bay. William Shirley was one of the Commissioners for setting the limits for Nova Scotia and other controverted rights in America and, in 1755, became General and Commander-in-Chief of H. M. Forces in North America. In 1758 he became Captain-General and Governor-in-Chief of the Bahamas Islands and in the following year became Lieutenant-General. In 1771 he died in Boston, where he had built Shirley House with bricks that he had sent out from England and which he then covered with boards. It was during this period that Selina, Countess of Huntingdon, leased Otehall as her country residence and a base for her preaching (Chapter 8).

William Shirley's heir Thomas was born in the Bahamas Islands and entered the army, becoming, in 1781, Governor of the Leeward Islands and Colonel of 91st Foot. Thomas became a baronet in 1786 and, in 1798, a General. He died and was buried at Bath in 1800, aged 74. Thomas Shirley had two sons both of whom went into the Navy. Only his second son, Sir William Warden Shirley, survived him, becoming second Baronet and owner of Otehall. He sold the manor in 1803 and died a bachelor in 1816.

The traffic was not all one way; men who had prospered abroad and wished to mark their success bought property in England. At Theobalds the vicissitudes of fortune had brought the formerly prosperous Attrees to the end of their line which in turn gave an opening to newcomer Captain W.H. Bacchus.[88] Bacchus was the younger son of a potter and glass seller. By the time he came of age his elder brother was running the family business, so William Henry, realising that he had few prospects there, bought a commission in the cavalry and made the army his career. After the Napoleonic Wars he was placed on half pay and turned to farming. Coming to live at Theobalds in 1823 with his wife and young son, he took his place among the gentry of Wivelsfield and it was here that his daughter was born although she was not baptised locally. By 1837, the slump in the wool industry made sheep farming in this country less attractive. At 55 he was rather old for an emigrant but he did have money to invest; £3800 from the sale of the estate to his brother-in-law Sir John G. Dodson of Hamsey, H. M. Advocate General.[89] Leaving his wife behind, Captain Bacchus and his children, Henry 16 and Eliza 9, set off for a new life in Australia. The journey to Van Dieman's Land took four months. Here he bought 2000 sheep before continuing to Port Philip and travelling inland towards Melbourne, to an area now known as Bacchus Marsh.[90]

John Marten Cripps the traveller and antiquary, whose seat was Stantons in East Chiltington, augmented his estate with new purchases in several nearby parishes, including Wivelsfield. Here he established a land base in the Slugwash Farm area, later expanding to Colwell. By 1828 he was the second largest owner in the parish.[91] His foothold in Wivelsfield was gained in an area of former commons and woods held of a variety of outside manors (Chapter 6). There was no strong local vested interest to hinder him. Cripps' estate broke up in 1885 on the death of his son Rush Marten Cripps and so allowed another new estate, Abbots Leigh, to make its debut.(Chapters 11, 14)

The general trend for 17th and 18th century families in Wivelsfield had been to expand estates when prosperity and opportunity allowed. Yet they also suffered from a common failure amongst the gentry of the period: that of not producing a male heir. Otehall, Theobalds and More House all passed down through the female line. In 1786 the childless John Fuller had bequeathed More house to his nephew William Tanner. In 1803 the childless William Warden Shirley sold Otehall to his cousin William Tanner, of the tanyard, then styled 'gentleman', and his son Anthony. When Warden Sergison died childless in 1811 Anthony Tanner, William's son, bought the Cleavewater/Franklands estate for £6,442.[92]   Anthony died in 1832 owing a considerable amount of money and the estate had to be sold, but the dynasty was firm. A further member of the family, Jane Tanner of More House, was the purchaser and the Tanners were secure, for a while, as Wivelsfield's first family.

Colwell about 1440, Clearwaters before 1560, Lockstrood 1560s, South Slugwash before 1590, Manns about 1600; Strood and Shoulders as yet undated.[1] There is also Hursthouse farm, or Asylum farm which was built with solid brick walls, stone window surrounds and a Horsham stone roof. A stone over the main door shows the date 1660.

Six former farmhouses of medieval or earlier origin [2] have completely disappeared:- Berth, Blackmores, Franklands Farm, Hole, North Hole and Scrases Farm.   Another five sites assumed to have medieval or earlier origins have been rebuilt, most of them in the 18th to the 20th century:- Bankside, Botches, Little Otehall, Rogers and Townings. Some of them may still contain parts of their earlier construction.   One or two farms evolved through new land-colonisation following the enclosure of common meadows in the 17th century (Chapter 6.) Furners in Slugwash Lane thus evolved into the freehold known as South Slugwash and is now Home Farm, while North Slugwash (Meadowlands) was created at a similar time. In the north of the parish North Colwell may have had a house there in 1637.[3] South of the Green, on what was part of the former Wivelsfield Common, the house at Whitebreads (Green Park Farm) might still contain its 17th century core and that at Coldharbour was re-built in Victorian times.

Each farm, varying from 11 to 50 acres, had a homestead with its own well, at least one barn, a barnyard and a pond for watering the animals. There was usually a garden and an orchard as well as the arable, pasture and meadowland, the latter near a stream if possible for good hay-making and grazing. The woods, shaws and coppices within the bounds of the farm, supplied 'free' timber for repair of buildings, and for fences and fuel. Unless some financial arrangement had been agreed with the lord of their manor the farmers were not allowed to sell wood for profit, nor any of their surplus crops or manure.[4] In practise, however, surplus was commonly sold in exchange for a small fine to the lord's steward, hay being the commonest cash crop from this area of the Weald.[5] It was a system designed for recycling the wealth of the soil and for subsistence rather than profit.   Some farmers such as John Dancy at Clearwaters in the 1770s, were craftsmen in their own right. Others would rely on local cottagers to produce tools and utensils, but between them all, Wivelsfield's local population was largely self-sufficient.

Re-cycling and conservation was the key to life inside the farmhouse as well as without. There was little waste. Beds, bed linen, household goods and clothes were lovingly handed down to the next generation, as were the favourite animals whose milk, fleece or hides would provide that extra source of comfort or income, to make life easier. Home produce was an essential part of the life style so that a spinning wheel, a dairy and a brewhouse would be found in every farmhouse.   In time the wealthier farmers began to accumulate some of the items we take for granted today, such as mirrors and clocks.

John Hother was the farmer at Home Farm in the 1590s, then known as Furners (Plate 19).[6] Lying in Slugwash Lane and described as one virgate, it had been formed from the outlying parts of Fanners. Hother's will, made a few years before he died in 1596, shows something of the life-style of a middling yeoman of the period.[7] The 'dwelling house' with the barns stables and other buildings were left for his wife for life together with the farm land. In return she was enjoined to bring up the children until they were 16 years, a usual and necessary provision in an age when men often died before they were 50 and there was no educational or welfare provision for children if a family failed in its duty. An aged mother was also entitled to her dues, to the effect that Hother's wife was excluded from *"all the East Meads which my mother Emmy Avery now holdeth as her jointure."* His beneficiaries were reminded of the customary conditions of tenure and were *"not to fell or top any oaks or beech trees on the Furners or Braxspere land except for repairs or fuel."* He must have owned a flock of sheep as he left one ewe and a lamb to each of his four younger sons and two daughters. There was also £10 apiece when they each attained 21 years, or earlier if the daughters married. His eldest son Thomas would inherit the farm on his mother's death, but in the mean time he was to have the farm vats, malt mill and furnace.

It is clear, therefore, that farmers such as John Hother had moved away from mere subsistence and had been able to put something by for a rainy day. There was money for the younger children and profit, perhaps in hops, to be made from the malt mill and furnace. Standards of comfort inside the house would have been low, by modern comparison, and the kitchen would still have been the only sitting room. Even so, Hother had perhaps used some of his surplus profit to improve his home. The efforts of farmers such as John Hother is a tale told in timber, stone, brick and tile, scattered around the parish and still there for us to read.

ii. Clearwaters

In the medieval period all the lands in the valley where the headwaters of the Ouse part from those of the Adur were all known as 'at Clevewater'; but in time this was realised to be confusing and the westernmost farm, firmly set on the banks of the Adur, came to be known as Clearwaters, to distinguish it from Cleavewater (See Chapter 3) to the east. It is thus impossible to say which of the two farms was home to the taxpayer *"Agnes of Clevewater in 1327."*

Clearwaters was a small customary holding of 24 acres, held of Ditchling manor and, as we saw in Chapter 1, its copyhold tenant was liable to service as reeve of the manor one year in every eight. It lay adjacent to Valebridge Common in Keymer but its rights of common were not on Valebridge but on Lunces common to the east. The earliest tenant to whom we can put a name was Roger Dancy, tenant in 1563.[8] Roger, aged 76 in 1593, was one of the witnesses in the Lockstrood tithe dispute discussed in Chapter 2.

xii. Clearwaters Farmhouse, late 1500's, showing the oven.

The original timber-framed house of three and a half bays would appear to have been built in the mid 1500s, with a smoke bay into which a chimney, of early type, thin bricks, was inserted later. This is shown by the sooted rafters which are not framed round the chimney stack. Before entering the house one sees the external curve of a fine brick-built oven and inside the original opening. A cast-iron fireback dated 1657, bearing the initials CAR has been cemented into the kitchen hearth but they appear unrelated to any known owner or tenant. The small panel framing, with heavy mid-rails and wattle and daub infill remains on the north west elevation but the other walls are now covered by tile hanging above a brick base. The mortices for diamond shaped window mullions show under the main beam in the kitchen, where it has been extended. A dining room with a bedroom above it, and a cellar beneath, was built on the south side making a T-shaped plan, with brick walls in Flemish bond of the 18th to the early 19th century. This date is confirmed, as the building was shown on the Tithe map as being this shape.[9]

There is a four-bay barn of very similar construction to that at Rogers, a nearby farm. The main difference is in the roof shape, that at Rogers being fully hipped, while that at Clearwaters has one half-hip and one gable end. Here the grooved posts for holding the threshing boards are still at one entrance and the present owners remember that the original timber threshing floor was there when they acquired the farm.

The Dancy family remained the copyholders of Clearwaters for about 300 years though often, when the heir was under age, it was sub-let. Thus in 1612 Simon Warden, yeoman, held it on a seven-year lease and when he died in 1617, by his will he left to his "...*loving wife four milche Kyne* [cows] *two young Bullocks sixteen sheep one white mare three Hogs with all the corn and hay in the barns*".[10]

When Thomas Dancy died in 1611, Richard his youngest son was only four years old. Three years later his mother Margery died and in her short will dated 1614 was included the bequest "... *Edmund Gillam shall have one black Cow with the white face*". Margery was known as Widow Dancy, while her sister, who had made her will in the previous month, was Widow Dane. They were the daughters of Edmund Nutley of Keymer, who by his will of 1591, left "...*to Margery ... 12 lbs of wooll and one pair of sheets*" and "*To Eden my daughter, wife of John Dane £5 and one pair of sheets*".[11] The latter left money legacies to the children of her two brothers, those of her two sisters and other members of the family, about £40 in all. She bequeathed her possessions as follows ... to Richard Dancy (nephew) "...*one featherbed, one chaffebed with joyned bedsteddle with all other commodities thereto belonging one great joyned chest .... to John Dancy* [nephew] *two pieces of pewter and a dozen of spoons five pairs of hempen sheets and one great chest ... to Elenor Showldar one russett petticoat and a green wastcote one linse woolsie apron, one neckecha or crosscosclothe and five shillings of money*".[12]

John Dancy, the tenant who died in 1774, was a carpenter. His youngest son, Josiah, inherited and paid "...*a horse coloured black worth £2 2s*" as his heriot. Ten years later Josiah obtained a licence from the reeve, John Attree, "...*to cut 14 oak trees about 7 loads for necessary repairs and not otherwise*". In 1794 a licence was granted to cut timber for sale - "...*40 oaks, one beech and one ash*".[13] In such cases the tenant was only allowed to keep half the profits and the lord of the Manor had the rest.

After Josiah's death and that of his second wife Sarah, there was a protracted dispute between two claimants for the copyhold tenure. One, John Dancy yeoman of Worth, presented at court the probate of his uncle's will, naming him as the heir and another nephew, William Dancy of Worth, a millwright, claimed entitlement by manorial custom of borough English, as the youngest son of Joseph Dancy, who was the youngest brother of Josiah. Eventually the court settled in favour of John Dancy in accordance with the will and not by the custom of the manor.[14]

iii. Rogers and the Berth

As in the case of Clearwaters, Rogers had certain rights on Lunces Common as a farm of about 18 acres held copyhold of the manor of Ditchling. The holding was originally 24 acres known as "parcel of Cleavewater" and "Hilland", but the north part, on Fox Hill developed separately as Scrases farm.[15] The rent for the 24 acres at 1d. per acre was much less than that paid for Clearwaters and shows that it was a newer holding, probably granted out in the 13th or 14th century by the Lord of Ditchling. The lower rents reflected the fact that new farmers had much clearance and soil-improvement to attend to in the initial stages.

Situated in the Adur valley Rogers farm had good potential to develop its meadow land. In 1599 its tenant, John Scrase, obtained a 'licence to cart', that is, to sell, 30 loads of hay. A few years later he paid 2s. to cart stones from the waste of Lunsford (Lunces Common). These may have been for use on his own premises, or again, perhaps to sell. When he died in 1608 the tenancy included a barn, which is almost certainly the four-bay structure standing today. It has been stripped to the timber-framing, the roof rafters of which are supported on clasped purlins with queen struts which must date it from the early 1600s. By 1610 a messuage was also included in the manor Records. The tenancy descended by the female line until in 1675 it came to Thomas Rogers, hence the present name, though in the records it was called Hollands or late-Scrases. He paid 4d. for a licence to pollard four trees.[16]

In the early 1700s, John Attree, a yeoman farmer, was the tenant. He also farmed the Berth, for which he is mentioned in the Church marks. As he shared a number of farm implements with Richard Button of Townings it is most likely that he and his wife Susan and their two daughters lived at the Berth, which lay opposite Townings at the crest of the 'long ridge' in Slugwash Lane. When he died in 1721, the heriot of the best beast, a cow, was valued at £10 10s. 0d.[17] According to the inventory taken at that time he owned four cows, two young heifers, one mare, one sow, two pigs and two 'shoots' or young hogs valued at £27 5s. 0d. Hay, wheat and oats were in the barns, threshed and unthreshed, with a bag of hops, hop-poles in the hop garden and faggots in the coppice.

xiii. Townings and the Berth, _circa_ 1900, from an old photograph.

In 1653 the Berth was a messuage with barns, stalls, stables, malt house and 24 acres of land.[18] The house in which the Attrees lived was a two storey house with a hall, kitchen, back room, bake house, milk house and brew house on the ground floor and three rooms over, plus a garret. The total value of the estate, as appraised by Thomas Pilbeame and Walter Vinall, was £100 19s. 6d.[19]

Singly, Rogers and the Berth were too small to be viable; but together, river valley and hill ridge, they were a balanced agricultural holding. Their combination recreated an early, Saxon order of land holding, which had since been lost. They remained with the descendants of John Attree until the beginning of the 19th century when the Berth was bought up by the Tanner family.

iv Lockstrood

Lockstrood was originally an area of 'strood', meaning 'green' and the full name arises out of association with a 15th-16th century family called Lok. It appears there were two properties there from around the last quarter of the 15th century, later merged. One timber-framed house survives today.

John At Ree and his wife Joan held a freehold property in Wivelsfield called Cokemanns in 1469, and in 1491 Joan, by then a widow, left it to their son John. [20] It is likely that this property remained with the Attree family for in 1575 John Attree was described as "of Loxtrode" on the day of his wedding to Agnes Wymarke. On architectural evidence the present timber-framed house was built about that time. In 1608, on the death of John At Ree, the property passed to his son John who was recorded in 1624 as tenant of a croft and four acres of freehold land called 'Lockstroode' held at 20d. annual rent. However, it was recorded as being in Ditchling parish, not Wivelsfield, a confusion perhaps still ongoing since the Lockstrood tithe dispute (Chapter 2). [21]

The small panel box-framing, with wattle and daub infill above a later brick base, is still visible on the north elevation. There is a later outshot to the south with modern additions on the east. The house was built with two storeys each divided into two rooms; an attic above is reached by a trap-door, the original wooden latch of which remains in place. The massive side purlins, strengthened by wind braces and one collar, support a tile-covered roof with gable ends. At one end, integral with the house, a large chimney stack built upon three courses of rough sandstone blocks, serves two hearths, one on each floor.

There is a well outside, together with a small bothy, later outbuildings and a barn, which was built about the same time as that at Rogers. The Lockstrood barn has three bays with also one side aisle and an end aisle, of which the hipped roof continues in a cat-slide to form a covered area for farm carts and implements. Other than the house, the barn was the most important and often the only building on the farm and thus was put to several uses such as the storage of grain and for threshing it on the floor in the draught from the two opposite doors. Part of the barn could be partitioned off to make stalls for cattle. Its most recent use has been as a cricket pavilion when George Cox, a Sussex County player, owned the house in this century. [22]

xiv. Lockstrood barn, *circa* 1600.

There was another cottage adjacent. In 1514 this was granted out as a freehold by the lord of Ditchling manor to John Mascall and his son Richard, described as "...a parcel of land called Westerowde", probably meaning 'west strood' as opposed to other areas of green away to the east. [23] The original grant may have been from the Lord's own land in the area but the Mascalls soon encroached on to Ditchling common and invoked the wrath of the local commoners. (See Chapter 6). By 1526 it was held by John Lok, who succeeded his father Thomas but by 1550 the tenement, barn, garden and two acres were in the occupation of Thomas Virgo. [24] It is likely to have been the dwelling occupied by Richard Shouswell, the curate of Wivelsfield from 1593-7. When it was sold in 1599 to William Page, of Newick, glover, for £37 it was described as abutting the land of John Attree on the east. [25] The remains of this cottage have been found in the field behind Lockstrood. The present 'Common Cottage' is a modern building lying a little further to the north.

Neither of these properties could properly qualify as a farm. They were both 'cottages', on land taken from the waste in classic Wealden fashion. However, also in good Wealden tradition, more land was added when it became available. John Turner, its occupant prior to 1713, had wheat, hay and oats, some in Lockstrood Barn and some on the ground, and a hop garden. His livestock numbered three horses and two colts, four cows, three oxen and 24 sheep. [26] In his shop in Church Lane (see Chapter 5) he sold hop poles. Another John Turner, perhaps a son, had succeeded him at Lockstrood by 1728. In that year the farm was valued at £10, the same as Bankside, an adjacent farm west of the main road. [27] Lockstrood's extra land lay west of the B2112 and was probably gained through enclosure of former commons. The enclosure possibly happened in Attree's time, giving him new assets with which to build his house.

In 1736 the two separate rents of 20d. and 2s. 6d. for Lockstrood were still being paid to Ditchling manor. For the rest of the century it was occupied by tenant farmers, the owners living outside the parish. However, by 1818 Lockstrood was once again owned and occupied by the Attree family, this time by James Attree who had been born and married in Ardingly. After his death, his son Thomas became a tenant farmer as the property was bought before 1828 by Richard Tanner to add to his More House estate. In 1840 it had 28 acres. [28]

v. Manns

On the eastern side of the parish, Manns farm was in the tenure of the Jenner family for about 300 years. Edward Gynner (Jenner) was the copyhold tenant of Manns prior to his death in 1557, paying 3 shillings, and an additional 12d. in lieu of the former customary payment of a cock and three days work at Stanmer at harvest time each year. He was succeeded by his youngest son Stephen who was still tenant in 1605. [29] He had been born in Ditchling and by 1611 was aged 64 and had lived in Wivelsfield for 38 years. [30] By 1632 his widow Agnes and son Henry had succeeded to Manns and other small properties in the vicinity and to a sizeable share, 23 acres, of the newly-enclosed common. [31]

The house that they lived in had been built as an open hall of two-bays with a wider two-storey service bay, under a steep pitched roof that originally would have been thatched. The small panel-framing with a deep middle rail still shows on the north elevation. The hall was floored over and a chimney inserted in the early 1600s, as by the time of the Hearth Tax in 1662 Thomas Jenner paid duty on four hearths.[32] Over the years a wide outshot was added at the back, another bay with a cellar at one end and at the other end a cow-house, later a dairy, which was entered from within the house. Other outbuildings are also shown on the 1829 map of the manor when Manns was held by the executors of Philip Jenner and was described as 51 acres, plus the common land and other lands which the family had acquired, making a total of 150 acres.[33] Two members of the Jenner family were churchwardens, Thomas, whose slab tomb to the north west of the church is dated 1681 and another Thomas whose name appears in the church burial registers for 1754.

Plate 14. Manns and the old 'strood' green. The grassy area in the foreground is part of the old green once enjoyed by the 'Stanmer' hamlet.

vi. Strood farm

Situated just north of Manns (Plate 27) this was called Neilands in the earlier records. It was the home of Thomas Pyltebeme (Pilbeam) in 1460 and a person of the same name in 1493 who paid 5s. annual rent for his 100 acres.[34] As in the case of Manns farm, the tenant of Strood had to pay an extra 12d. to absolve him from three days harvest work at Stanmer. Thomas Pilbeam was tenant in 1605. In 1633 his successor Edward Pilbeam paid an extra 8d. for his newly-gained 35 acres of common land.[35] A Mr Pilbim appears on the list of Church Marks for 1697. Of the few inventories, mostly early 18th century, existing for Wivelsfield, the two wealthiest farmers were Richard Pilbeam who died in 1722, leaving an estate valued at £119 6s. 5d. and John Attree of Rogers and the Berth (above). Pilbeam's stock of two sheats and two hogs at £5 10s. was small by comparison with Attree. His home, fully described with room furnishings, was perhaps more opulent.[36]

xv. Part of the inventory of R. Pilbeam of Strood.

Downstairs there was a parlour with a table, nine chairs and a pair of andirons (indicating a hearth), a kitchen, a back room, a drinks room and a buttery. The kitchen goods were valued at £12 17s. and with three tables, two forms, seven chairs, the usual cooking utensils, he owned a clock, a dresser, a spinning wheel, a lanthorn as well as four candlesticks, two window curtains (the only mention found of these in any Wivelsfield inventory), two coffee pots and a parcel of books. In the four rooms upstairs, together with two feather beds and steddles complete with curtains and belongings, he had chests, two tables, two glasses (mirrors), a cord mat, a close stool (commode), a tea kettle, eight silver spoons and six silver teaspoons.   In the back chamber he stored six pairs of sheets, two dozen napkins, six table cloths and one dozen towels in a chest, which together with a bed were valued at £7. In the outbuildings there were a brew house, a milk house, a malt house and a bake house in which was a 'bunting hutch' or food safe.   There was also a granary, so that he had no need to store his grain upstairs in the house as was the usual custom.   There was a barn containing unthreshed oats and wheat and a "wean house" for the wain or wagon; a dung cart, two barrows, three old ploughs and a lead lip (for sowing seed).   The two ricks of hay were valued at £15, wheat on the ground (in December) £3 and old hop poles in the garden.   There were small debts amounting to £12.

The Pilbeams owned Strood until the 1760s, after which it passed to Mr. Garton. Before 1808 Miss Jenny Tanner of Morehouse had bought Strood and rented it to a tenant farmer.

viii. South Colwell

South Colwell, which included Northland Wood, now a housing estate in Haywards Heath, was an outlying copyhold tenement of the Manor of Middleton, near Westmeston. It may be assumed that the farm site was inhabited by 1296 when the king's tax was paid by one Robert of Kolewell. He was followed in 1327 by Isabel and John of Colewelle while in 1379 Thomas Colwelle paid his poll tax.[37]

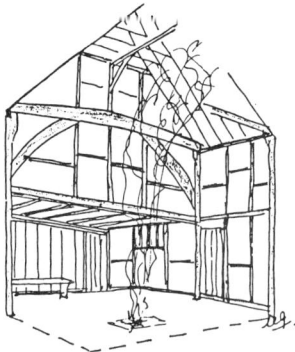

xvi. The smoke bay at South Colwell, *circa* 1560.

The present timber-framed building, of small panel type, dates from not later than 1450 judging by the simple style of the dais beam moulding. The house was built as a two-bay open hall with a service bay which shows some of the original, very heavy floor joists, and another bay was added to the other end at a much later date. Heavy posts with checked rootstocks and enormous braces support the 12-inch deep, cambered tie-beam across the hall, with a tall crown post above. This forms part of the later stud framing for a wattle and daub partition, which extends to about seven feet above the ground floor, making this into a smoke-bay, which was the earliest method of channelling the smoke from the open hearth out of the hall. At the same time in the 1550s, a floor was inserted across half of the hall.

The next improvement in the 1600s was to build, inside the smoke bay, a brick chimney stack with a salt cupboard in the inglenook and a second hearth in the room above. Three early windows, two now walled up, but all having two diamond-shaped mullions would have been unglazed. The steep pitch of about 51 degrees suggests that the roof was originally thatched. Externally the house now has a tiled roof and tile-hung walls above brickwork.

A fascinating set of bills tell a 20-year story of upkeep and repair from 1706 until 1725. [38] In 1706-7 South Colwell was in the hands of absentee owners. Its farmer was Edward Carter, tenant to Edward Lewis of Capel, Surrey. In that year Carter paid for two loads of straw and for a thatcher who laid six squares of roofing. Payment was also made for 1,000 tiles and 300 bricks, suggesting that part of the timber-framing was then tile-hung. There are bills for glazing some of the windows. Other work done at the time was pitching the stable, mending the barn walls and making a new oven. In 1716 damage, which had been caused by high winds, had to be repaired (Illustration xxxv). Straw was supplied for two days thatching and another 400 tiles, lime and in addition hair bought from Mr Burt, the tanner, were required. The daub for wattle infill panels was made from clay, cow dung and hair from the red Sussex cattle. By 1723-4 Nicholas Vinall was the tenant and he paid Benjamin Dobson with his three assistants, for mason's work and also for some more tiling, glazing and thatching.

Plate 15. South Colwell *circa* 1956.

In 1758 Mr. William Marten of New Close in Keymer bought South Colwell. On his death he left it to his nephew John Marten who was in possession in 1788.[39] By 1797 the farm of 69 acres and 45 acres of woodland was inherited by the latter's great-nephew, John Marten Cripps, together with 149 acres of North Slugwash which also included a large area of woodland. By 1819 his whole estate, in several parishes, totalled about 3,000 acres.[40]

Extra partitions and a staircase were added in the 19th century but the house remained basically the same until it was sold in 1956 as Lot 4 of the Abbots Leigh Estate. After this it was so sympathetically extended that it is difficult to detect the modern addition.

ix. Their worldly wealth

In 1637, apart from the larger estates looked at in Chapter 3, there were 51 land holders in Wivelsfield.[41] Twenty nine of these held land that was worth £5 a year or less and would have supplemented their income by crafts and trades. Their number included Thomas Scrace at £4 and John Scrace at £3 10s. who were perhaps the farmers of Rogers and Hilland. Only three of Wivelsfield's farmers, Edward Weller, Thomas Pierce and Henry Jenner had land worth more than £20 a year and these all seem to be from the 'Stanmer' hamlet whose wealth had been boosted by their common enclosure. Henry Jenner of Manns farm was worth £25 in land and he had built a (wind)mill on his allotment from the common. The remaining 19 local farmers had land worth between £5-£15 a year. Richard Dancye, for instance, at Clearwaters, was valued at £9. England's lesser yeomen were well represented in Wivelsfield with 30 of the landholders occupying their own lands and only 21 tenant farmers in the parish.

In the 18th century the smaller farmers maintained a solid land base in the parish despite the expansionary policy of some of the larger estates. In 1728 there were 45 independent landholders and seven persons owning a house only. Between them they owned nearly half the rateable land-value of the parish. In 1785 the number of smaller landowners remained the same at 45 but only nine of them occupied their own land. There were 22 tenant farmers, some of whom rented more than one farm from different owners. Houses were not always listed, but of those that were, only four were owner-occupied.

In 1818, apart from the larger estates, there were 45 further landholders in Wivelsfield. Nine were owner-occupiers of houses without land, but the remaining 36 were independent landholders. Twenty two of these were occupying their own land.[42] Although the Tanner family were by then strengthening their hold, the independent small farmer still played a viable part in the economy of the parish.

Their personal wealth, standard of living and farming lifestyle can be judged from their probate inventories. In 1728 Edward Carter had a mare, bridle and saddle valued at £2 2s.0d.; £3 3s.0d. was owing to him from Thomas Young for a cow and a further £2 2s.0d due making his total possessions and money amount to £49 7s. 0d.[43] His farm, Bankside, was valued at £10 a year in 1728 and he, or another person of the same name had an additional holding worth £2.[44]

At Whitebreads, a farm of about 11 acres (now Green Park Farm), John Walls had more livestock, three cows, one mare and a sow valued at £11: two harrows and a plough at £1 which together with his household goods made a total value of £29 5s. 0d.[45] According to his will made in 1730 the copyhold tenement of Whitebreads was to pass to his wife Elizabeth (nee Whitebread) and after her death to their son Joseph, who was charged with the payment of £30 each to his sisters Elizabeth, wife of William Burgess and Philadelphia. If Joseph refused to pay this they could claim the money from the rents and profits of the copyhold land. John Walls' lands were valued at £6 in 1728. He also held a copyhold cottage and lands called Jeffreys, which after his wife's death, were to pass to his daughter Sarah Walls.[46]

Thomas Geale, who died in 1719, was a 'husbandman' whose goods amounted to only £28 10s. 0d, whereas another husbandman, John Hilton, had goods valued at £25 7s. 0d. but he held securities of £157.[47] The inventory of one Daniel Pannett showed his chattels were valued at only £13 2s. 0d. in 1730 but £25 was due to him on a bill. He owned two pigs and a grindstone valued at 16s. and also had beans, peas, cabbage and faggots worth 10s. 0d.[48]

The only 19th century inventory for Wivelsfield is that of George Hemsley who was the owner/occupier of North Hole Farm. This was originally part of the 'Stanmer' hamlet and was also known as 'Sherries' after the Shereve (Sheriff) family who had lived in the hamlet since medieval times.[49] It consisted of a messuage, barn and ten acres, for which was owed the annual rent of 1s.8d. He also paid an additional 1s. in lieu of a rent of two hens, signifying a very early contract between North Hole and the lord of the manor. Hemsley also held two more fields of $13\frac{1}{2}$ acres and his entire land holding was valued at £10 in 1818.[50] The farm house still existed in 1910 but the site is now deserted.[51]

George Hemsley was living at North Hole Farm in 1818 and was still there at his death in 1835 aged 65. The inventory then taken gives a picture of the traditional Sussex farmer of the period. He owned the following wearing apparel:- *"three round frocks, one pair of boots, one pair of shoes, one hat, two pairs of small clothes, three shirts, three pairs of hose, three waistcoats, one coat, one jacket and sundry hankerchiefs"*. He had about $9\frac{1}{2}$ acres, growing 5 acres of oats, 3 acres of wheat and $1\frac{1}{2}$ acres of peas and he grazed one cow. The farm

most of them sprung up in the 16th and 17th centuries.   Estate improvements and the new wealthier lifestyle of the rising Wealden gentry brought new opportunities lower down the social ladder. For example, Richard Illman, a cottager living at Birch Green in 1597, worked as a 'stone healer'.[3] There was evidently work to be found locally in replacing thatched roofs with stone, and this in turn enabled him to acquire his own cottage.

The problem of population growth without the means of support was addressed during the Tudor period by a series of Acts aimed at ensuring each rural family had enough land with which to support itself.[4] Cottages had to have at least four acres. But the Acts were ignored and cottages continued to be erected illegally on commons and wayside wastes with inadequate amounts of land attached. In the clay Weald around Wivelsfield it was normal in the 16th and early 17th century for a new cottage to have about half an acre of land. The same cottage in the early 19th century, however, would often be found to contain two acres or more. Fences had gradually been pushed out in the intervening period.

Locations such as Church Lane provided little opportunity for expansion and the plots remained small. In other areas, such as Jefferies Green, or at Birch Green in the north of the parish, there was opportunity for accretions and additions, gradually reducing the greens down to tiny remnants (Chapter 6). Population pressure does not seem to have been a great problem in Wivelsfield at first, but was clearly becoming a worry by 1660, some 30 years after the last-remaining large common had been enclosed. John Faulkner, a weaver, of 'Jenners' sold "...*a cottage and a little peece of land late taken out of Wilsfild common*" to one Richard Wickham "... *upon condition that the said Richard Wickham shall not surrender nor convey the same nor any part of it to any person that shall dwell out of the parish of Wilsfeld*".[5]

Much poverty existed in Wealden parishes, and can be measured in the 17th and 18th centuries by size of the poor rates. Wivelsfield's place in the scale of poverty will be discussed in Chapter 7. Compared with some of its neighbours the parish was reasonably well off, but there was nevertheless an underclass for whom we have few names and of whom we know little. For instance, saving an entry in the parish register in 1609 we know nothing about "...*Gorge the well dygar...bureyed the xix of desembar*".[6]

The craftsmen with whom the present chapter is concerned were usually ratepayers, though their land was often minimal and, in 1637, valued at only £1 or £2 a year.[7] To be called 'carpenter' or 'wheelwright' presupposed that they had mastered their trade, or at least owned their own cottage and workshop. In the more industrial concerns, such as tanning and brick making, only the site manager or the farmer-employer was credited with the trade to his name.[8] The rest of the workers, though skilled, were technically labourers. Others in the parish, equally skilled in various aspects of what we should now call 'country crafts' such as hedge laying, hurdle making or charcoal burning, lived out in the woods, rented rooms in cottages or were billeted in farmers' hay-lofts. Often working at different tasks round the seasons they owned no property and rarely left any record of their goods and chattels.

xviii. Excerpt from the 1637 revaluation.

By contrast, those whose lives we glimpse in this and the previous chapter, through the inventories of their goods, occupied roughly the same place in society as the average householder today. Though exact comparisons are impossible, if we multiply the values of their goods by 1000, we start to comprehend their modern equivalent. John Walls, for example, whose total worth was £29 5s., had "... *One feather Bed Stedle Curtains and Healing* [its roof] *all as he stands -- £1 10s. 0d.*" The modern equivalent of such a four-poster, fully equipped, would be at least £1,000.   Straight comparisons are impossible because our range of goods and dependencies are different, but an average rate-paying household today will contain around £20,000 of goods.   The rate-paying cottager of the early 18th century had about £20 worth of goods, over and above the value of his house and land. He was not rich, but neither was he poor.

The cottager with land produced the same range of food as did the farmers, but on a smaller scale.   On his 'croft' or small field the cottager grew, for his own use, crops such as corn, oats, pease, hops and flax.   In his garden he grew roots, fruit, vegetables and herbs. On his plot of land he would also graze an animal or two, to provide milk, meat, wool and skins. In the Wivelsfield area of the Weald he would usually exercise rights of pasture on the local commons, to supplement the grazing, though legally he was not always entitled to such rights. He usually owned a pig and, when it was killed, he cured it in order to preserve it. The offal was often shared with the neighbours. Bees were kept for honey which was the main sweetner used before 1750 when beet began to be grown for sugar. Cane sugar, cultivated in foreign countries, was far too expensive for all but the gentry.

The poorer craftsmen would have diversified by doing seasonal work; bark-stripping for the tanning industry, coppicing, hedging, ditching, haymaking and harvesting for the local farmers. Their wives and children would have helped. Documentary evidence for women's work rarely appears, but in a collection of bills paid by Richard Webb of Fanners in July 1745 the following entry was included:-

"...pd. to Goody Bull for 17 & a ½ [days] *a haying & half a Day a Winnowing -- 9s. 0d.; Then pd. to her Daughter Elizabeth for 17 & a ½ a haying --4s. 4¹/₂d.; Then pd. to her Daughter Ann for 15 & a ½ a haying -- 2s. 7d.; Goody Bull and her Daughters begun Hay. the 8th and Ended the 31st and Then Ended Carrying"* [9]

Payment for goods supplied or for work done was often in kind with little money changing hands. For example, the miller would keep a bushel or so of the farmer's corn as his payment for grinding the remainder into flour. This form of barter was illustrated in 1745 by John Parsons' bill to Richard Webb of Fanners. Parsons was the local innkeeper but he also worked as a shoemaker. From July 16th to September 4th he had 4 separate bushels of wheat at 2s. 6d. per bushel totalling 10 shillings from Mr. Webb. Richard Webb's accounts indicates how he was paid:-

"...11th September Recd. ye full Contents of this Bill. Then pd. to him for a payer of pomp shoes 3s. 6d. in money 2s. 6d. and in work 4s. 0d." [type unspecified].[10]

Mr. Parsons had paid for his wheat with a pair of shoes, money and work.

ii. Craftsmen's cottages

Before the 16th century small houses or cottages were built to last for only two or three generations. Flimsy, timber-framed structures with wattle and daub infilling and thatched roofs, they were often erected by the occupier himself. From the second half of the 16th century onwards they began to be better built and in Wivelsfield some of these have survived until today, though altered and extended over the years. For example, near the Green are Baldings, Jenners and Oak Cottages. Similar houses have disappeared completely as, for instance the old parish poor house on Lunces Hill and 'Bulls of Fanns' in Slugwash Lane, next to Baldings. Others, such as Dumbrells and Stream cottage, were rebuilt in the 19th century.

The life-styles, and therefore the houses, of 17th and 18th-century craftsmen were essentially the same as the small rural farmers.[11] The main living room was the kitchen, with its large fireplace for cooking and a bread oven to one side. Subsidiary rooms were the milk house or dairy, the brew house and/or drinks room where barrels were stored. There was sometimes a wash house, another store room or back room in an outshot, that is under a lean-to roof at the back of the house. A very steep, ladder-like staircase gave access to the rooms upstairs which were called chambers after the room beneath, such as the kitchen chamber or milk house chamber. In earlier days there were no sitting rooms or parlours, as there was little time for leisure activities, but by the 18th century John Coleman, a shopkeeper, had a parlour, in common with the local farmers.

Typical furnishings for properties of this type in the 1700s are shown by contemporary inventories and would have included:- in the kitchen several chairs and a table, a settle, pewter dishes, bowls, spoons and candlesticks; pot-hangers or a jack, bellows and andirons, iron cooking utensils, an iron kettle and tubs. Fifty per cent of the households for which inventories exist had a clock. There were no floor coverings as we know them, only rushes laid on bare earth or brick surfaces. Upstairs the main items were feather and chaff beds with steddles. These had healings (canopies) and curtains to keep out the draughts and, for warmth, blankets and coverlets. There were chests for storage of sheets, pillowcoats, napkins and the few spare clothes which they had. Any valuables such as silver spoons were kept in the main chamber, which was usually above the kitchen and thus the warmest upstairs room. Many folk had either a woollen or a linen spinning-wheel, sometimes kept upstairs but often in the kitchen for instant use.

The cottages in Church Lane were not wayside encroachments like so many in this part of the Weald but were developed on land provided by the Otehall estate. Four fine timber-framed houses, two on either side of the churchyard, were erected in the period 1560-1675 and still exist today. Each appears to have been built originally as one house and has since been divided into two dwellings. There is no apparent evidence of a medieval community in the vicinity of the Church.

**Tapestry and
Wren cottages**

Tapestry and Wren cottages, on the east side of the churchyard, are the oldest remaining pair in Church Lane and were built on land granted out of the Otehall estate. The plan was L-shaped with a large elaborately-stepped brick chimney stack for the ingle-nook fireplace. The house was constructed of huge roughly chamfered timbers and the tiled roof supported by side purlins and wind braces which date it to the 1560s. In one ground floor room there remains an older, finely carved dais beam, which is likely to have come from another house of the open hall type and to have been re-used. Might it have come from Great Otehall which was rebuilt at this time? In 1766 one William Bran was occupant of a house called "Ye Bell", which may have been this. A later owner was Walter Chatfield a victualler and maltster after which the house was referred to as "late Chatfield's".[12] It remained as one dwelling until the 19th century when it was divided in two. It has a small brick-built cellar containing a well, both of which keep a constant temperature. It

xix. Chimney at Tapestry
Cottage *circa* 1580.

also shared a well with the adjacent house, now Verger's Cottage. This still exists under a paving stone in the garden of Wren Cottage.

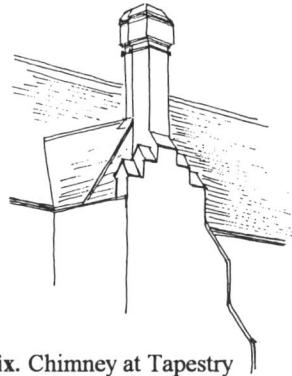

Verger's cottage

In 1525 Thomas At Ree (of Great Otehall) made a lease to Nicholas Hurst granting him two parcels of land on the east side of the churchyard for the rent of "...one red rose at Mid-summer".[13] From the location and dimensions this refers to the land on which Verger's Cottage was built in the early 1600s. In 1637 "...Henry Hurstes house", valued at £1, was perhaps this. Both structures, Tapestry/Wren and Vergers were shown as part of the Great Otehall estate in 1641.[14]

**Glebe and
Chimney cottages**

On the west side of the Churchyard, now divided into Glebe and Chimney Cottages, stands what in early deeds was called the Church House, but as far as we know it was never occupied by a vicar or curate. The site was a field in the Otehall estate in 1641. This accords with the style of timber-framed construction of three storeys. The top storey is half in the roof which has half-hipped gabled ends and cannot have been built before the early 1600s. The earliest documentary evidence dates from 1668 when Thomas Godman gent., owner of the Great Otehall estate, leased a messuage called Church House, together with a barn and 47 acres of land, to William Best of Wivelsfield, merchant, for 21 years at a yearly rent of £36 10s.[15]

Moonrakers and Windham cottage   Next door to Church House was another house developed by Thomas Godman around the same time. It was leased in 1689 to John Turner of Wivelsfield butcher, as a new house in Wivelsfield with stable and half an acre of land abutting the west side of the churchyard.[16] Known as "Butchers House" in 1697, it was from here the liability for churchyard repair was measured by the "Church marks". In 1780, William Bean the Parish Clerk, paid twelve shillings for Butchers House. By 1840 it had been divided into two dwellings which today are called Moonrakers and Windham Cottage (see Plate 21). Their gardens are minimal. Could John Turner's half-acre of land have been taken in Victorian times to provide space for a vicarage and garden?

The houses in Church Lane were thus the result of expansion by the Great Otehall estate - expansion with an eye to sales profit or new rent income. They were not the usual 'ad hoc' encroachment of local greens and wastes by owner-occupier cottagers. In 1766 "ye shop house", "late Turner's" and "the Butchers shop house" were all in the hands of undertenant John Picknoll but from 1788 the three properties had separate tenancies. They all remained part of the Otehall estate until the early 19th century.

Baldings   Near the Green, in Slugwash Lane in 1583 Walter A Wood "of Wysfield, bucher" bought an acre of land called Baldynges for £8, on which he built a small, low two-storeyed house of two and a half bays, timber-framed, using heavy timbers roughly splayed. The original box-panel construction with daub infilling, is visible on the north side but the other walls have since been covered with tile-hanging above a brick base. Later another bay and an outshot was added to the rear. At one end a very tall elaborate chimney-stack was built of thin, therefore early, bricks, appearing to be contemporary with the house. He mortgaged the house for £22 and still lived there in 1624, at which time it was bought by his son Walter for £30. Walter Wood senior died

xx. The hearth at Baldings, built 1584.

in 1629 but a Walter Wood, presumably his son, owned it by 1637. By 1728 Baldings was part of the Morehouse Estate and in 1760 Mrs Frances Day, the last direct descendent of the More family, transferred it to the Trustees of the Baldings Charity (See Chapter 12). In 1766 the occupier was John Randels. By 1838 the occupier was John Newnham, a carpenter, whose family connections remained there until the 1900s.[17]

Jenners   Near Baldings stands Jenners, a similar small house of the same period. It is a two-storey house of three and a half unequal bays, with a large, internal, brick-built chimney. The east and north walls show a considerable amount of the original box panelling with daub infill, but here the ground floor panels have been replaced by later brick infilling and the whole of the south side covered by tile hanging above brickwork. In one bedroom is a fine, cambered tie-beam and the tiled hipped roof is constructed of principal rafters with collars and side purlins. This freehold property was first known as 'Gunns', from an early owner. It was probably the freehold house mentioned in a rental of around 1590 held by one Walter a More and described as "...once William Gunnes". The Gunne family had been in the area since at least 1460.[18] In 1676 John Faulkner, a weaver, died and left it to his wife Elizabeth for her life and afterwards to their son John. In 1695 the house called Gunns had a barn, garden, orchard and the same amount of land, two acres as it did in 1838. In 1703 the property was held by John Farley of Keymer and was presumably sublet, but a dishturner named Samuel Smith who died in 1729 perhaps lived there. He also owned the copyhold property next door, now called Verandah Cottage.

xxi. Jenners, *circa* 1600.

In 1751 Ambrose Gallard, a carpenter, paid Samuel Smith's nephew and heir £85 for Gunns, but had to take out a mortgage for £60 at 4% interest. Ambrose died in 1790. William Homewood held the property in 1798. About 1800 Gunns, by then called "late Gallards" and "late Faulkners" was acquired by Richard Pannett and his wife Emma who were tenants of Fanners which stood to the west of it. [19]

Oak cottages   South of the Green, in Eastern Road, Oak Cottages
were copyhold of Ditchling Manor and were built as
one three-bay house with a central open hall, at an
earlier date and using poorer quality timber than at Baldings. The
paired rafters, some with collars, supported a tiled roof with one hipped
and one gabled end. In the early 1600s a central
chimney-stack with a bread oven was inserted
when the hall was floored over and an outshot
built on the north side.   Two of the original
windows remain, each with two diamond shaped
bars, but one has been plastered over and the
other, still visible, is now blocked by a later
chimney-stack built against the gable end.

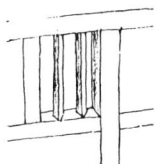

xxii. Window bars at
Oak Cottages.

In 1676 the Lord of the Manor granted a cottage and garden at 6d.
rent to Richard Shoulder, who died in 1705 leaving the cottage to his
widow Mary and p.m. to their son, another Richard, a shoemaker.
Unfortunately both the son and then his mother died in 1706. By 1760
it was owned by Cooper Sampson of Ditchling, surgeon, who was
recorded as the occupier in 1766.[20] This was during the period of his
pioneer experimenting with small pox vaccination.[21] Cooper Sampson
moved to practice in Eastbourne and it was later sub-let to one
Abraham Knight who was there in 1780. By 1788 the cottage had been
bought by Ambrose Jenner in whose family it stayed into the early
1800s. By 1838 the cottage had been extended and divided into 3 small
dwellings.

iii. The Wivelsfield Tannery

The preparation and tanning of hides appears to have been the most
important craft carried on in Wivelsfield, starting in medieval times.
The Tanyard was situated opposite the Fox and Hounds Inn on what is
now the main B2112 road.

The craft was one of the oldest known to mankind and a process that
took about 18 months from beginning to end. First the hide had to be
cleaned in a water pit to remove any blood and also to swell the fibres.
It was then put into the lime pits, firstly into a mellow solution of old
lime in water with hen manure and dog excreta, next into a less-mellow
solution and thirdly into a solution of almost-new lime. The length of
time depended on the type of leather required. For hard sole leather,
eight to ten days in the strong lime but for soft pliable leather, such as
for harnesses and shoe uppers, up to six weeks was needed in the old
mellow solution.

The main purpose of liming was to loosen the hair and outer portion of the skin. This was done by a beamsman using special knives, working in the Beam House - the beam being a steeply sloping wooden work table with convex top, over which the hide was thrown for de-hairing and fleshing. Before tanning, the hide was cut up, as different parts took up the tanning at different rates and the odd uneconomic pieces were sent away to make glue or gelatine. A vast quantity of oak bark was used and had to be kept dry in the Bark Room, before being finely ground in the Mill House - a very dusty process. The powder was added to cold water in a leaching pit, then transferred to the tanning pits. First the hides were suspended in a weak solution, then moved from pit to pit into gradually stronger solutions, keeping the hides from touching each other. Afterwards they were moved into another set of pits of much stronger tanning fluid where they were laid flat before a final wash in a weak solution and being hung up to dry slowly in the Drying Shed.[22]

Plate 16. Jefferys Green today: the tanyard and its 65 pits lay beyond the houses on the right.

Tanned leather ended up stiff and badly coloured so had then to pass through the hands of a currier to make it suitable for the shoemaker and other craftsmen to use. Currying was a separate, highly skilled craft but so far no mention of a currier has been found in Wivelsfield. Glovers were recorded in the 17th century, Richard Dancy of Clearwaters and William and Anthony Page of Lockstrood. Shoemakers or cordwainers included Richard Knight in 1640 and, in 1705 Richard Shoulder of Oak cottage. In Church Lane the Bean family provided a shoemaking service continuously from the 1740s to the

1850s: William Bean the father, 1731-1806, William Bean his son, 1758-1828 and Stephen Bean 1777-1850s.[23]

In 1380 the poll tax return lists three tanners in Ditchling which at that date included Wivelsfield. In 1492 John Michelborne alias Mascall took possession of Franklyns manor and the land on which the tannery stood was part of this holding.[24] John's son Richard Mascall, was prosecuted in 1528 for badly tanned hides.[25] There were very strict laws governing the processes of tanning; buying and selling of hides had to be on the open market, the finished ones being stamped by the licensing officer before sale.

There was a murder at the tannery in 1532. The coroner's inquest records Richard Mascall as a master tanner. Mascall lived in Wivelsfield, perhaps at Lockstrood about $1\frac{1}{4}$ miles south of the Tanyard.[26] The Michelbornes were people of substance and branches of the family held property in several other local parishes.[27] On the death of Richard Mascall in 1540 his son John Mascall of Plumpton, sold Franklyns to Edmund Pope.[28]

The "common tanners of leather" in Wivelsfield from 1578-1594 were John Averye and John Kydd.[29] There being no other tannery they must have been employees of the Pope family who owned the tanyard. Ralph Pope was mentioned in the will dated 1597, of his cousin Richard Shouswell, curate of Wivelsfield who was then living at Lockstrood.[30]

When the Pope family sold Cleavewater in 1626, part of the estate was described as "...*a messuage, barn, stable, tanyard and 11 closes of land (32a.) in the occupation of Thomas Wood*". By 1635 William King had succeeded him in the tanyard.[31] The Church mark in 1697 registered Walter Burt, the tanner. The complicated process of tanning produced many by-products and one which was essential in the building of timber-framed houses with wattle and daub infilling, was hair. Mr Burt, in 1716, supplied five bushels of hair to Edward Carter for repairs to his house, South Colwell, at 10d per bushel.[32]

It is interesting to note that Josiah Turner, a tanner, who died in 1721, had other interests which gave him self sufficiency. The profits of his trade had perhaps given him money to invest in land. In his barn were 14 bushels of wheat, oats and pease. He owned farming implements and a wagon, plus two cows, four calves, one old horse, three geese and a gander. The total value of his property at "late Anchorland", next to the Tanyard, was £58 14s. 0d.[33]

There is confirmation that the tanners had apprentices, for in 1745 an indenture states that John Wood, son of George, was to serve five years with Richard Floyd, tanner of Wivelsfield for the payment of £15. Floyd was probably in charge of the Tanyard for Nicholas Relfe, who owned it in 1728. He was appointed in 1747 by the J.Ps. of Lewes, to inspect cattle, houses, farms and markets. He recorded outbreaks of "distemper" in the surrounding villages north of Lewes but Wivelsfield seems to have escaped.[34]

By 1759 John Fuller, who in 1769 inherited More House from Mrs Frances Day, had the Church mark for the Tanyard. The 1785 Land Tax was paid by his nephew William Tanner, described as a tanner of Ditchling and Wivelsfield. It was presumably he from whom John Burgess, a fellmonger, breeches-maker and glover of Ditchling, bought skins in 1785 and 1786, having noted in his diary that he walked to the Tanyard at Wivelsfield. Burgess also went to Lewes to pay for licences to dress leather and to sell gloves.[35]

Tanner was indicted at Quarter Sessions at Horsham in 1788. William Carter gent, Collector of Excise, stated, "*that one William Tanner of Wivelsfield, Tanner, on 24th June last at Wivelsfield, did take 9 hides out of the Wooze and Liquour wherein the same had been tanned and did hang up or dispose of the said Hides to be Dried without giving or sending Notice in Writing to the proper Office for the Duties payable to such Hides of the time when the said William Tanner should so take the said Hides two days before and dispose of them in Horsham*". He pleaded 'not guilty', but to no avail, and he was fined £20 ".[36]

Plate 17. 'Bark harvest in Sussex' *circa* 1904. From a postcard in the possession of Bob Chimley.

On William's death in 1809, his son Anthony inherited the estate. By this time the Tanners styled themselves "gent.", but Anthony, in need of money, borrowed £305 on the Tanyard at 5% interest.[37] On his death in 1832 his financial situation had deteriorated and his will stated that all his property must be sold. The Tanyard was put up for sale by Auction on June 4th 1833, described as follows *"...a most desirable freehold property... consisting of a roomy Dwelling House, late the residence of Mr. A. Tanner, deceased, with excellent Gardens, Orchards and Pleasure Ground, a Summer House, Chaise House, Stabling for five horses, Granary, Cart Lodge, Cow Lodge, Farm Yard, Bark Barn, Mill House, two Drying Sheds, Leather Beam, Lime House and Tan Yard, well supplied with water, and containing sixty-five Pits, also five pieces of Rich Meadow land, 8a. 3r. 36p., subject to annual quit rent of 1 shilling to the Manor of Franklands and 6d to the Manor of Otehall. The purchaser to have option of taking the Pits, Bark Mill, Stock in Trade and Implements at fair valuation"*.[38]

Anthony Tanner's executors were not successful in selling the tanyard itself. The trade had shifted to large urban centres and rural tanneries were no longer viable . By 1844 the yard itself, 1 acre 19 perches, was still in hand. It does not appear to have been operational. No tanner existed in the parish in 1841 but John Cook, who occupied Cleavewater, was farming the 'Tanyard Meads'. Anthony Tanner's "roomy Dwelling House" had disappeared but the pits were later incorporated into the garden of Hurstwood House, which was built in 1869.[39]

iv. Shops, workshops and the village Inn

Shops in the 16th and 17th centuries were usually what we would term a workshop, that is, the actual place of trade or craft, to which the public had access in order to make purchases. However, the cloth trade seems to have had outlets in the Weald that were perhaps shops in the modern sense. In 1589 Walter Ashefold had a shop "in the house of Roger Dansie" at Wivelsfield. On 20th November that year the shop was burgled and various items were stolen: 10 yards of red woollen cloth, six hats, three yards of cotton, three yards of russet woollen cloth and eight ells of canvas to a total value of 29s. 6d.[40] Names of tailors and weavers living in the parish between 1593 and 1840 have been found.[41] In 1745 John Anscombe was paid 6s. 1d. for supplying 21 ells of 'towen cloth' to Richard Webb of Fanners.[42]

It was good for trade if a shop was at the meeting place of the community. Wivelsfield, in common with many other Wealden communities, had several road intersections and small greens where shops and workshops might favourably be placed; but two natural meeting places took precedence, the Church and the Green.

Church Lane, as we have seen above, was developed in the 16th-17th centuries and soon became a trading centre. The earliest shop for which details exist was that of John Turner, a butcher (Moonrakers & Windham). It presumably sold meat but there was also hardware, including 1500 hop-poles. This, together with Turner's farming concerns at Lockstrood, secured him a place among the 'comfortable' middle class and he died in 1713 worth £160 12s. 6d. John Colman who died in 1741 was also a shopkeeper in Church Lane, the most likely house being Verger's Cottage. He was a draper and grocer. Upstairs in his garret he stored his surplus stock including brooms, bee-hives and tubs. He appeared to have no land but kept a horse and a hog, which indicates that he must have rented sufficient space for a stable and a sty. He was worth £86 9s. 8d., £33 18s. 0d. of which was "in the shop" but this came from trading and not from a manual skill.

The east end of the Green, the junction of roads from Plumpton, Chailey and Lewes, became the venue for the annual fairs and the natural choice for a cluster of shops and workshops (see Plate 5). Of these the blacksmiths shop was perhaps the earliest. One Thomas Whitebread, blacksmith in 1630, bought eleven acres of land he had been renting, perhaps using money earned from his trade.[43] It lay opposite what is now Blacksmiths, formerly 'Goldsmiths', where the blacksmith's shop was sited. The 17th century diarist, parson Giles Moore, wrote in 1666 of taking a sick horse to Wivelsfield, to Thomas Buckwell the farrier.[44]

A blacksmith would have had no need of a shop in the modern sense but only of his workshop, where the majority of his products would have been made to order as builders and other craftsmen required them e.g. bolts, nails and hinges, also the repair of tools. John Knight was the blacksmith living at the Green in the early 1700s. When he died in 1726 he left his son all the tools of their trade, which were kept in the shop. This son, also named John, received Richard son of John Awcock as an apprentice blacksmith for five years.

This second John Knight died in 1778. He kept a mare colt but otherwise had no farming interests. As he travelled to undertake shoeing and running repairs on other people's premises he needed his horse for transport to the outlying estates. He had £37 16s. 0d. in cash. His total estate was £107 5s. 6d. but £35 of this was securities for money owed. Though farmers had regular work for the blacksmith, they often paid their accounts months in arrears. The practice continued well into the present century as Robert Millam's account book shows.[45] Millam was the blacksmith operating at the same place on the Green as the Knight family and all the others had done before him.

The blacksmith's skills were essential for other men such as the wheelwright to complete their own work. At Wivelsfield the two craftsmen traded next door to each other. Wheelwright Thomas Renfield died in 1732. The surname is alternatively spelt Renville or Renvell. He had for sale items of drapery such as muslin, also butter, soap, brandy, candles and corks as well as the effects of his own trade. He was thus a craftsman but also a tradesman and left goods totalling £229 9s. 8d, a large sum for his day. John Renville, Thomas's son, was also a wheelwright. He died in 1749 owning wheeling stock and tools valued at £27 15s. 0d. He also had unspecified shop goods amounting to £132 13s. 6d. and money on the book worth £10. Four years before his death, he had received one John, son of Jesse Attree as apprentice wheeler, for a term of seven years.[46] One wonders what happened to the apprentice at his master's death.

In 1613 it was stated that an unlicensed alehouse had recently been suppressed and its keeper sent to prison "...*and there is none there now*".[47] In 1638 one Edward Weller a cooper (barrel-maker) lived in the parish.[48] In 1766 William Bran's house, "Ye Bell", and David Price's "...*house called the chequer*" were possibly ale houses, the former perhaps in the vicinity of the church. "Anchorland", near the Tannery, may possibly have taken its name from a public house nearby called the Anchor.

xxiii. Part of the inventory of John Parsons.

It is likely that the Fair Place had seen an alehouse or two over the years. In 1747 one John Parsons died, described as an inn-holder and cordwainer (shoemaker). His inn may have been an earlier building in the vicinity of the present Cock Inn. Parsons' inventory showing 17 pairs of sheets suggests that he accommodated passing travellers. In his three bedrooms he had a total of five beds so possibly the three in the Brew House chamber were a source of income. Nothing therein could be removed. The Parlour contained several tables and only one arm-chair; shelves held drinking glasses and earthenware utensils. This room would have been where drinks were sold and any other seating was likely to have been benches fixed to the walls. In his cellar there were seven barrels, bottles and pots. He had a "Sign and Sign Post" outside the inn. This was valued at a £1 but would have been worth far more to John, as it attracted travellers to his trade. The total value of his estate was £47 2s.6d. of which £5 was on the book. He kept a cow and a few sheats (young hogs) but otherwise was not farming and there was no mention of any tools of the cordwainer's craft. The earliest date found so far for the name "the Cock" is 1798 when Jane Brooker was the landlady.

There is a will of Stephen Elliott of Wivelsfield, grocer, who had his shop at Hamlyns, on the Green and died in 1811.[49] His mother Mrs. Elliott, daughter of John Renville the wheelwright, was mentioned from 1780-1815 as the owner of the premises. He left his stock in trade, furniture and securities, to his niece Mary Tanner of Ditchling. The executor John Tanner was Mary's brother and he was also a grocer, which would give a reason for leaving grocery stock to her. Stephen's nephew, another Stephen, also Tanner by name, inherited his uncle's wearing apparel. Even among the comfortably off, clothes were highly prized and worth inheriting. Stephen Elliott's estate was worth around £450. Allowing for any inflation which may have occurred between the death of John Colman in 1741 when he left £86 from a grocer's business, when Stephen died 1811 his must have been a flourishing concern.

v. Their place in the community

Many cottagers and small farmers in the Weald lived poised between credit and debt and their fortunes were interdependent. The two groups each occupied a similar position in society and each allowed the other credit until profits could be harvested.

There was good fortune for some. John Ashfold, for instance, a thatcher, had only a cottage and one acre; but the enclosure of the common in 1626 resulted in an extra 10 acres coming to his son's inheritance in 1634. The son was then able to sell the extra land to pay his father's debts, thereby ensuring his own future security.[50] Thomas Whitebread, the blacksmith in 1630, had the means first to rent and later to buy a piece of the enclosed common. In the following century John Turner, a butcher and Josiah Turner, a tanner had each managed to invest in a little land, thereby increasing their income and status.

Others were already farmers who were willing to diversify. If their land contained good clay they could enter the building trade. By setting up kilns and re-deploying their seasonal workers to do all the heavy manual labour involved they could become 'brickmakers'. Thomas Hurst of Hurst House farm was one such.[51]   In 1644 Giles Moore, rector of Horsted Keynes paid him 30 shillings for bricks. The Hurst family continued in the trade, for in 1708 Henry Hurst and in 1748 Henry Hurst the younger were styled 'bricklayers'.[52] The terms brickmaker and bricklayer were interchangeable at that period.

Those who had risen through the trade as workers, to become site managers, usually looked for land in which to invest. In this way Wivelsfield gained the Burgess Hill brickmaker, George Taylor, manager of the 'Meeds' yard. He bought Puddledock farm and was living there at his death in 1746.[53] The rise in the building industry brought in its wake opportunities for other workers, carpenters, masons and plasterers as were employed at South Colwell in the early 1700s (Chapter 4). The Hurst family, as brickmakers, provided themselves with a fine brick-built farmhouse (plate 2) which still graces its hill slope in the north of the parish. They now ranked among the landed families of the parish. (See Chapter 3, table 1.)

Lower down the scale was Edward Fairhall, a 'bricklayer' perhaps working for the Hursts. He was also a husbandman. On his six acres of land there were two acres of oats and four of wheat. His livestock included a cow, a heifer and their calves, one colt, three sheep, three lambs and two pigs. He had a woollen wheel, a linen wheel, two bushels of flax seed and six nail of tow. Evidently he or his wife earned extra income by spinning. With all these extras, Edward's total estate was valued at £39 4s. 6d. in 1726.

There was a role in community service for traders who could read and write. David Virgo a tailor, was Parish Clerk in about 1650. Although literate his records were noted as being difficult to read. Richard Mills who died in 1722 aged 89 was a tanner by trade and had been Parish Clerk for 42 years.[54] When he died he possessed a hog and two pigs, his total wealth only £14 3s. 6d. His son, another Richard Mills, a tailor, followed him as Parish Clerk. He died in 1743 worth £27 14s. 6d., having no livestock and no farming interests but presumably a small income from the parish. He had a gun and no doubt shot the odd rabbit or bird and there was a linen wheel in the kitchen.

Later, in 1766 William Bean, a shoemaker, held the office of Parish Clerk and was paid 10s. 0d. for keeping the accounts. He became Head Borough (constable). He was followed as Parish Clerk from 1806 - 28 by his son William, also a shoemaker, who in turn was succeeded by his brother Stephen, another shoemaker. That William Bean senior was lending money is shown in the court books of Ditchling manor.[55]

parcels of the waste. It was often the lord of the manor himself, anxious to extend his park or home farm, negotiating with the 'commoners' to buy them out. This could cause friction, rancour and lucrative rewards for Chancery lawyers.[6]

Several downland communities had once had access to meadow and pasture in the Weald alongside those who themselves lived in the Weald. As we have seen in Chapter 1, the Wivelsfield people in 1333 won the fight with the people from Stanmer, near Brighton, regarding the use of common pasture called 'Stammeryngferth' (later known as the 'Bishoprick'). The downlanders thus began to lose their grip on the wealden areas they had formerly freely used, while the wealdeners' stakes increased. If then the big landowner in the Downland swallowed up his smaller neighbours by enclosing their arable and pasture, as happened at Stanmer from 1625-1650, enclosure could be ruinous for the local small farmers. They had lost their former Wealden outpastures and in losing their arable and sheep-down at home they were reduced to the status of landless labourer.[7]

Enclosure at Wivelsfield was not ruinous for the local farmers. On the contrary, they courted it. The vital difference between places like Wivelsfield and Stanmer was that, although Wivelsfield had one or two prominent landholders, the smaller owners were never ousted. The community remained a vibrant mix of squires, farmers and craftsmen.

Those who did lose out at enclosure were the smaller cottagers whose claim to right of common had never been established or formally ratified. Rights of common evolved early, often in the Saxon period, so that newer cottages did not always officially lodge a claim to common rights. While there was still plenty of waste land to go round they would use the commons without challenge. This involved out-pasturing a few animals, gathering firewood, cutting furze and bracken as fodder and bedding for animals; and cutting heather for rough thatching and to fill truckle beds. After enclosure they lost these amenities and began to turn elsewhere. Those with rights in nearby commons which remained open, such as Ditchling and St. John's (Burgess Hill), became hawkish. They railed bitterly against 'foreigners' from other manors, or against new cottagers in their own manor, using their commons.

The new fields of an enclosed common were readily bought, sold and exchanged by local farmers in the 17th, 18th and 19th centuries so that today the parish contains several 'new' holdings, such as Home Farm or Green Park Farm, which, as self-contained farms, are much younger than estates such as Otehall or More House. Their land is just as old, but their separate identity is far newer.

ii. Wivelsfield village green

For the origin of the former Green in the Green Road area of Wivelsfield we must first look to its location. It occupies the length of the valley between two ridges, the 'long ridge' on the north and the clay-woodland ridge on the south. By the late Saxon period, or earlier, the two ridges would have contained boundary ditches and fences marking out people's areas of interest - a meadow here, some crops there, a private woodland beyond. People wanting to travel from east to west would naturally choose the valley in between. With several drove roads and the Iron-Age track (fig. 5) all crossing the east-west route, the area must soon have become trodden down, a natural stopping and meeting place. The west end of the green was forked, circumventing a detached piece of the lord of Ditchling's 'free chase', presumably fenced and gated, the wayside waste here later being known as "at Kydd's Gate" (Stream Cottage).[8] The bottom of Eastern Road and the bridle path westwards would once have been part of this green. It is interesting that the word 'strood', meaning green, has survived at the far west and at the far east of the green, as if to mark its limits, Lockstrood in the west and Strood farm in the east.

The western part of the Green was in Ditchling manor and, apart from Fanners, 'Bulls of Fanns', and Pepperhall, no one lived in the vicinity until the 16th century. The eastern end, by contrast, in Stanmer/South Malling/Lindfield manor, had the 'Stanmer' hamlet on its north side. From the 1300s onwards the hamlet expanded. The original, large farms were divided in order to provide new holdings and it was not their own 'strood green', but the longer green (Green Road), that was favoured for new houses. By 1600 the community had multiplied to around 10 households, though they were all still on the north side of the green, the 'Bishoprick' common being on the south.[9] This part of Wivelsfield green would thus have been a focal point for the people of the hamlet, for meetings, sports and pastimes.

What must have started technically as a trespass, or at most carried on with the permission of the lord of the manor, ultimately matured into a customary right enforceable through the courts. In due time the desirability of a fair arose. Most fairs had their speciality; sheep fairs, horse and cattle fairs, cloth fairs, cheese fairs and goose fairs. There were also 'mop' or hiring fairs, usually held at Michaelmas or Martinmas, when the rates of pay for the coming year were fixed by the magistrates.

In 1813 Wivelsfield Fair was said to be held on 29th June, the feast of St.Peter and St.Paul - an important day for the hamlet before the Reformation, its own chapel being dedicated to St. Peter (Chapter 2). The fair may once have been a livestock fair, but in 1819 it was only for pedlary.[10] Even so, it may well have accommodated those looking for jobs, perhaps displaying the emblem of his/her trade - the shepherd

his crook, the waggoner his whip, the dairymaid her pail. It was held at
the junction of the roads in from Lewes, Plumpton and Streat (Plate 5)
and, as we have seen in the preceding chapter, became a focal point for
shops, workshops and an inn. Fairs also brought showmen, strolling
players, travelling menageries, cheapjacks and prize fighters. The
Cock, reputedly once the 'Fighting Cock' was well placed to serve all
comers.

Plate 18. 'Wheelwrights' at the Green *circa* 1905.

In 1830 the green was still open and the fair place was still in its old
traditional position.[11] These things were to change before the century
was out, a story whose finer details must await a future study.[12]

iii. Jefferys Green

Jefferys Green (see Plate 16) lay towards the north east of the parish
at the bottom of what is now Fox Hill on the main B2112 road. It lay
on the east of this road at the junction of Hurstwood lane, which once
connected with tracks westwards to form a crossroads. Crossroads
then, unlike their modern counterparts, would have been excellent
meeting places. Jefferys Green seems to have been a focal point in the
parish in the late-medieval period and possibly earlier.

The green was formerly known as Gyffords, corrupted to 'Jeffereys Green' by the 17th century and alternatively, 'Cliffords' Green. Modern maps omit its name altogether.[13] In 1504 the area was identified as "Gyffordes crosse", meaning cross roads, and "...a common called Herstwode" was said to lie east of this - perhaps another name for the green.[14] There were various small meadow plots and houses in the vicinity including, in 1547, "...the house and land once of John Gyfford" and a "...plot of land once built upon called Le Croucheplace" - meaning 'the crossroads place'.[15] Isabel atte Crowche lived adjacent in 1441 and John Gyffard " of Wyvelesfeld" was there in 1485.[16]

The area was clearly a focal point. The tannery was close by. The oddly named "malerose wysche" in 1370, later "malleyrose mead" may be a corruption of 'malhereuse' and may thus allude to the tannery. A sump meadow full of evil-smelling wastes, or perhaps tannery pits themselves, may well have been called 'malhereuse', implying a wretched and unhealthy condition. A place name of French derivation here could reinforce the earlier suggestion (Chapter 5) that this was the location of Ditchling's medieval tannery and would perhaps imply its existence early in the medieval period, when French was still being spoken by the lords' henchmen.[17]

Jefferys Green had been cut down by encroachment to almost nothing by 1800.[18] This remnant, together with some wayside waste in Hurstwood Lane, was enclosed and parcelled out to private owners in 1861.[19] Today the footpath west from the main road, the Fox and Hounds public house and a tiny triangle of grass opposite in Hurstwood Lane are the only memorials to this former crossroads and green, a once-important focus in parish life.

iv The common meadows

Meadows were once a significant common-land resource in Wivelsfield. Wealden streams are particularly variable in their flow. A parched summer trickle can turn into a swirling torrent in winter, flooding all its bordering grasslands. The lush hay that follows in Spring makes them a valuable part of the farming economy. It is noticeable therefore, from studying patterns of land-holding from manorial records, maps and deeds, that the stream-side meadows and low-lying wetlands had once been a shared resource.

Meadows along the River Adur on the west side of the parish were held in three main blocks, the Clevewater/Clearwater estates (Ditchling and Streat manors), the Theobalds/Antye hamlet (Houndean manor) and the Otehall/Lunces estates (Withdean manor). In the centre of the parish the riverside meadows west of Otehall chapel, shared by the Otehall and Morehouse estates and Lockstrood, were called "Keerish" in 1641. In these areas there are glimpses of an earlier common land system.[20] Between Green Road and the 'long ridge' was a meadow called "southwishe". The owner of Pepper Hall, nearby, had five acres of meadow in the area in 1333, but these were already "set out with metes and bounds" by 1322. There had clearly once been a 'common' in which several owners had a stake, but any system of common cropping or use was petering out by the 14th century. In 1583 Townings farm was still entitled to a parcel of land "in Southwishe".[21]

The long Ouse valley east of Cleavewater contained meadow land belonging originally to Ditchling, Clayton, Plumpton, Falmer and Stanmer. The latter two, being downland manors, had little or no meadow land at home. It is perhaps no accident that the trans-wealden Iron Age track, (fig. 5) runs right through this key meadowland area. If the Downland needed hay then the crop had to be got out of the Weald after harvest and local drove roads may have been avoided as too miry for cart wheels.[22]

The character of the land in which these meadows occur is found in the local name Slugwash, 'Slough of the moist meadows' (Slugwash Lane, Home Farm area). There would have been two crops of hay each year in these meadows, followed by good grazing for cattle until Christmas. Manorial rents in the early 17th century reflect the desirability of such meadows, the average for arable being one shilling per acre, but twice that for meadow, at two shillings. Further, if a tenant was found ploughing the river meadows, he was liable to have his land taken away from him by the lord's officials.[23]

The common use of this meadow area was still apparent at the end of the 16th century. It contained three areas known as the Breache, the Moor and the Hammes, in each of which several different manors had a stake (see Plates 4, 19). But by then people were beginning to streamline their farming and the old common-land system was cumbersome. It was annoying to have pieces of meadow here and there, on both sides of Slugwash Lane, and on both sides of the 'long ridge'. And so they met, came to agreements, exchanged parcels and divided up the old customary holdings, collecting together as much as possible in one place, preferably near their home farm.

One Thomas Button, yeoman of Lindfield, the Mores of More House and the Lucases of Fanners drew up deeds of exchange and partition in 1583 and 1600.[24] These deeds tell us that the Breache lay north of Townings and west of Slugwash Lane and that its total area was 64 acres. Thomas Button's lands "...lying in the Breche" would from now on be his own, to use and enjoy "...in severalty". Thomas Lucas, of Fanners, had 16 acres "...in a common field or meadow called the Breache". These he gave to Francis More of More House. In 1840 there was an area called Low Breach, the property of Richard Tanner of Morehouse, and also Button's Breach which belonged to Townings. They lay west of Slugwash Lane opposite Moors Farm.

The Moor lay on the east side of Slugwash Lane. It was described in 1600 as "a common meadow called the Moor". Within it there were areas called "lands" and we have the name of one of these, "broadland". The old holding called Haywardes, a copyhold of Balneath manor, had been entitled to "four parcels in the moor". One of these was described as "the fifth land in the moor". The parcels were quite small, one being only eight 'pauls' (poles) wide. It is interesting that 'Haywardes' had a large stake in these meadows. The homestead, now 'Townings', was probably that of "Walter the Hayward" - the hay-warden - in 1327.[25] In areas where hay is still grown in common fields the first assault on the standing crop is by the commoners and their families treading out their allotted share.[26] One can imagine the arguments, the attempted sneaking of an advantage, were there no supervision or control.

Plate 19. Home Farm and Meadowlands from 'the hamms', 1994.

The third area of meadow, the "hammes" lay north of the Breach and the Moor and extended north to the river course which itself was called "Hamme brooke" in 1600. The area has had a very long pedigree of human association and is the starting point of the mid-8th century Saxon charter, the "humahamme". (Chapter 1) These were perhaps smaller and older meadows than the Moor and the Breach, both of which names suggest that a wettish but heathy open landscape was observed by the first colonisers. *Hamm* is Old English for (meadow) 'enclosure' and it seems plausible that the first English settlers found river meadows here already in use. The farms in Wivelsfield having an original share in the 'hamms' were Strood, Manns and Shoulders, the Berth, (Haywardes) i.e. Townings and Fanners.

By 1600 the different allocations had already been gathered together in one place to create a modern-type rectangular field scape. John Button (of Haywardes) owned a field called "the Little Hamme" and Thomas Lucas of Fanners also owned a field of the same name, his being 10 acres in size. The 'Stanmer' hamlet owned further fields called the hammes. The broad area of the hammes had perhaps been reorganised into a fieldscape earlier than the Breach and the Moor.

North of the river two farms took shape in the late 1500s or early 1600s, South Slugwash or Home Farm and North Slugwash or Meadowlands. Their interlocking tapestry of fields, apparent still in the 19th century, betrays an earlier common-land use of the area they occupied. Meadowlands still had long thin fields slicing down to the riverside, an echo of the old system which insisted that each user had his fair share of wetlands. Although the farm had been created as an agricultural unit, with its own name and one private owner, its riverside fields were still shared out between Ditchling and Balneath manors.[27]

In 1837 a copyhold, held of Balneath manor, was described as "... a hovel and land called Moors".[28] The 'hovel' or small barn later evolved into a brick-built dwelling which, improved and extended, still stands today in Slugwash Lane. Its name, Moors Cottage, and its location commemorate the former 'moor' where a system of common land use had run for perhaps 1000 years before the changes of the 16th century brought in a new order.

v. The Bishoprick

On the clay ridges south of 'the Green' at Wivelsfield numerous local communities held their own share of wood-pasture commons. Wivelsfield's share was an elongated rectangle, penetrating south for about one mile ending just north of what is now North America Farm. ('Wivelsfield common' on fig. 8; and see fig. 2, between D,E,F and G.) It would have been separated from the neighbouring commons of Plumpton, Streat, Westmeston and Middleton by embankments and other landscape features, to discourage people from using others' commons. The bounds of Westmeston common, for instance, ran in 1582 "....[from] *the Newecrosse ....northward to a decayed hedge, the*

common of the Buysshoprick of Chichester lyenge along the easte:
thence northward to a dyche   leading   to Wyllsfelde pitt....."[29]
Wivelsfield's common was perhaps known locally as 'the Bishoprick',
because, as Church land, people assumed it to belong to the Bishop of
Chichester.[30] Its immediate lords were in fact the worthies of the
religious community of secular canons at South Malling, the
Chancellor, The Precentor, The Treasurer and the Dean, until the
Reformation sent them packing, The bounds of all these commons,
Plumpton, Streat, The Bishoprick and Westmeston, have become the
parish boundaries.

The 16th century had seen great upheavals in the locality.
Private profiteering was rife and was not helped by the example set
from above. The Crown for instance happily sold off a rich source of
profit they had gained from Lewes Priory, the Great Ham wood in
Chailey.[31] The Earls of Abergavenny did the same with their demesne
woods Shortfrith and Frekebergh, vast tracts, stretching for miles.[32]
Taking their cue from those above them, some farmers and lesser
gentry began to enclose commons illegally and to cut down trees. But
others objected. Around the year 1530 Richard Mascall, the tanner of
Wivelsfield, had enclosed part of Ditchling Common near his house at
Lockstrood. (See also Chapters 2 and 5) In Edward VI's reign (1547-
1553) the enclosure was 'riotously' thrown down by 'rebels', that is,
other locals slightly down the social scale who had lost valuable
pasture by his action.[33]

In 1595 Plumpton Common, which lay along the east side of
the Bishoprick, was legally enclosed by the lord of its manor who
bought out the copyholders.[34] Such actions would have been enviously
observed by others in the locality who saw the new owners
converting the land to profitable agriculture while they were still
restricted by the old customs of common pasturing.

The tenants of Wivelsfield once had the right to gather necessities,
known as 'estovers' over all *"...the Lord's waste in Wivelsfeld called
Le Bishops and Stanmyr Frith"*, but sometime in the 16th century they
relinquished these rights *"...in the Lord's wood, reserving the
aforesaid common to each and every of the aforesaid tenants for
their beasts ...and common estovers of thorns and bushes."*[35] This
tells us that the commoners were not stinted or restricted as to how
many animals they could put out to graze. It perhaps also implies that
the local people had enough supplies of firewood, or they would not
have relinquished these rights. The official commoners of course were
mainly local farmers with adequate amounts of their own land. Smaller
cottagers still trying to establish a right by custom, would not have
been given a say in the matter.

In 1582 the neighbouring commons of Westmeston and Streat were
a mixture of furze, bracken and trees, very similar in fact to the

appearance of parts of Ditchling common today. Westmeston common was "*...dispersedly sett with okes and bushes amongst which growe some furzes*" while Streat had "*bushes and furzes ...set in divers places with okes of sundry ages*". These commons were not over-pressured and had not been completely converted from woodland pasture to open heath by over-use. The oaks and other timber trees were all carefully valued for the lord of the manor's private purse.[36]

The Bishoprick, by contrast, may have been relatively treeless by the close of the 16th century. The final collapse of the religious colleges in 1546 must have induced a "free for all" attitude to its timber resource for in 1552 it was reported that:

"Nicholas Pencost, John Estefeld and Edward Gynner acknowledged that they had cut down various oaks in certain land in Wivelsfelde called Le Busshopryke and further said that several other tenants of the manor had cut down trees at the same time"[37]

In 1560 William Shereff did the same thing and faced forfeiture of his property (probably Hole farm) as a punishment. In the following year Thomas Button, Roger Pylbem and Roger Shereve were also brought before the court for having "*... cut down oaks, both timber and other wood and converted it to their own uses.*" Their properties were forfeited to the lady of the Manor (Queen Elizabeth I), but were returnable on payment of a fine to half the value of their profits on timber sales. [38] It was loss of money, not loss of trees that irked the Lady.

Plate 20. The Bishoprick in 1994: houses in South Road stand on part of Stanmer's former 'swine pasture', later the 'Bishoprick' Common.

In the first few decades of the 17th century the desire to enclose became a fever that quickly spread through the Weald of Sussex. 500 acres on the heaths of Chailey parish were enclosed in Houndean manor in 1621, an act which would have profited the holders of Theobalds and Antye which were held of that manor.[39] Standing against them were "...*strangers* [probably new cottagers living off the common] *having no right of common there who labour by indirect means to hinder the enclosing thereof*".[40] 'The Bishoprick' was next to go in 1626, while not far away to the west there was an attempt in 1633 to enclose vast acres of common in the manor of Keymer.[41] In 1636, just south of the Bishoprick, goaded no doubt by that common's recent conversion, someone tried to divide Middleton common with hedges, but these were "riotously levelled".[42]

The Bishoprick's fate as an open common was sealed in the following manner. In 1626 a court of the manor of South Malling Lindfield was specially convened for the express purpose of enclosing "..a common or waste called Wivelsfield common".[43] Preceding this there may well have been informal talks between tenants and the agents of lord of the manor to establish a general consensus for the idea. If there were objectors we do not hear of them.

The homage, that is, the executive committee representing the tenants at this court were Wivelsfield landholders, the majority of whom seem to have been residents: Walter Lucas, gent., Thomas Newman, Edward Walker, John Wood, Richard Virgoe, John Dumbrell, Thomas Piers and Edward Pilbeam. The Lord of the Manor, William Newton, gent., attended in person - quite an event, as manorial courts were usually handled by lords' agents. The homage took their places and the rest of the meeting was made up of other Wivelsfield tenants - Henry Jenor, Stephen Potter and the widows of John Faulconer and John Stone. The most likely venue for the meeting was a local inn - perhaps sited where the Cock Inn now stands.

The proceedings were simple. The resolution to enclose the common was put and was unanimously agreed. Everyone present made a personal promise to carry it out. A plan of enclosure was to be worked out at a future meeting. There were perhaps smiling faces, drinks ordered and schemes and dreams exchanged or kept secret. Three tenants had not turned up. Was it illness, indifference or were they objectors offering a mute protest rather than countering their neighbours in public?

At the next meeting the enclosure plan was presented and agreed upon. By established custom the lord of the manor had one third of the common and the tenants had the other two thirds between them. Of their two thirds, each tenant received an "allotment", or share,

proportionate to the size of his holding and this created plots ranging
in size from five to 35 acres. These were all in the centre and north of
the common. The lord received 100 acres in a block at the southern end
of the common. This evolved into a farm first called The Bishopricke,
later Hundredacre Farm, but is now Park Farm.[44]

The enclosure was evidently a long-winded affair and was not
finished until 1630. The new plots were to be held by customary
(copyhold) tenure, the same as their existing holdings but with one
important exception. All the woods and underwoods on their new plots
were to be theirs to fell and sell as they wished, for their own gain: no
more fines and forfeitures. The poorer people in the locality turned
elsewhere for succour. In 1633 Francis Button, Thomas Harris and
John Whitbreade and in 1693 William Hobbes of Wivelsfield were all
reported for using Ditchling common.[45]

> *"The law doth punish man or woman*
> *who steals the goose from off the common,*
> *But lets the greater villain loose*
> *who steals the common from the goose. "*

xxiv. Field pattern of 'Bishoprick' after
enclosure. Ref. O.S. 6 inch, 1874.

So runs the old rhyme.   In
Wivelsfield the 'villains' were the
farmers and craftsmen whom we
have already met in the two
previous chapters. Taking a stand
for middle England they had
erected their battlements, moat and
drawbridge. They fenced, ditched
and enclosed their common. In so
doing they warded off the larger
predators, the aspiring gentry.
Their action also cast out the free-
riders: the newer cottagers,
seasonal workers and travellers
were debarred.

As the old common disappeared
a generous selection of alternative
names were paraded before the
lawyers - "...*Wivelsfield common
alias Bishops Rith alias Thornett
alias Shortriet, or whatever it is
called...*".[46] People busily bought,
sold and exchanged their new
plots or 'severalls' (because they
had been severed from the whole).
'Perkins severalls' and 'Walkers

severalls', for instance, were later acquired by the Fanners estate. 'Whitbreads', now Green Park Farm, started up in this way. [47] The house lies with the former common behind it to the south. It no longer fronts the green, for that fell to a later wave of enclosure enthusiasm. Henry Jenner got 23 acres of the common, in respect of his existing holding, Mann's farm. He built a windmill on the new land, on the hill ridge. [48] It lay near a spot called Coldharbour in 1766, on which the house of that name was later built.

Enclosure turned the 'Bishoprick' into a grid of rectangular fields in a hotch-potch of scattered ownership, still apparent in the 1870s. [49] It is strikingly different from the older Wealden field patterns in which boundaries marry more naturally with the landscape. Today, by contrast, most of the internal hedges have gone and the area is again an open sward: but modern wheat production and high-yield grasses have replaced the former rough pastures of the old commoners of 'Wivelsfield hamlet'.

vi. In the north of the parish

The north of the parish lies on a High-Weald sandstone ridge. Remnants of waste, formerly portioned out between various manors, evolved as small greens. They were all on the top of the ridge along the important east/west ridgeway track (now the A 272).

Lyoth Common   The name Lyoth is a combination of Old English *leah* meaning 'green sward' and *hath* which means 'heath'. In the 1600s it was sometimes referred to as Lywood common. [50] Lying in the far north east of the parish it was used by local tenants of Middleton, Balneath, Plumpton and Streat manors, each of whom would originally have had their own area carefully delineated. In 1600 it would have covered a larger area than in 1840 when only a remnant patch was shown as common. [51]

By studying the field names in 1840 it is possible to see not only where the Common may have extended in earlier times but also how it was enclosed and became part of various farms. To the south of the highway there are "Common Field" and "part of Common Field" also "part of Common" all farmed by Colwell, whereas North Slugwash farmed "part of Common" and together with Colwell Farm shared a large wooded area called Common Wood. What little remained of Lyoth Common was to the north of the road and here the Tithe map shows the large Northlands Wood shared by Slugwash and Colwell Farms, five fields, a barn and a house called 'late Bennets'. The enclosing of this common was probably gradual and would have happened after c.1600 when the old manorial holdings such as

Haywardes and the Berth were split up, the meadows enclosed and new holdings created.

Between 1601 and 1834, as we shall learn from the following chapter, the parish was obliged to house its own poor. At that time commons such as Lyoth, being well removed from polite society, were seen as ideal sites. Two separate poor houses were located here, on open ground, each with its plot of land. In 1841 one was occupied by a carpenter, his wife and two lodgers and the other by an agricultural labourer, his wife and three children. The house 'late Bennets' was in the occupation of an agricultural labourer, his wife and six children. An order for the sale of the Parish Cottage on Lyoth Common and one on Lunces Hill was made on September 25th 1843 by the Poor Law Commissioners and a Conveyance was executed by the Guardians of Chailey Union, Thomas Attree and John Cook, churchwardens, Henry Wells and John Martin, overseers of Wivelsfield, to Richard Tanner of Morehouse, gent. for £62. By 1851 further encroachment had taken place.[52]

Birch Green   Birch Green was within Franklands manor, and lay where The Birch Hotel now stands (see Plate 32). Encroachment had started there in the 1500s for in 1597 Richard Illman, a maker of stone roofs, lived there, probably related to the Illman at Haywards heath (below).[53] In 1814 a cottage and premises at Birch Green in Wivelsfield, an encroachment from the waste, was said to have been formerly used as a millwright's shop.[54] In c. 1840 there was a small area of green left. It linked south to Jefferys Green via Hurstwood Lane.

Otehall Common   This common, held of Otehall Manor, was part of
on   Haywards Heath. It occupied the north west
Haywards Heath   corner of Wivelsfield parish, a narrow strip of the common extending south to link with Jefferys Green. It was the remnant of what had formerly been the northern outpastures of Lunces/Otehall manor, the majority of which had been enclosed some time in the medieval period to create Hurst House farm. Its earliest mention was around 1295-1300 when the heir of Osbert le Luns granted it to John of Ottehale and called it a common of pasture and heath "called Hothlaghe near Heyworthe in Wivelsfield".[55] This remnant was eroded in 1540 when Thomas Godman, lord of Otehall, created a new freehold tenancy in his manor by granting out a parcel of land on "Haywords Hoth" common to be held at 12d. rent. It abutted west and south onto the road leading from Cuckfield to Lewes and north onto a further piece of Otehall common.[56]

A few years later, in 1547, Godman made a freehold grant of a different parcel "of my waste land at Haywardes Hothe in the parish of Wevylsfeld", four acres in extent, to be held at 6d. rent. It abutted north " on to a certain ride upon the said common of Haywardes Hothe called Fellryde", east and south to "...my waste land aforesaid" and west to "...the highway leading from Lewes to Cokefeld".[57] Richard Illman, the tenant, still held these four acres in 1592 when he bequeathed them "...for the fatherly love" to his son Henry Ilman, alias Hesslinge. [58] Full manorial dues were nominally owed to Otehale for the tenancy. In 1638 a dwelling called Shoulders was shown in the plot. The boundary of Otehall Common, referred to as Wivelsfield Common, was shown as west to the highway, north west to a stream and Fellride Bottom. It was marked on the north and north east by some 'boundary' oaks.[59] In 1681 the Hurst House estate owned a kiln, presumably a brick kiln, on Haywards Heath, but it is not known where this was.[60] By 1840 Haywards Heath itself was still unenclosed. The Wivelsfield end of the heath appeared much the same as before though the enclosures there amounted to eight acres containing six fields. There was a large pond and a homestead, which had been renamed Hodsells. The final enclosure of Otehall Common occurred in 1861 (Chapter 14).

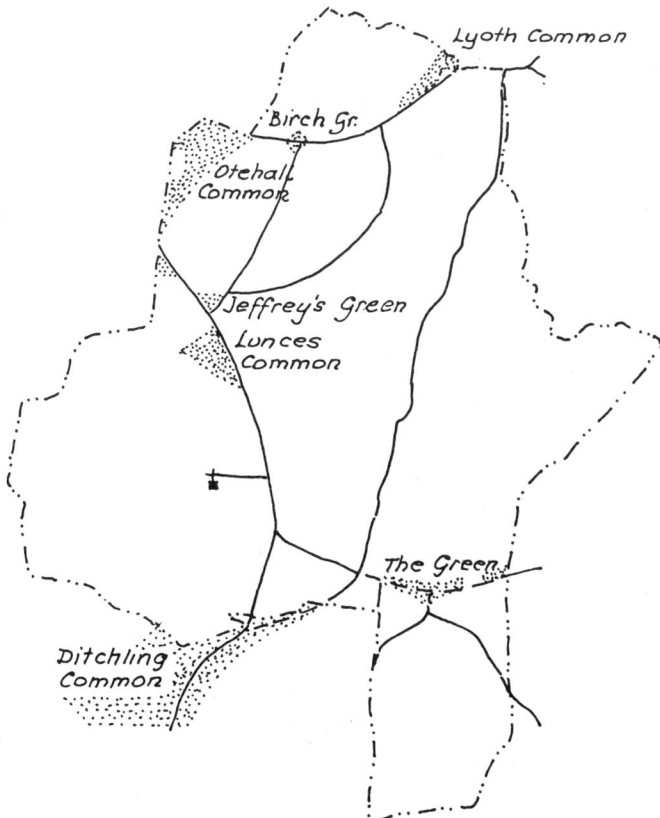

Figure 9. The commons in 1840, from the tithe map.

vii. Lunces Common

By comparing figs. 8 and 9 it is clear to see that between 1600 and 1840 common meadow and common pasture within the parish had been drastically reduced. Lunces common survived in 1840 with around 11 acres, which it retains today as the only Registered Common in the parish.

The common lies west of the B2112 at Lunces Hill, just south of Clevewater. In 1800 there was also a narrow strip east of the road.[61] To the north it once extended to Jeffreys Green, which in turn linked up with Otehall manor's part of Haywards Heath. Lunces Common remains open today (see Chapter 14) because it was part of the manor of Ditchling and not, as its name seems to imply, of Lunces. If it had belonged to the Lunces/Otehall estate it would have been enclosed in 1861, if not earlier, along with the rest of the waste in that manor. Being in Ditchling's domain, it was outside the control of local residents.

This ancient common of Lunces, together with the main part of Ditchling common away to the south, was once part of the royal manor of King Alfred the Great. Ditchling Common and, by implication, Lunces common, were thereby involved in one of the earliest charters concerning common land in Sussex. For after the Norman conquest Earl William de Warenne, having received the Saxon kings' holdings at Ditchling, then used them to help endow his new priory of St. Pancras at Lewes. His son William, around the year 1090, stated: *"let the Monks who live at Dichening* [Court Garden Farm] *have pasture for their beasts and cattle in all the pastures in which my men have common".*[62]

It has been suggested that masonry in the fabric of Wivelsfield Church was taken from Lunces common (Chapter 2). If so, the licence to quarry would surely have been granted by one of these early Earls de Warenne.

Lunces Common would not then have been known by that name. It lies on the route of the drove-road from Lunces Hall to the outpastures of that manor and, just north of the common, this route crossed the river. The 16th-century name 'Lunsford Common' therefore seems to connect medieval association and the modern name, which is perhaps a contraction of Lunsford.[63] In 1504 a deed relating to the Cleavewater area mentions a *"...garden called Lyncolneshawgh* [2 acres] *abutting west on highway leading from the common called Luddilliswyrde to Gyffordes Crosse, north on the land of John Gyfforde.... and south on Luddilliswyrde common".*[64] This appears to identify Luddilliswyrde common clearly with what is now known as Lunces Common.

'Luddill' would have been a local resident and the suffix -*wyrde* means an area of thickets or bushes.

The size of the common at that time is not known but a timber-framed cottage, known as the 'Old Cottage' still stands within its enclosure on the open common, implying little further encroachment since it was built. It was built of wattle panels with lime plaster between the timber framing, oak beams and 12 inch wide floor boards. In 1800 it was recorded as 'late Walkers'.[65] In 1833 this cottage was for sale by auction and was described as a copyhold of Ditchling manor, having "... an excellent orchard and two gardens, situated at Lunt's Hill opposite Clevewater, containing 2 rood 34 poles". Three large walnut trees were to be included in the purchase price.[66] It was liable to a 'best beast' heriot which marks it as an established member of the manor and which would have guaranteed its rights of common, rights it still possesses on Lunces Common.

xxv. The old cottage, Lunces Common.

Rights of common for the Old Cottage are for the taking of gorse, furze bushes, underwood and peat over the whole area of the common. Other rights on Lunces Common existed for Rogers Farm, Scrases Farm, Clearwaters and part of Clevewater, all held of the Manor of Ditchling. The bridleway which leads from the common to Clearwaters Farm is the drove by which the cattle from Clearwaters came to graze.[67] A boundary ditch still exists between the common and Rogers Farm house and also between the common and the former Griggs Farmhouse; this would have prevented cattle from straying. Griggs Farm, though situated at the edge of the common, was not part of Ditchling manor and therefore had no customary rights there.

By 1606 a quarry had been established on the common. At that time Merifields (now Middlefield Cottage, Fox Hill) was owned by the Hogge family, the well known Sussex ironmasters, and was used to house the foreman and workers from the quarry. In 1608 John Scrase, who had been admitted in 1598 to Rogers (Chapter 4), was granted a licence to take stones "...from the waste of Lunsford".[68] The old barn which stands behind Rogers farmhouse is thought to have been built about 1610. Recent conversion work on the barn revealed a foundation of roughly hewn blocks of sandstone. Were these the very stones used by John Scrase? It is more than likely that this is so.

Pauper children had always been a significant problem, as a selection of extracts from the records of 1770 show:

"Feb 20: John Buckman [of Little Otehall] *to keep Sarah Holcombe and to have two pounds, two shillings for next year.*

Master Buckman to have George Huggett and to have one pound one shilling for next year .

Mr Fuller [of Morehouse] *to keep Ben Cork for his board*

July 12: Master Farncombe [of Lunces] *to keep James Lawson & to have at nine pence per week to Easter next.*

Ann Butcher went to John Chatfield [of Lockstrood] *at sixpence week.*

Aug 23: Mary Tharp went to Master Mainard for one shilling week."

The overseer was of course concerned to reduce the number of individuals dependent on poor relief. Even if work was not available for the father, or he was unable to work, at least it might be possible to train the child to be useful to local farmers. What is more, the farmer would be getting some cheap labour. In 1771. for instance:

"Feb 20: Master Jeffery to have Ben Cork next year and give him fifteen shillings for next year

Master Russell to have George Huggett and to give him five shillings next year"

Ben Cork had learned enough with Mr Fuller to become a useful worker. George Huggett had graduated from pauper child to paid worker, but still under the overseer's jurisdiction.

We can trace further annual increases, George getting £1 10s. in 1772, changing later that year to a weekly wage of 1s with Master Johnson; John Tharp's pay doubled from 1773 to 1774 to £1 10s. There are other examples of youngsters who were thought to be good workers. Sarah Tharp was paid £2 and John Huggett £2 2s. for the year 1774 when they were with Joseph Farncombe. Of course, apart from giving a helping hand to these pauper children, this type of employment reduced the cost to the parish.

Sometimes, we can sense that the parish officers were not so keen to keep a particular child within the parish. On 29th April 1771, it was agreed as follows:

"John Weller to have Mary Jeffery and to have nine pence per week certain and if the girl proves well and he get her a place out of the parish he is to have 3 pence per week more for the year".

If successful, this would mean that the parish would save the cost of maintaining at least one pauper.

When parents were unable to maintain their children the Overseers, in their zeal to reduce the cost to the ratepayers, trawled their net among other members of the family. In April 1789 William Brigden, a farmer living in Cuckfield, was ordered to pay 2s 6d for the maintenance of his three grandchildren, then a charge on the Wivelsfield officers. As owner of Lockstrood in Wivelsfield, Brigden would have been known to the parish officers as a man of means and his family duty was therefore unavoidable. [26]

When children were put out to work it was usual for indentures of apprenticeship to be drawn up. Unfortunately none have survived for Wivelsfield. Typically these documents ensured that for the seven years the young person was under his master's roof he was properly instructed, fed and well cared for; and in return he was bound to serve his master faithfully "...*in all lawful businesses according to his power, wit and ability; and honestly, orderly and obediently in all things demean and behave himself towards his Master*". Apart from anything, the arrangements ensured that the the apprentice "...*be not any way a Charge to the ...Parish*". Jasper Turner, apprenticed at Billingshurst to a husbandman in 1682, was to receive at the end of his term "....*a good new Suit for the Holidayes, and another for the Working-days*" [27]

The parish also continued to help people to stay in their own homes by contributing towards the rent: "*April 3rd: John Broad half a year Rent. T Waller 15s. 0d. Henry Bristows Rent £1. 10s. 0d. October 17th: to Sarah Holman for Rent 5s. 0d.*" On November 25th Dame Huggett received £1 5s. 6d. for "*Boarding & Nursing Mr Harker*"; and on December 23rd Edward Carter was paid 2s. for a bedstead.

All these entries would seem to indicate an increase in the proportion of out-relief, but the workhouse was still playing an important role in the care of paupers. The list of recipients of monthly dole had mounted to eleven, at least some of whom would have been inmates. They included three men and a boy, but with none of the 1767 names still appearing. It looks as if John Budd's wife was then a widow, referred to as Dame Budd, and she received weekly pay of 1s. in addition to 1s. per pound for her spinning, in contrast to the regular rate of 5d. per pound. Did she do her work on finer material, or was this a hidden subsidy? In her place, we now have John Ashdown's wife receiving regular monthly payments - another absconding husband perhaps.

The workhouse had to pay a tithe of five shillings on November 11th. The tithes of the living had been impropriated to the owner of Morehouse - none other than John Fuller, the Churchwarden of 1786 and the Overseer of 1766. Did he actually demand his rights, even from the parish paupers?

One thing is certain. The well was still going strong, because on July 18th John Geaven was paid 1s 0d for "mending a well Buckett". Was it the same one that Widow Hoal supplied on March 1st 1767? The accounts for the intervening years make no reference to any similar repair, so perhaps things were made to last in those days. At least we know where the well was, for in 1874 it was marked 'D.W.'[deep water] immediately to the north of the present school buildings.

viii. To the very end

"When constabulary duty's to be done"

W.S.Gilbert

By 1786, John Fuller had been succeeded as Overseer by John Leaney, and William Bean, the Clerk of 20 years earlier, had become the Headborough as well. This office was synonymous with that of constable, or else his deputy, depending on the part of the country and the period; in any case, the more familiar modern term eventually took over. Until the various Victorian Acts empowered larger authorities such as the counties, the parish was responsible for maintaining law and order through the manor court (and even after 1842 the Vestry could still appoint a constable).

Apart from the more obvious involvement with misdemeanours and felonies, the headborough of the sixteenth century was responsible for eliminating beggars, apprenticing poor children and housing those in need. Even after the Elizabethan poor laws he could still be responsible for paying the overseer's wages, for giving doles to vagrants in possession of the necessary papers to allow them to continue their travels, and for burying any pauper who had mismanaged his affairs so badly as to die within the parish. Before the establishment of a regular poor rate, the constable or headborough levied the rate on the authority of the constable of the hundred, the next rung in the administrative ladder, between the parish and the county. So it can be seen that his involvement with the poor could be considerable.[28]

At the workhouse, as everywhere else, illness was part of the web of life and death came at the end. It was often the constable who had to attend to all matters pertaining such as: January 20th *1766 "moveing*

the people in the Smallpox." "February 9th: Dame Renvell's Bill for
the Smallpox 18s. 3d." and "paid Lidya Lutman for nursing in the
smallpox, 12s."

In 1767, between January and Easter, several entries referred to
payments to Dame Holcomb "in Illness" of one or two shillings.
Thomas Chatfield the "docter", also received his dues and the
appropriately named Thomas Carter, *"fetching and carting during the*
smallpox".

The mention of smallpox might lead us to think that an epidemic
occurred during the year we are looking at. Of course, many people
recovered, and these will not be recorded in any collected figures, but
certainly there is no evidence that more than the usual number died at
this time. In 1766 the deaths from all causes in Wivelsfield totalled six,
in 1767 the number was nine; the average for each of the 20 years
1760-1779 was seven. It could be that the workhouse suffered its own
mini-epidemic, which would not be surprising, in view of the probable
primitive, cramped and unhygienic conditions.

"1765 Sept 30: Paid to Master Gallard for a coffen	*8s.*	*0d.*
1766 May 26: .....*to bury a child.......*	*0s.*	*1d.*
Oct 8: paid Widow Lawson going to the Docter		*6d.*
Nov 18: paid Thos Chatfield for taking care of		
Ben Jones Wife	*12s.*	*0d.*
paid Wm Bean for diging the grave	*3s.*	*0d."*

Even after burial, the overseers work continued:

"1767 Mar 21: paid for crying the sale of Lidya	
Pearce's clothes	*2d.*
1771 Mar 25: Linda Pearce purse and wearing apparel £2 18s. 4d.	
June 27: rec. at the first sale of Widow Avery,	
after paying crying [i.e.for the advert]	*£4 13s. 8d."*

The accounts presented at the Easter meeting show William Bean,
who in earlier years had written up the accounts and dug the grave, in
his new role as Churchwarden - clearly a busy man. But they all seem
to have been busy men, rotating the various offices within a small
group, probably as means of maintaining control in a parish which did
not benefit from, or suffer from, the influence of just one resident
landowner.

While clearly the practical attitudes of the larger landowners had a
major effect, was it in part because of the dedicated and thoughtful
management of these lesser (?) men that, when food riots occurred
elsewhere in, for example 1766, or 1795 with the so-called revolt of the
housewives, or in 1830, when the Captain Swing disturbances affected
nearby parishes such as Bolney, Cowfold, Poynings and Cooksbridge

with arson and damage to machinery, Wivelsfield did not get involved?[29]

Plate 21. 'Moonrakers' and 'Wyndham', where the Parish constable lived in the late 1700's.

Wivelsfield's old parish workhouse in Church Lane, ministered by its dutiful officers, spun on to its final years. In 1834 everything was to change. The parishes were to relinquish their individual control of the poor within their bounds and instead 'Unions' of several parishes were to take over. One vast central workhouse in each Union was to replace the 'homely' cottage workhouses in the parishes. Wivelsfield was to be in Chailey Union.

When the details were being worked out, prior to the passing of the Poor Law Reform Act of 1834, the local Assistant Poor Law Commissioner, William Hawley, encountered many objections from parishes unwilling to relinquish control. For example, five of the parishes to the west of Wivelsfield had to be forced to accept the Cuckfield Union of 15 parishes. By contrast, there were no objections to the scheme from the 11 parishes in the Chailey Union, even though Ringmer, Ditchling and Wivelsfield had been managing their own in- and out-relief previously. Indeed, it can be inferred that the "...landed proprietors and influential ratepayers" subscribed to the view that "...the devastating blight of pauperism [was] rapidly consuming the property of the owners of the soil and undermining the moral condition of the poor".[30] They were willing to seek new solutions.

At the time of transfer of control to the Guardians of Chailey Union in 1835 there were 17 paupers in Wivelsfield workhouse, with ages ranging from 57 years down to 10 months. Direct involvement of the parish officers ceased in March 1836, when the workhouse was given up, and the able-bodied women and children sent to Chailey. But what a prospect for the inmates themselves. Even though their previous standard of living must have been minimal, at least they had been housed in cottages in their own parish, with opportunities of visits to and from their more fortunate neighbours. Now they were faced with isolation in another village some distance away, in a building the size of which they had probably never even dreamed of in their worst nightmares.

xxxi. Henry Booker, first pastor of Bethel Chapel. Copyright Rev. R. S. Payne.

CHAPTER 8

CHAPEL AND CHURCH 1672-1851

"Whoso would be a man must be a nonconformist"

Ralph Waldo Emerson *Essays: self reliance*

i. A climate of Non-conformity

In the Commonwealth period the parishioners of Wivelsfield had, as we have seen, installed a minister of their choosing against the wishes of the patron. At the Restoration of the monarchy in 1660 Parliament feared that religious extremists might provoke another civil war. Therefore legislation was passed declaring that the Church of England was to be the only denomination allowed and that any deviations were punishable offences.   Thomas More, Wivelsfield's patron, had responded by throwing out the commonwealth pastor as a "schismatical, fanatical fellow", and thus, for a while, Wivelsfield's own civil war continued.

Parliament's wariness was partly due to the fact that the new King Charles II's wife, Catherine of Braganza had failed to produce children and James, Duke of York was an ardent Roman Catholic convert. Charles, who had strong leanings in the same direction was therefore prepared to be more tolerant of dissidents and recusants. In 1672 he published a 'Declaration of Indulgence' whereby non-conformist meetings or 'conventicles' and their preachers might be registered and allowed to continue if approved. This was reversed by Parliament the next year and the 'Test Act' imposed penalties on those who would not demonstrate allegiance to the Church of England.

In 1685 after the death of Charles, James became king and made a bid to reintroduce Roman Catholicism as the faith of the realm, but failed. Finally he was forced to flee to France and Parliament invited William of Orange and his wife Mary to accept the Crown, as joint rulers.   Both had legitimate claims as grandchildren of Charles I. William and Mary were strict protestants and in accepting the Throne they aimed to preserve that faith. They were therefore willing to give religious freedom to Protestant non-conformists but not to Catholics. To these ends in 1689 the Act of Toleration was passed. Roman Catholics remained excluded but the way was now paved for protestant non-conformists to worship openly in their own chapels.

From the Restoration of the Monarchy in 1660 to the Toleration Act of 1689 Protestant non-conformity simmered away in mid Sussex.[1] Ejected ministers, such as John Oliver at Wivelsfield, went underground. Meeting with their supporters in private houses, they preached, travelled and spread the word.[2] Though we lose track of John Oliver and his advocate Thomas Hunt after 1660, the names Olive/Oliver and Hunt reappeared locally in the 18th century in connection with the Otehall chapel.

The earliest-known conventicle of non-conformists at Wivelsfield was in the house of Thomas Hurst, probably Hurst House Farm.[3] The preacher, one Thomas Hallett, applied for a licence to meet there in 1672. Described as 'from Ireland' he had 'resigned' as rector of Streat in 1662, perhaps ejected. A few years earlier, in 1669, Hallett, noted as being "at Wivelsfield" had been listed as one of the preachers of a conventicle held at Westmeston in a house called Blackbrooke (Blackbrook Farm). This conventicle was attracting "above 200" non-conformists who were "many of good estate". A significant proportion of them must have been drawn in from the surrounding area.[4] Among the regular preachers at Blackbrook was Edward Lulham, a previous vicar of Ditchling until ejected in 1658. By 1672 Lulham had registered his own conventicle at Kenwards in Lindfield, as 'presbyterian' but Hallet's at Wivelsfield was 'Congregationalist'.[5]

The increasing numbers asking for recognition caused the authorities in 1676 to take a Religious Census of Sussex. They feared *"the consideration of the number of dissenters hath been an argument as if their party were too formidable to be suppressed"*. The number of non-conformists of 16 years and over in Wivelsfield was registered as 18 compared with 82 conformists - 18% of the adult population. No Roman Catholics were listed.[6]

ii. Baptist Dissenters in mid Sussex

The strongest non-conformist movement locally was that of the Baptists, known originally as Anabaptists. In Ditchling there were 18 'middle sort' , that is 'middle class' supporters of the movement in 1672. Half a century passed before they, and their descendants could obtain their own place of worship; but eventually, in 1730 one Edward Tanner [7] sold a house "...butting east on a footpath leading to East End Lane" to Robert Chatfield, eldest son of Robert Chatfield of Streat, yeoman. Chatfield was to hold it in trust "... *that the premises will be a Meeting House and Burying Place for the Baptist Meeting...in and around Ditchling without disturbance and molestation*".[8]

The Chatfields were a land-owning family from the Westmeston and Streat area. Among the first trustees of the Ditchling Meeting House in 1740 were William Marten of Clayton, Michael Marten of Keymer, and Michael Marten of Ditchling, all described as 'yeomen'. They were in fact substantial yeomen, owning, from west to east, New Close farm and Franklands in Keymer, and Fragbarrow farm in Ditchling, three profitable farms now on the south side of Burgess Hill, as well as other land in other parishes.[9]

The chapel drew people in from a wide area including several families from St. John's Common and from 'Whalebridge' [Valebridge Common], a general term which included Clearwaters farm in Wivelsfield. John Dancy from Clearwaters was ordained an Elder at Ditchling in 1737 and was registered a preacher. In 1802 the congregation included Mary Dancy from 'Whalebridge'. Members also lived in the northern part of Ditchling common, notably the brickmaking family the Billinghursts (who supplied the Wivelsfield well bricks in 1766) and their successor Francis Foster.[10]

The Webb family of Fanners were involved in 1713/14 when "the house of Ambrose Jenner" in Wivelsfield was registered "...for worship of Ana Baptists", the preacher being Nathaniel Webb.[11] Nathaniel, a blacksmith, had his workshop on the Green, but lived in Ditchling. Wivelsfield in 1724 was recorded as having eight anabaptist families resident in the parish.[12] It is clear that Baptist families intermarried, as would be expected. Michael Marten of Newclose farm in Keymer had married one Anne Webb of Falmer while his sister Mary, who lived at Franklands, had married Richard Webb of Fanners.[13] From the records of Ditchling Meeting House it can be seen that Thomas Mercer, Panet Drew, Joseph Mercer, Mary his wife, Mary Panet, Henry Booker and members of his family were all received into membership of that chapel between 1739 and 1751.[14] Mary Mercer, one of two daughters of Martin Richard Webb, inherited Fanners in 1749. Her husband was Joseph Mercer of Isfield. It is no coincidence that members of the Pannett family were her tenants at Fanners. The description of local dissenters in 1669, "many of good estate" still held good a century later in Wivelsfield.

It seems clear, therefore, that though the Ditchling General Baptist meeting had members from Wivelsfield, they had met at Fanners before the founding of the Ditchling chapel in 1730 and they perhaps continued to meet occasionally at Fanners and at other local venues until their own place of worship could be built. In 1763 they were still at Fanners. A "..meeting in the house of John Pannet in the Parish of Wivelsfield for Baptists" was registered in that year, for six members.

But a member of the Ditchling chapel had been moved to strike out on his own; and his action soon brought Wivelsfield Baptists their own place of worship.

iii. The Bethel Strict Baptist Chapel

Plate 22. The Bethel Chapel *circa* 1900.

Henry Booker was a member of the Ditchling Baptist movement whose home was at Ditchling. One day in 1762, a bricklayer friend told him of a preacher who had made a great impression on him. This was George Whitefield whom the Countess of Huntingdon had engaged to preach in Brighton. When Henry Booker heard his message it caused him to feel that he "did not esteem the (Ditchling) Community to be a true Christian Church" and he threatened to "tear the church to pieces". Understandably, Ditchling withdrew communion from him on the twentieth of October 1762, as was declared by Brother Fry, Chairman. Ditchling's loss was Wivelsfield's gain. Henry left Ditchling with several members of that church, joined with friends in Wivelsfield and registered Fanners as a meeting place in 1763.[15]

In 1764, John Simmons, who previously had been minister of Ditchling, was appointed pastor of Wivelsfield. Again there was a difference of opinion and when a split followed in 1765 he left, taking half the congregation with him. In 1768, Henry Booker, who had moved to Wivelsfield and was living at ''Great Bankside' (Bankside farm),[16] took over as pastor to the remaining group. They met in his house and it was perhaps at this point that the meeting moved from being general to being strict Baptists. By the time of his death 31 years later, there was a congregation of 41 members.

In 1779 the group was admitted at an Assembly to the Kent and Sussex Association and in the following year Wivelsfield obtained its own, purpose-built Baptist Meeting House. It was sited on land almost next door to Booker's home which causes one to speculate whether it may have been he who provided the land. It is a square brick building under a tiled roof. Inside is a simple, very light, room with high level windows on two sides and with the wooden pulpit opposite the entrance door. The present sturdy wooden pews came from the Ebenezer Chapel in Brighton. Some of the original pews are now in the low gallery which is over the entrance vestibule. A door leads into the attached cottage, which was once the home of the pastor, but is now used for church rooms and connects with the modern hall built in 1977.

Eight baptisms were recorded in 1780, some of whom may have been adults rather than infants. However, until after 1815 only three more persons were baptised in the next 22 years. Either the chapel had its ups and downs or the provision of the new building had caused a flurry of new recruitment.

Pastors held office intermittently from 1799 to 1840 and on occasions when there was no pastor, a preacher from Brighthelmstone, such as Rev. William Savory in 1837, helped with the services. John Sarjent was in charge from 1802 until 1814 and during his time numbers increased. William Coppard who was appointed in 1816 died only two years later and numbers began to drop again.

The fortunes of the Bethel chapel were revived by the arrival of the Baldock family into Wivelsfield. Thomas Baldock came from Wadhurst in 1840 as minister and took up residence at the Meeting House. The first to follow Thomas and his wife to the village was his brother John. He had been a tenant farmer in their home village of Wadhurst but his landlord having died, the farm was in the hands of executors. In the 1840s, being too old to start up again when the farm had to change hands, John, his wife Maria and one of their sons, William, came to work for Mr Brattle also born in Wadhurst, who had just bought Manns Farm. Left behind with his Uncle William, was young John Baldock, the other son. Thomas Baldock continued as the pastor at Wivelsfield until his death in 1873.

A burial ground was provided with the new Chapel in 1780. Prior to this the Wivelsfield Baptists may have used the Ditchling Chapel for burials, or the local parish Church. At the Bethel burial ground the earliest legible inscription is in memory of Mary the wife of John Knight, who died in 1811. The tombstones give evidence of strong family connections within the group and by far the largest monument is to Henry Booker. Much in evidence are names of the Baldock family, who came to play a prominent role in Wivelsfield affairs as we shall learn in the ensuing chapters.[17]

iv. A missionary comes to Wivelsfield

"Surely Oathall is a highly favoured place,

where the Lord himself delighteth to dwell"

Rev. William Romaine, 1761[18]

In 1765, as we have seen, there was a split among the Baptist flock in Wivelsfield. It was a time of intense activity among local dissenters. A new contender had joined the field and those involved in trying to establish a non-conformist chapel in Wivelsfield, were torn between staying with the Baptists or following the newcomer, the Countess of Huntingdon.[19]

Around the year 1760 Francis Warden, the trustee for the Shirley family who owned Great Otehall, heard that Selina, Countess of Huntingdon was seeking accommodation in rural Sussex. She had been born a Shirley. She was a widow, her son Lord Francis having inherited the title in 1745/6 on the death of his father, Theophilus 9th Earl of Huntingdon. Two sons aged 11 and 13 had died of smallpox in 1743. Of her remaining four children only one daughter, Elizabeth, married and outlived her.

Great Otehall was offerred as a residence for the Countess. The house had already a long association with non-conformity. Remembering that it was the Godmans of Great Otehall who had supported the Commonwealth minister John Oliver, it is no surprise to find that in 1714 the *"...house of Ashdowne called Whathall* [Otehall] *", had been registered "...for Presbiterians at the request of John Ollive".*[20] Olive was also active in Lewes where he appears to have been succeeded by Samuel Olive, probably a son.[21] The Countess found the registration system offensive and in 1763, after her arrival, it was recorded, *"...Mr. Ollive desired... to take off the licence for Oathall and says Lady Huntingdon desire it should be done."* Her followers, she believed, were still part of the established church and therefore there was no need for registration.

xxxii. Selina, Countess of Huntingdon. Copyright the Cheshunt Foundation.

John Olive's Calvinistic beliefs insisted that by 'Predestination' only 'elect' souls could be saved; a faith which Countess Selina, at first influenced by the preaching of John Wesley, expounded and expanded in the drawing rooms of her friends. Genteel society was entertained with preachers rather than with the card table. Yet it was the artisan classes who took up the message and became 'hearers'. She founded the first Chapel of her 'Connexion', in North Street, Brighton, and drew a large congregation. Here she had engaged preachers such as George Whitefield, by whom Henry Booker of the Baptist Chapel had been influenced. This chapel was demolished in 1969.

Members of the Brighton congregation who came from north of the Downs had begged the Countess to arrange meetings nearer to their own homes in the Weald. Wivelsfield became that new meeting place. As a first step in providing a place of worship in Wivelsfield the Countess turned the large hall of her temporary home into a chapel, keeping the upper rooms for the use of herself and visiting preachers. On the north side of Great Otehall can still be seen the oriel window from which her personal chaplain, the Rev. William Romaine preached.

There, in 1761, he gave communion to a congregation of a hundred people, drawn in from Wivelsfield and further afield.[22]

The Countess clearly regarded her own role as that of a mission-ary, for having sown the seeds of a chapel in any particular locality, she moved on, leaving the local inhabitants to use her money to build and organise their own chapel. The Test Act of 1672 had stipulated that dissenters, Protes-tant as well as Roman Catholics were debarr-ed from holding public office or attending uni-versities. This Act was not repealed until 1828. In 1768 she set up, at Trevecca House in Breconshire, a train-ing college for non-conformist ministers. Her first students were six men from Oxford

Plate 23. The oriel window, Great Otehall.

University who had by law, been expelled as dissenters. One of these, the Rev. Thomas Jones was from 1778 until his death, the first minister of Otehall Chapel and the Countess' personal chaplain.

v. The Otehall Chapel

Otehall Chapel was the second chapel to be founded by the Countess, the Brighton one being the first. However, many of her later foundations erected their own buildings before Otehall Chapel was built in 1778. It stands on the northern tip of Blackmore's farm, at the junction of Ditchling Road (B2112) and Green Road, a vunerable corner. Until 1993 in front of the chapel were to be seen the remaining three of a group of 11 Scots pine trees, which were once a landmark in the village. As is usual with non-conformist chapels the building was a simple one. It had brick walls and a tiled roof with the manse, the minister's house, added to the south end of the building in 1789. The

Rev. Jones was the first minister from 1778-1808 and, after his death, his widow remained in occupation until her death. There was a stable but this came to an abrupt end when hit by a vehicle. In 1956 the Manse itself was demolished and replaced by a new building, the 'Huntingdon Hall' and vestry. The chapel porch had to be rebuilt as the result of a car leaving the road and knocking down most of the structure.

The style of the inside of the chapel is typical of 18th century, non-conformist meeting places, with the pulpit as the focal point and a simple table instead of the altar found in the established Church. The pulpit at Otehall Chapel is a valued possession. It was transferred from Great Otehall and was that from which Whitefield, Romaine, Venn and other famous clerics preached. What the media is in the late 20th century, the pulpit was to the people of her time. The Countess' movement had been inspired by the belief that all sinners, high or low, were equal in the eyes of God; a comforting message, no doubt, to the ordinary working people who listened below her pulpit and went out again to tell their neighbours.

Otehall Chapel has also inherited the chandelier which was used by the Countess in her private chapel. This is indeed a privilage of which the congregation is proud.

A trust deed dated 31st December 1831 allows us a glimpse behind the scenes in the running of the chapel. The first party, perhaps trustees acting on behalf of the 'Connexion', were Mr. John Hunt of Brighton and Rev. Robert Taylor Hunt of Kennington, (then in Surrey), father and son. John Hunt was also a Wivelsfield landholder who in 1818, perhaps through his 'connexion' with Wivelsfield, had purchased the Little Otehall estate for £4,650. The second party was headed by the Rev. Samuel Franklyn of St. Thomas in the Cliffe, Lewes; there was also John Avery the elder, John Avery the younger both of Chailey, yeomen, James Jeffery of Ditchling, yeoman, and James Baker of Keymer, smith (who worked the smithy at the top of Fairplace Hill, Burgess Hill), for the other part. The second group represented Otehall Chapel. The Rev. Franklyn perhaps had a supervisory role from the Connexion Chapel in Lewes, there being no ordained minister at Wivelsfield since the death of the first minister, the Rev. Thomas Jones in 1808.[23]

The Otehall Chapel trustees were to pay Rev. and Mr. Hunt 10s. for the "...*messuage with chapel or meeting house stable yard and garden adjoining Blackmores Farm*". This was behind what is now Baldock's Garage. Rebecca, the widow of Rev. T. Jones, was still occupying the house. The agreement made, was that for her lifetime she should be allowed to remain the tenant but should she leave or die, the premises would become the home of the minister.

was at least on the doorstep. Indeed, in the latter part of the 18th century the patron was none other than the John Fuller named above. After his death in 1786 the patronage of the Church and the tithes remained for another century with the owners of More House and/or Great Otehall. While this arrangement clearly reinforced the establishment role of the parish Church, it also seems to have ensured there was a ministry.

Philip Shore, M.A., the incumbent 1705-ll, has a memorial inscription in Woodmancote which describes him as:

> *"learned yet polite, facetious yet sincere*
> *A poignant wit on Fools, on knaves severe"* [26]

It was during the curacy of William Lamb that:

"Richard Miles an Dorithy his wife murdered an was Buried hear June ye l 1734". These were the innkeeper and his wife from the Royal Oak on Ditchling Common, victims of Jacob Harris, a pedlar. The sad event still has its memorial, 'Jacob's Post', on the common near the Inn.

In 1745-6 the curate was commemorated at his burial as *"...Edword Pouell qurot* (curate) *at this time and amerywon"*. Can this mean 'a merry one'? Edward Powell was appointed in 1740 and although his life may have been merry it was also short. He was aged 33 years when he died.

The Rev. Rowland Lewis was incumbent at Wivelsfield from 1749 to 1772. In 1761 he had married one Mary Comber in the next parish of Lindfield. In 1780 he was allowed a stipend of £20 a year. As he had by then retired, this must have in fact been a pension. It was granted by:

"John Fuller of Wivelsfield, Esq. Impropriator of Impropriate Rectory and Patron of the Curacy or Church of Wivelsfield, with the approval and at the direction of [the] *Governor of* [the] *Bounty of Queen Anne for the Augmentation of the maintenance of the poor Clergy to Rev. Rowland Lewis, Clerk Curate of the Curacy or Church of Wivelsfield* [an] *Annual rent charge of £20 payable out of the impropriation or impropriate rectory of Wivelsfield and out of tithes".* [27]

When Anne became Queen, following the death of William III in 1702, among her many concerns was the welfare of her clergy, especially those in want. The old medieval dues of "First Fruits and Tenths" which the Pope had always collected from the English clergy had been annexed to the Crown by Henry VIII and converted into a fixed tax which amounted to some £16,000 a year. Anne, moved by two of her bishops, gave this money in 1704 to form a fund known as

Queen Anne's Bounty from which stipends of the poorer clergy might be augmented.

In the 19th century George Dixon served the parish for 34 years as Perpetual Curate from 1829 to 1863. The Chancel's Victorian east window is dedicated to his memory. The major scenes depict the Adoration of the Magi, The Crucifixion and the Resurrection whilst below are illustrations from the life of St. John the Baptist.

Not only the clergy, but also the parish clerks gave long years of service, the Mills and the Bean families whom we met in Chapter 5. Richard Mills had been "...clerke to this parish fourty two years" when he died, aged 89 years, in 1722. His eldest son, also Richard, was appointed in his place and was followed by the shoemaking family, the Beans, as clerks. Though the Chapels had claimed many of Wivelsfield's trading classes, they had not claimed them all.

xxxiv. Print of the church, 1830.

There were few alterations and embellishments to the church in this period. One significant addition, however, was the installation of a west gallery across the front of which was inscribed "The bounty of Mrs.Frances More, to this parish, 1716". The erection of galleries for singers and musicians became common during the 18th century but it is not known if this was the reason for this particular gift.[28] At sometime a dormer window, perhaps to light the gallery, was inserted in the nave roof above the north doorway. This is clearly shown in an undated colour-wash drawing of the Church, possibly by A.N.Somer about 1830. However it was not until the Victorian enthusiasm for 'restoration' that major work on the fabric was considered.

vii. Gathering in their flocks

"Wherever God erects a house of prayer,
The Devil always builds a chapel there;
And 'twill be found upon examination,
The latter has the largest congregation."

Daniel Defoe, *The True-Born Englishman*

In 1633 the Bishop of Bath and Wells wrote "*I finde that by Church ales heretofore many poor Parishes have cast their Bells, repaired their Towers, beautified their Churches and raised stocks for the Poor.*" These 'church ales', as we saw in Chapter 2, had been the principal fund-raising activity for every parish, a gathering for food and drink which also included sports, dancing, drama and other festivities. These occasions regularly raised amazingly large sums even in sparsely populated areas. There were, however many objections to church ales on both religious and moral grounds. Once they had been suppressed Church rates became compulsory and difficult to collect.

Each year the Vestry had met to decide rates for Church repairs, restoration, enlargement and improvements such as heating but since these rates were compulsorily levied on all households non-conformists felt particularly aggrieved. They had no allegiance to any parish Church and no wish to support it when they had their own places of worship to build and maintain. This great source of irritation to non-conformists generally resulted in many Bills being introduced into Parliament, all un-workable until under Mr. Gladstone's Bill of 1868 Church rates were finally abolished.

One wonders, therefore, whether the rash of west galleries that appeared in parish churches in the 18th century, was a bid by the established Church to staunch the flow of support that was running in the free churches' direction. A recent study of village music in Sussex, has shown that the musicians were mainly the village craftspeople and traders.[29] They represented that section of society that was turning to the independent churches. Did Wivelsfield's west gallery, provided by the patron's maiden aunt in 1716 help hold back the tide?

Evidence of the tug of war between Church and Chapel in Wivelsfield is apparent in the Will of Joseph Farncombe. In 1706, having recently bought Lunces, he lay dying. His much-wanted son, Joseph, was only about a year old. His wife, Anne, was the daughter of Michael Marten, a prominent non-conformist. His wife's younger sister, Mary, had married the non-conformist Richard Webb of Fanners. Farncombe insisted, from his death bed, that his wife Anne should have:

> "...the tuicion and bringing up of my children.." and sufficient money for the task "...provided that she bring them up in the Faith practice and Profession of the Church of England into which they were Baptized...". Moreover, "...if either my Said Son Joseph or any of my said three daughters when they come to Years of Discrecion forsake that Church into which they were Baptized ..(they shall)..forfeit those legacies herein respectively to them bequeathed...". [30]

The three daughters were Sarah, Anne and Elizabeth. Ann married John Dancy of Clearwaters who was ordained an Elder at Ditchling Chapel in 1737 and she presumably lost her inheritance. Joseph, the son, held on to the established faith, and to Lunces.

General Baptists were not adverse to the occasional Church service. John Burgess, the diarist, recorded on 10 April 1789, "...Went to Keymer church...it being Good Friday..." and on the 25 August, " ...went to Weavilsfield Church and to Furncomb for Wip sticks...". [31] The Otehall chapel continued on into the 19th century enjoying firm support. Its register for the period 1795-1836 shows the distance which people travelled for baptism at Otehall Chapel. They came from as far away as Holborn, Bethnal Green, from Capel in Surrey and from most of the surrounding Sussex villages including Maresfield, East Grinstead and Clayton. This was long before railways or cars were even contemplated and must have involved not only dedication but considerable expense.

Stray references occur in this period to other meetings as in 1815 when George Anscombe, a weaver lent his house "Shoulders" for worship of Protestant Dissenters, but there is no record of which sect used it. [32]

In 1829 a Religious Census shows that the non-conformist churches were still thriving in the Weald of Sussex, though they were still very thin in the Downland. [33] In Wivelsfield the Otehall chapel, 'Independent Calvinism', claimed a congregation of around 250 souls while the Bethel, 'Particular Baptist', spoke for 'about 80. [34] This apparently shows that somewhat more than half the residents of the parish 'belonged' to a Chapel rather than the Church for in 1821 the parish contained 537 persons, while in 1831 there were 559. [35] However, the

figures were considered by a churchwarden to be far too generous and
he credited the two chapels with no more than 30 and 50 members
respectively.   There was an 'out-chapel'   attached to the Otehall
meeting, situated at Yokehurst in Chailey, whose members may have
been included in the higher figure. The two chapels shared a minister
who had to be transported between the two sites for services.
Unfortunately a disagreement arose as to who should provide the horse,
and so the dual ministry ceased. [36]

On 30th March 1851 another Religious Census was taken of all those
attending services on that day.[37] The date of the church or chapel
building was recorded (1) together with the seating capacity (3),
whether seats were free or worshippers were required to pay pew rent
(3), time and frequency of service (4,5) and the name of the incumbent
(6). Wivelsfield responded as follows:

The Parish Church: 3) 200 total; 4) morning: 150, total 150; March
30 is an average; 5) alternately morning and afternoon; 6) George
Dixon, Perpetual Curate.

Otehall Chapel: 1) Before 1800; 3) free 200, (total 200).

Independent: 4) morning: 53 Total 53; 6) William Gravett, minister.

Particular Baptist: 1) Before 1800; 3) free 200, (Total 200); 4)
morning 80 + 32, total 112; afternoon 200, Total 200; 6) Thomas
Baldock, Minister.

Comparison of the three places of worship is interesting as each was
said to seat 200 people.   At Otehall Chapel where only a morning
service was held, 53 of the congregation were present. The Bethel
Chapel held two services, one in the afternoon instead of the more
common evening session which we have nowadays. At evening service
in March, as there was no gas or electric lighting, the buildings would
have been gloomy in the light of flickering candles or oil lamps and it
would have been dark to return home. There was morning service in
the parish Church on 30th March 1851 and 150 made a point of
attending. The Bethel Chapel under Thomas Baldock, was evidently
very popular, for he could get 80 people to the morning service plus 32
children and then in the afternoon back they came, plus 88 of their
friends and neighbours. There was presumably some effort on the part
of each establishment to educate the children of their congregations
(Chapter 12).

Comparison of the names on the gravestones at the Bethel Chapel
with those found on a list of subscribers towards alterations and
refurbishment at Otehall Chapel in 1870, shows that many families

who gave allegiance in their lifetime to the Otehall Chapel were buried at the Bethel. Otehall Chapel had no burial ground of its own and a free-church burial ground was presumably preferred to that of the parish Church. Alongside members of the Knight family, strict Baptists, can be found memorials to the Averys, Gravetts, Bishes and Richard Short, loyal members of Otehall Chapel.[38]

One can imagine a village funeral, the mourners clad in their home-spun, hand made suits and heavy boots, (only the men would have followed the bier, the women remaining at the home of the deceased to comfort those left behind.) The women may have worn pattens, to keep their feet out of the mud. Did those from Otehall Chapel have their funeral service there, or was it held at the Bethel? Whatever happened, obviously there was friendship, not rivalry between the two chapels. There were no chapels of rest where the body could remain until the funeral, for the undertaker, not funeral director, was the local wheelwright or carpenter. If the deceased was expected to die, it is likely that the coffin would have been ready before death actually occured.

It is unsurprising that the memorials found in the Bethel graveyard commemorate people who earned their living by the skill of their hands. Before all males were given the vote such families had no say in running the country. By giving their allegience to the non-conformist chapels they were able in this sphere to be in charge of their immediate situation. Their descendants have remained loyal to the chapels. The Countess of Huntingdon had horrified her noble friends by telling them that in the sight of God the poor were of equal status with the rich. Yet she was no feminist and followed the custom of her time by excluding women from holding office.

Wivelsfield's place in the history of Non-conformity is considerable. The parish, though a rural not an urban area, still has two 18th century chapels in use. Finally in 1861, after the building of the Asylum the Wivelsfield Road, now part of Haywards Heath, began to be developed (Chapter 11) and a Congregational Chapel was opened there. In the Parish Church are to be found memorial windows and monuments given by local landowners, the Mores of More House, and the Tanner family. Later memorials were donated by such as Lt. Col. Holden-Rose's family. Here we see where the landed gentry worshiped. It may appear to be a contradiction that Richard Webb, like the Colonel, had owned Fanners, yet was a Baptist. In the Weald of mid Sussex the non-conformist movement had sprung up freely, with lively vigour, out of the independent landed estates of families such as the Chatfields the Martens and the Webbs. In Wivelsfield its fortunes became bound in with the local brick and tile trade , the Hursts in the 17th century, the Billinghursts, Averys and Gravetts later. These workers and entrepreneurs mined the clay and returned its wealth to their much-loved chapels. And the chapels continued to hold their ground through the energies of local tradespeople such as the Knights and the Baldocks and those who have followed in their footsteps.

CHAPTER 9

WIVELSFIELD AND THE WIDER WORLD

i. The network of roads

"A rolling road, that rambles round the shire"

G. K. Chesterton, (1874-1936)

We have seen in Chapter 1 how a network of local trackways had developed during the medieval period to meet the needs of a growing community. These routes were, even then, part of a wider network. Our school history lessons told us that in 1066 for Harold was able to get from Yorkshire to London, gather an army and reach Hastings in 13 days at most.[1] Rapid movement through the Weald was commonplace a century later. For example, in 1199 John landed at Shoreham on Tuesday 25th May and was crowned at Westminster on Thursday 27th. A sheriff's account for January to October 1326 details frequent transportation of supplies from the Weald for Pevensey Castle, much of it heavy enough to need carts and waggons.[2]

Because the Royal court had no fixed abode in medieval times but travelled the country, attending to the business of the realm as it went, a network of roads was maintained throughout England in the status of 'King's Highway'. These were usually the through roads between towns and the more important manors. The earliest recorded law on roads was Edward I's Statute of Winchester of 1285, which expected highway maintenance to be carried out by the manor, defaulters being fined. Not only the King but his chief subjects would travel these roads regularly. For example the earls de Warenne, who held the Rape of Lewes, also had land in Surrey, Somerset and Norfolk which would be regularly visited.[3] Green Road and the main B2112 in Wivelsfield were each described as a 'highway' in the 14th century. The earl's entourage would sometimes have travelled this route when commuting between their castles at Lewes and Reigate, stopping off, perhaps, to do

highway repairs. Other parishes in Mid Sussex were called to account at the Assizes held between 1601 and 1625.[17] Similarly, Quarter Sessions from 1652 to 1682 heard a number of presentations about road maintenance[18]. During neither of these periods was any concern expressed about Wivelsfield. Was the parish beyond reproach; or were its roads of little interest to through traffic?

xxxv. Materials and labour at South Colwell, 1716. An example of 'ordinary folks' handwriting.

Timber-framed buildings could have been constructed from materials found within the parish. When brick and stone began to be used more in the seventeenth century, the contractors had to go farther afield, although of course they kept the distances and therefore the cost to a minimum, using local sources as much as possible. From the Journal of Giles Moore, Rector of Horsted Keynes, we learn that George Ashfield of Wivelsfield supplied 2 loads of lime in 1657; and that Thomas Hurst of Hurst House farm in the north of Wivelsfield parish supplied and delivered over 7,000 bricks and 2,000 tiles, as well as lime, between 1664 and 1668.[19] The parson and the brickmaker haggled over prices twice in the first month, but they seem to have resolved their differences, as the relationship continued for four more years.

In 1653 another John Attree bought 95 acres of land for £650, including "...*woods and trees growing upon the waste & highway*".[20] This would have been a commercial enterprise, and the timber would have needed transporting elsewhere. In 1698 Thomas Godman obtained permission to move timber, some for conversion into [char]coal, from his land at Otehall by means of "...*teams, carts and waggons with free access & cartage.*"[21] Not all of this business was the concern of Wivelsfield parish. In 1688 Lindfield churchwardens and overseers allowed John Attree and Richard Button, for 36/- per acre, to "...*ffell cutt down faggot up coard, coale take & carry away the wood & under wood*" from "*the coppice ground or woodland* [in Wivelsfield] *of one Stephen Pilbeame a poor child kept & maintained by the said parish of Lindfield*".[22] The inference is that the money was used for Stephen's keep. Timber was moved after death as well: in 1580 the will of John Adeane required "...*that ther shalbe vij Tonne of Tymber cutt down in my land called Lunces land and carried to Weghdeane* [Withdean] *in the parish of Patcham imeadiatly after my decease for the repayring of the housses there.*"[23]

Lords of manors had, time out of mind, carted timber out of their woods for sale, but in the 17th-century Weald almost every small farmer started to do it, having bought the timber rights from their lords. The farmers of Wivelsfield hamlet secured their timber rights in 1626 at the enclosure of their common (Chapter 6). In 1672 the lord of Middleton manor sold all timber on the combined 210 acres of North and South Colwell to the tenants.[24] Commercial, rather than subsistence farming had received a massive boost through enclosure of commons and sales of woodlands. A felled wood became a tilled field only after supplies of marl, lime and other improving agents were brought in from elsewhere.

Wivelsfield's ample woodlands clearly therefore kept the roads busy in the 17th century with the transport of felled timber, coppice wood and charcoal. The tannery, as we have seen, was a major enterprise in the parish, drawing in its regular supply of oak bark and raw skins as well as sending out its finished products. New pasture fields, won from the waste, fattened larger amounts of cattle than before. These were driven out on the hoof for sale to local or London markets. Giles Moore of Horsted Keynes came to Wivelsfield not only for bricks and lime. In 1664 he used George Chatfield as a carrier, while Thomas Buckwell, a "bullock-leach", was called upon frequently between 1665 and 1670 "...*for Bleeding & Drenching my Mare*".[25] Chatfield and Buckwell, both of Wivelsfield, would not have relied solely on the Rector of Horsted Keynes for their income; they must have been using the roads on a regular basis. Despite winter's bottomless mud or summer's hardened craters, the roads in a wealden parish such as Wivelsfield were a vital part of the local economy.

iii. The increase in private travel

"Supper is a turnpike...to get to bed"

Oliver Edwards, 1778

Much travel between parishes in the 17th century had been on official business, such as overseers attending on justices for warrants, and headboroughs executing those warrants. It had also been for commercial reasons, as we have seen, involving cattle drovers, higglers and carters. These motives for travel have continued to be with us. Young men and girls still worked as living-in farm servants, although decreasingly as the eighteenth century progressed. This decline was offset by the increase in the number of men working as day farm labourers, or in harvest gangs in the 'closed' Downland parishes.

By the middle of the eighteenth century a new voice was loudly heard, that of the private traveller. Prefering the comforts of his carriage rather than old-fashioned horse-back, he met with extreme problems in the wealden clay. Our roads were not meeting the potential demand, at least from the gentry. In 1749 Horace Walpole was writing to an Old Etonian friend: "If you love good roads, be so kind as never to go into Sussex."[26] In 1751 Dr. John Burton asked: *"Why have the cattle, pigs, women, and other animals longer legs in Sussex than elsewhere? Is it not because of the difficulty of pulling them out of so much mud and through its holding power, that the muscles are extended and the bones grow in length?"* The Sussex roads were *"...full of sloughs and holes and covered with standing water"*.[27] For a local example, Governor Shirley needed six horses, each as powerful as a brewer's dray, to pull his carriage from Otehall through the mud and deep potholes, suffering misery, pain, and even danger during his journeys.[28]

In 1691 the justices had appointed Surveyors of Highways to take over from the parish officials, and allowed the levying of a highway rate not exceeding one shilling in the pound.[29] Sadly, we have no records of the activities of Wivelsfield's Surveyor of Highways, and so no first hand account of the problems of maintaining the parish roads. Even so, the Overseer's accounts for 1766-7 (Chapter 7) indicate regular carriage of goods such as bricks and mortar for the workhouse. If this was possible, it is likely to have been due to the roads being made passable for general commerce. From the end of the seventeenth century general carriers, using 'long waggons' with four wheels as well as smaller two-wheelers, were regularly plying between the market towns and the outlying villages, carrying a bewildering variety of goods, from alcohol and fruit to earthenware and clothing and furnishing materials. It was mainly the trade in perishables such as malt and fine cloth which brought heavy waggons on the roads in winter, thereby hastening their deterioration.[30] We also know that people were still travelling to markets and fairs, as well as about their daily business.

Plate 24. The old road from Otehall to Wivelsfield Church. Now a tranquil 'green lane' footway, not a carriage way for gentlemen. Sally Burton and Sarah Warne befriend a local horse, 1985.

Many journeys would of course have been carried out on foot or on horseback. People would walk as much as 20 miles in a morning. Richard Budgen's map of 1724 shows his preferred route from Lindfield to Bramber via Wivelsfield, with 18 'milestones' marked as guides for travellers, not actually indicating distances.[31] In 1761 Mr Cooper Samson, surgeon of Ditchling and living at Wivelsfield Green, announced in the newspaper the names of the people he had vaccinated the previous year, some coming from Godstone in Surrey and Ashford in Kent, the latter over 50 miles away.[32]

It was now that the need for something more than parish initiative became evident, and the move towards turnpike trusts started to gain momentum. Turnpikes were so-called from the pole which originally prevented cattle straying and which could be turned like a gate to allow lawful access. Once fully established it meant that those who used the roads contributed to their maintenance, rather than the parish inhabitants, many of whom did relatively little damage to the surface. The first Turnpike Act had been passed passed a century previously in 1663, but the scheme was not introduced into Sussex until 1749.

The Turnpike Acts listed the tolls to be levied, and followed a general form: for passenger vehicles (including hearses) drawn by six horses the charge was commonly one shilling, drawn by a smaller number from ninepence down to threepence; goods waggons and carts drawn by six horses cost 1s 6d; droving charges were also itemised. Toll gates were numerous and led to long delays. In addition the keepers had to be paid, either directly or by leasing the tolls, which in turn led to abuses. Some travellers went to great lengths to avoid paying by bumping through fields, or forced their way through the gates without paying. The keepers were accommodated either in parts of existing buildings or in purpose-built cottages. Acts relating to Wivelsfield were passed in 1770 (Ditchling-Lindfield-Turners Hill to Newchapel, now the B2112) and 1771 (Buxted-Cuckfield, now the A272).[33]

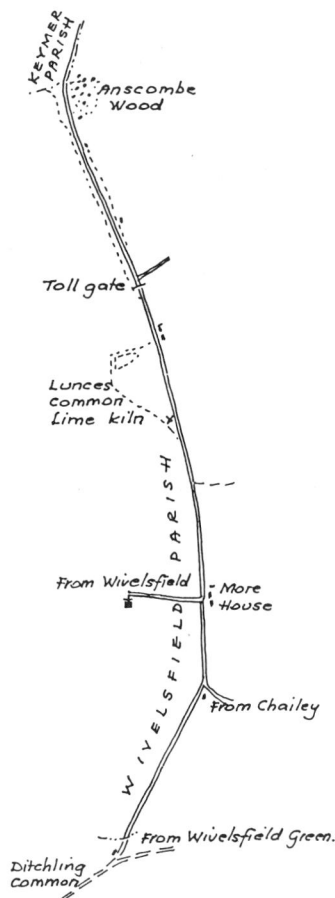

Figure 10. The Clayton to Godstone turnpike, 1824, Wivelsfield section.

The actual implementation often required the acquisition of land, and this took place through a series of indentures between the Turnpike Trustees and the individual landowners. Those for our parish were entered into in February 1778, and involve small parcels of land owned by William Brigden at Lockstrood as well as part of the Pepper Hall estate. The Trustees paid a nominal amount for the land, followed by an annual peppercorn rent. The reason given in each case was that if it was thought "...*proper to widen or alter the way or path or any part or parts of the road thereby directed to be repaired for the better accommodation of Coaches Carriages and passengers it should ...be lawful ... for them the said Trustees or any seven or more of them ... from time to time to treat contract and agree for the purchase of any Lands Ground and Hereditaments lying contiguous to or near the said Road and for the loss or damage the Owners Proprietors or Occupiers thereof....shall sustain....[and] the Trustees should become the Purchasers for the best price....*"[34] This "best price" was five shillings for two small parcels of land, in each case less than 2 acres. Presumably William Chatfield as Treasurer disbursed these sums. At least the cost compared very favourably with figures for other areas, where as much as £120 an acre has been recorded, plus compensation for the removal of buildings.[35] James Attree's will of 1812 refers to his land at Lockstrood "...heretofore part of the Old Road *"having been purchased "...from the Trustees for repairing the Road from New Chappel to the top of Ditchling Bost Hills".*[36]

Breeches maker John Burgess of Ditchling is an interesting example of a local resident for whom travel was an important part, not only of his working life, but of his cultural life as well. His diary shows that he was travelling from his home in Ditchling to most nearby parishes, and many further afield.[37] In return, he frequently received visitors from other parts. For example in the twelve months from late February 1785, when his diary starts, there were about 120 comings and goings involving other parishes, from the immediately adjacent to as far away as Wisborough Green and London. Of particular interest to us in Wivelsfield are the following entries:

> *"March 25 ..to Mr. Knights with a pr old B[reeches] 2/- then to*
> *Mr Tanners at ye tanyard....*
> *July   23 ....to Weavelsfield to Mr. Knights*
> *Febry 2   Went to Weavelsfield to Mr Beans"*

In addition, Burgess must have passed through Wivelsfield on his way to Scaynes Hill, Lindfield, Godstone and London. Much of his journeying resulted from his deep involvement with the Baptist communion, as he records on a weekly basis his attendance at Meetings in other chapels. In this regard he may not be typical of his fellow tradesmen; and, unlike the gentry he was on horseback, not in a carriage. He could cover a lot of ground in a working day:

> *"July 5th* (1786) *Went to Weavelsfield to ye tanyard. With 2 dozen leather to Scains Hill. With some old breeches and Bot an old Coat. Gave 2s 6³/₄d. for it then Went to Chailey with some wool 4¹/₂lb. for dame atheirl came home* [to Ditchling] *then went to St. John's fair etc."*

St. John's Fair was away to the north at Burgess Hill; "etc" usually involved a pipe and a few jars, but clearly there were no ill effects because he was off to Lewes the next day. Though he would perhaps have made use of the new turnpike road up to the Wivelsfield tanyard, the absence of a turnpike elsewhere was no impediment to his travels.

One aspect of personal travel can be looked at through the marriage registers. Until after Hardwicke's Act of 1755 these were not kept with any consistency; it was Rose's Act of 1812 that required the details we expect today; and only in 1837 with civil registration did we finally achieve standardisation. This means that any analysis of earlier entries must be suspect because of possible incompleteness. However, we can get some glimpses of the marriage horizons of brides or grooms from the recording in the registers of parishes other than Wivelsfield.

The overwhelming number of marriages during the whole of the period from 1696 to 1880 took place between individuals living in Wivelsfield itself or the immediately surrounding parishes. Taking the marriage totals of the first 20 years of the eighteenth century we find that out of 30 weddings 34 brides or grooms came from other parishes, but 26 of these were from just across the boundaries, and none from further afield than Maresfield, a matter of 10 miles away. A century later there were 64 marriages in a comparable period. Only 24 individuals did not give Wivelsfield as their residence, and half of these were immediate neighbours. The other 12 do show some signs of a little more adventure, one coming from East Grinstead, one from Waldron, and two actually from another county, Halden and Tenterden in Kent. Only these four were from more than 10 miles away. If we look at particular instances during most of two hundred years we find that distant partners were almost always classified as "gentry". The small number of exceptions occur after 1860 among the staff of the asylum, three of these coming from a small area in Northamptonshire. All in all, mobility was not something which the average inhabitant of Wivelsfield indulged in unnecessarily.

The Highways Act of 1813 refers to the "...*Purpose of amending, widening, repairing and keeping in Repair the Road....through the several parishes of Buxted, Maresfield, Fletching, Newick and Chailey to Beadles* [Bedales] *Hill in the Parish of Lindfield, and....through the Parish of Wivelsfield to the Town of Cuckfield....*", the approximate route of the present A272.[38] By 1824 we have the route of the extended Clayton to Godstone turnpike clearly mapped along what is now B2112.[39] From the north to south, tollgates were sited at Anscombe Wood (Haywards Heath), at Cleavewater farm, south of the junction with Hurstwood Lane (thus catching the traffic to and from Scaynes Hill) and at the Royal Oak public house on Ditchling Common. (See fig. 10.) Later evidence indicates that a route to Lindfield via Hurstwood Lane and Scaynes Hill was also turnpiked.

The improvements were naturally welcomed by those engaged in commercial transportation, there being ample evidence of use. For example, loads of lime were transported regularly from Clayton to Theobalds.[40] Not everyone approved of the turnpikes. Some locals felt they were an invitation for undesirables to invade their seclusion; the mire was a protection against foreigners.

xxxvi. 18th century carrier's wagon: from an aqua-tint by J. P. Pyne.

In 1813 the Reverend Arthur Young thought that "...*the turnpike roads in Sussex are generally well enough executed: the materials are excellent: whinstone, the Kentish rag, broken into moderate size pieces.*"[41] The rapid expansion of the turnpike network over the country as a whole was in part possible because of the techniques of road building and maintenance put forward by Thomas Telford and John Macadam. The latter emphasised the need for proper drainage and the use of an exact size of stone. Both men and women were employed breaking stones to the correct dimensions, before placing them in position in two layers six inches deep, with an interval in time to allow for consolidation of the first layer. Perhaps it was the opportunities afforded by this lengthy procedure that encouraged the locals to both take materials and dump rubbish. It was the responsibility of the road surveyor to stop this happening.[42]

For the time being, however, until the railways presented a challenge to the roads, the turnpikes were established, and brought with them their own inefficient bureaucracy. Under an Act of 1820[43] Trust Clerks and Treasurers were required to make returns to central authority. In this particular year the income for the whole length of the Newchapel to Brighton road was £450, the expenditure £370; there was a capital debt of £3805 and no settlement of accounts because there were four separate Treasurers for different stretches. The separate reports of

Clerk and Treasurer are identical in every respect.[44] Regular accounts were being presented by 1823-4, tolls in that year amounting to £666. Day labour cost £537, team [direct?] labour £410, contract work £19, tradesmen £70, rent of quarries £178 and salaries £125.

Plate 25. Cleavewater and the B2112, *circa* 1910.

The toll house itself was also rented for £10 per annum. Total expenditure was nearly £1400, while receipts only brought in about £700.[45] In spite of the turnpikes, Sussex continued its reputation for poorly kept roads, as in 1825 only £70 was spent per mile, less than half of the expenditure in Surrey.[46]

By the 1880s it was obvious that the turnpikes had long since ceased to be a viable commercial proposition. As we have seen, even in the "good" years such as 1823-4, they were costing almost twice as much as they received in revenue, and the Trusts were wound up. Under the New Chappel Lindfield and Brighton Road Act 1862 the Trustees in 1885 released to James Albert Freeman, William Kensett and William Hammond, as joint tenants, "...*All that piece or parcel of land situate in the Parish of Wivelsfield in the County of Sussex on the West side of the High road leading from Lindfield to Wivelsfield and heretofore forming part of the Cottage or Toll house called Cleavewaters Toll house with the appurtenances thereto belonging but not included in this Conveyance the said Cottage or Toll House which is to be pulled down....*[47] Although five shillings seemed to have been the 'going rate' in 1778, a century later it cost the tenants £50 to recover the land for normal use. What is more, the Trustees had the power to have the rented toll house pulled down.

Local roads remained the concern of the parish until the end of the nineteenth century. Regular Vestry Meetings between 1857 and 1894 appointed Surveyors and fixed Highway Rates, and there were occasional references to specific problems. In 1860 Wivelsfield and Westmeston agreed to share the cost of repair of a disputed stretch of Hundred Acre Lane, the dispute going to arbitration in 1867; in 1862, when Hurstwood House was built, permission was given for the road leading to Colwell to be realigned near the former Tanyard, subject to the local landowner undertaking "*....repair for four years and not [interfering] with the present road until the new one is in a fit state for traffic*". Legislation in 1878 transferred responsibility to Highways Districts, and Wivelsfield became one of 11 parishes in one such District, but parish concern continued. In 1890 Charles Stewart Cox was permitted to move 525 yards of the road passing Coldharbour on similar terms. In 1892 an extra payment of £25 was demanded because of the increased traffic involved in the construction of Abbots Leigh (now known as Abbots Leigh Place), and in 1894 yet another road diversion was approved, this time where the Birch Hotel is now.[48]

Soon after the flurry of activity to improve the roads of Sussex there came efforts to develop another means of communication, water. The main tributary of the Ouse is the nearest navigable river to Wivelsfield, but at no point does this enter the parish. It is perhaps ironic that the improvement of its navigation in the peroid 1790-1815 enabled bricks to be transported cheaply to the site of the great viaduct to carry the new railway over the river; for this too was to avoid Wivelsfield, though the parish boundary runs alongside the track at Valebridge and the name 'Wivelsfield Station' (in Burgess Hill) still confuses strangers to the area.

Certainly some of the hundreds of "navvies" who worked on the construction of the railway found accommodation within the parish, as we shall see in Chapter 10. One of the eight route options for the London to Brighton line would have come through the parish on its way from East Grinstead, but it was not to be, and Wivelsfield had to wait for the widespread use of the internal combustion engine to become more closely involved with the wider world. This comparative isolation affected the population, which increased only slowly until this century.

iv. The arrival of the Post

"It is a place with only one post a day....I always
fear creation will expire before tea-time. "

Rev. Sydney Smith

The arrival of the railway had one immediate effect. Haywards Heath station, though not within the parish, was nevertheless near enough to allow the mail from distant parts to come more quickly and more frequently. In 1846, before any sub-post offices were established in the parish, letters came via Lindfield, a boy being paid by Wivelsfield parishioners for bringing them. In 1851 the Census tells us there were 18 'wagoners' in the parish. (Chapter 10). Some, at least, of these may have played a part in delivering the local mail. In 1856 Lindfield inhabitants made representations to Rowland Hill at the General Post office that siting the district office in Cuckfield disadvantaged those settlements to the East of the railway (including Wivelsfield of course), delaying delivery by several hours. Their suggestion was that the office should be moved to Haywards Heath, being more or less half way.

Needless to say, Cuckfield fought back. A much longer list of signatories sent a request for the maintenance of the *status quo* on the grounds that Cuckfield was a more important centre. What is more, they believed in "going to the top", for their letter was addressed to the Postmaster General himself, the Duke of Argyll.[49] Who won the battle in the short term is not clear - perhaps a compromise solution was achieved which satisfied nobody; for in 1867 the mail came to Wivelsfield by pony and trap from Hurstpierpoint. A telegraph and money order office had been established near the railway station at Burgess Hill by the 1870s and by the 1880s letters came to Wivelsfield from Burgess Hill.[50]

The "Penny Post" was established to meet the needs of an increasingly literate population. Can we discover when and how this literacy spread in our rural community? Clearly, individuals such as John Burgess in Ditchling were literate enough to keep a diary. Yeomen farmers and successful tradesmen could write. For others wills were written by a village scribe or by a literate friend of the testator. Parish officials were required to maintain accounts, to witness documents and to present evidence to justices, and either they or a clerk put these matters in writing. However, these activities in themselves do not give any clues as to general communication or mobility. Let us use the marriage registers again.

"I wish I was a poet and could write a fine hand; I'd write my love a letter that she could understand" runs a traditional song of the mid 19[51]th century. How widespread was illiteracy in the 19th century? After 1812 the basic literacy of wedding couples can be judged from their use of actual signatures as opposed to their "marks", as well as from any discernible change of occupations from manual to clerical. From 1813 to 1880 there were 307 marriages in Wivelsfield, 155 before 1850 and 152 after that date.

In the earlier period 73 men and 92 women out of a total of 310 individuals signed by mark; in the subsequent 30 years only 35 men and 25 women were disabled to this extent. Expressed as percentages a 53% illiteracy had been reduced to 20%. We must remember that this is a measure of a very basic level of literacy. It does not imply that many were writing letters frequently, but the increase in postal activity was becoming widespread. For example, in Oxford in 1890 Flora Thompson was employed as an assistant straight from school aged fourteen, indicating a relatively busy village office.[52]

Plate 26. William Kenward, the oldest working postmaster in England, 1906.

In 1855 here in Wivelsfield William Kenward was the person who received the mail, at his premises in Church Lane, and he was still doing so in 1895, adding subpostmaster to his original trade of harness maker as well the jobs of school attendance officer and parish clerk. Other sub-offices were opened at the Sussex County Lunatic Asylum by 1881, run by William Gates. He was a picture frame maker who, by 1899, had changed the name of his premises to "The Haven". At Wivelsfield Green in the 1880s grocer and draper Trayton Randall carried out postal duties in addition to his own shopkeeping. Mail arrived twice daily and the 'pillar letter box near Wivelsfield Green' was cleared twice daily.[53]   By the early 1900's it is recalled that deliveries were being made to individual houses.[54]

By 1909 Wivelsfield had its own money order and telegraph office run by William Avery at the Green. To this, by 1922, had been added the dashing innovation of a 'Public Telephone Call Office', run by Mrs. Adeline Morfee. By now the bulk delivery point had changed again, this time to Haywards Heath (eventual victory for Lindfield?), but local arrangements continued much as before and in Church Lane and at 'The Haven' the same families continued to run the offices. The Church Lane office closed in 1944 with the death of Thomas Kenward, while Miss Gates ran a stationer's business at The Haven at least until 1938.[55]

The need for three mail offices derives geographically from the development of separate communities within the parish, the two Saxon settlements first mentioned in Chapter 1 and the mushrooming growth within and surrounding the new Sussex County Asylum which opened in 1859, developments we shall follow in ensuing chapters. But it assumes an increasingly literate population, needing or wishing, and able, to communicate in writing in sufficient volume to justify this country-wide network.

The overall impression is one of rural semi-isolation for most local people for several centuries, barring the trips to market, port, county town or manorial court that business or local duty demanded. Long distance travel was always part of the essential life-style of the landed classes and continued to be so. They eventually abandoned horseback in favour of the carriage as a favoured mode of personal transport, and this in turn placed road improvement high on the national agenda. Better roads enabled the gentry to maintain their contacts with others of their class, both in the country and in London. Such roads were also available, on foot, for those who moved about the county and further afield, looking for work; but for those with roots and employment locally - farmers, husbandmen, labourers and their families, there was no need to stir far. By the mid 19th century, however, the old patterns were changing. The development of Brighton, the rise in tenant farming and the coming of the railway had brought new faces into the parishes of mid Sussex. Their impact on Wivelsfield was considerable, as we shall see in the two chapters that follow.

CHAPTER 10

THE COMMUNITY IN 1841 AND 1851

"The old order changeth, yielding place to new"

Alfred, Lord Tennyson, *Morte d' Arthur*

i. The evidence

All the preceding chapters in this book, are to some extent, the result of detective work. Small pieces of evidence are teased out of a variety of different sources, compared and tentatively slotted together in order to start the jigsaw. Very often, however thorough the detective work, there is simply not enough contemporary written evidence to allow us to complete it.

For the 19th century, however, a more comprehensive picture can be drawn. In the preceding two chapters the gradual improvement of travel facilities and increasing personal mobility were shown. Literacy, born from the desire to read the Bible for oneself, was strong among the free churches and ushered in a nation-wide movement for the education of working-class children. Throughout the century the written word gradually proliferated in forms that held up a mirror even to the smallest local communities - poll books and electoral rolls, local trades directories and newspapers. For the decade 1841-1851 a microscopic view is possible in many parishes, by using and comparing two particular sources, the parish Tithe survey and the Census returns of 1841 and 1851.[1] Both these sources were a result of Acts of Parliament. Both were surveys, one of land, the other of people. Put together, they shine a clear light into the communities of their day and provide us with a wealth of detail.[2]

The Census is ongoing. Once every ten years since 1801, (except war year 1941) a population count has been made of each parish or local government district. Between 1801 and 1841 the information was statistically summarised, without giving the names, addresses, ages and occupations of people in each dwelling. In 1841 and subsequent decades these details were recorded. From then on the regular counts have survived and have become progressively more informative. Copies on microfilm and microfiche are kept in local record offices, the originals being retained in the Public Record Office.

From 1841 each parish was listed in households and the following details were recorded:- firstly a reference number was given to the premises, then each head of the household named, followed by the family and any others sleeping at the house on the night of the count. The occupations of the inhabitants where known were given and their age - actual age of those under 15 years old, approximate age, within five year bands, of those over 15. By 1851 each person's place of birth, age, marital status and relationship to the head of the household were noted.[3]

The second important source for the period around 1840, the Tithe Survey, is completely different from the Census in that it was a 'once only' survey. In 1836 the Act of Parliament had been passed in order to commute the old tithing system into money payments and therefore, if no adequate survey already existed, each parish that paid tithes had to be measured. Many Midland parishes already had adequate Enclosure surveys, but Wivelsfield, in common with most parishes in East Sussex was surveyed. The basic survey work was done in 1838, resulting in a "Book of Schedules", but the map itself was not drawn until 1844. At a scale of 20 inches to the mile, it numbers all buildings and fields. It is beautifully drawn in ink on thick paper and kept in a roll, but when laid out flat it is about five feet wide by eight feet long and can be seen at the East Sussex Record Office.

The infield measurements, that is the actual land used for farming, amounted to total acreages of the different tithed areas within the parish are as follows:-

	acres		acres
arable land	1,061	meadow and pasture	856
woodland	788	furzeland	70
hop gardens	7	market gardens/orchards	3

The total of 2765 tithed acres for the whole parish was augmented by a further 148 acres of roads and waste and 1 rood 38 perches for the Church and churchyard. The total acreage of the parish was 3103 acres.[4]

Given these two sources, the Tithe Survey and the 1841/1851 Census Returns, it has been possible to obtain a fuller picture than before. The landed estates of the parish, the farmers and craftsmen and the communities living by the Green may now be observed in detail.[5]

ii. The farmers of the parish

It was shown by the Tithe Map and the 1841 Census Return that there were 17 farmers in Wivelsfield.   Two formerly-independent estates had come into the Tanner family dynasty, Otehall and Cleavewater. The latter was still under Anthony Tanner's executors, with a farm bailiff from Harrow, Middlesex, in occupation. Otehall was in the hands of a tenant farmer, as were Lunces and the Theobalds estate .

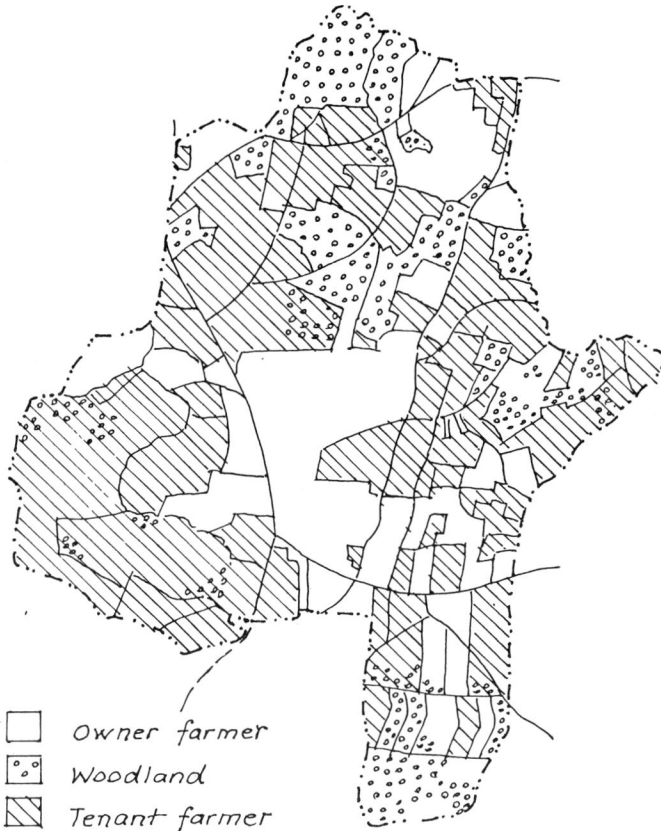

Figure 11. Land tenure in 1840.

Only two of the farmers were owner-occupiers. The principal of these was Richard Tanner who owned the More House estate including Pepper Hall (340a.). He also farmed 23 acres of Great Otehall for his sister Jane and the whole of North Colwell (91a.) for his aunt, Jenny Tanner. The second, William Brattle owned Manns, with Wilderness, and the north part of Hole farm; and he farmed the rest of Hole as a tenant (owner of 175 acres and tenant of 82 acres). He had bought Manns and Wilderness from the executors of Philip Jenner and had acquired North Hole after the death of George Hemsley (Chapter 4) in 1835. The third owner occupier was Joseph Farncombe. He owned Fanners (34 acres), together with 'Walkers', (53 acres) a part of the former 'Bishoprick' common.

Tenant farmers ran the other 14 farms, which varied in acreage from the large Theobalds estate, down to several of 20 acres or less. Of the tenants only one was a woman, Mary Jane Jenner, who described herself in the 1841 census as a farmer. She and her sister, both unmarried, occupied Bankside, a farm of 27 acres of which 22% was meadow and the remainder arable. There was no woodland. Clearwaters Farm of 45 acres was still in possession of the Dancy family but was farmed by John Dancy who was not the owner. It was made up of 20% meadow and pasture, 72% arable and a further 7% woodland, shaw and orchard. The woodland in the parish was mainly under the control of the larger estates, timber, underwood and sporting rights being valuable sources of income. William Brattle's woodland at Manns and Wilderness amounted to 29% (51 acres) of his total 175 acres. 59% of his land (102 acres) was under cultivation. The tenant farmers of the parish generally had a larger percentage than this under the plough. The remainder of Brattle's land was 10% meadow (18 acres) and there was a further 2% on which he grew hops, the poles for which were cut from his coppiced woodland.

By 1851 the only owner/occupier was William Brattle, a bachelor aged 55, employing 14 men. His name does not appear on the 1841 Census but by 1851 he was in residence. With him was an employee named John Baldock aged 65, his wife Maria aged 44, a dairywoman, and their 12 year old son William who was working as a labourer on the farm. All three had been born in Wadhurst, as had their employer. A trail from Wadhurst to Wivelsfield had earlier been marked out by John's younger brother Thomas Baldock who had been officiating as the Minister of the Bethel Chapel since at least 1841.

Richard Tanner of More House died in 1845 aged 43, leaving the estate by his will, to his brother William Tanner of Patcham, gent. On the census night of 1851 there were only a groom/gardener, his wife the cook and their daughter the housemaid, in the house. Presumably the land was farmed by Nathaniel Randall, the farm bailiff, who was living in Pepper Hall. About this time, William's eldest daughter, Philadelphia married her cousin William Farncombe of Bishopstone. The couple lived in More House from 1854 until she died in 1869, producing six children all of whom were baptised in Wivelsfield Church.

The other large farm, 225 acres, was Theobalds, owned by Sir John Dodson, Queen's Advocate, D.C.L., an absentee landlord whose family came from Hurstpierpoint. He married Florence Campion of Danny and his son established Coneyborough in Barcombe as his main home. Theobalds was farmed by John Hollingdale, aged 56, Plumpton born and his wife Mary, who was born in Wivelsfield. He employed five men.

In 1851 there were four estates of 100 to 200 acres in the hands of tenant farmers. Great Otehall was owned by Jane Tanner, the only female owner and tenanted by John Stone. Hursthouse in the north-west of the parish was farmed with Strood in the south-east by Fred Knight, born in Wivelsfield. He was also a master blacksmith. North Slugwash, including Lower Ham and Moors Farm was farmed by George Heaver from East Grinstead and owned by John Marten Cripps of Stantons, East Chiltington, who also owned South Colwell and woodland in Wivelsfield, together with land in other parishes. Little Otehall was owned by John Hunt, a trustee of Otehall Chapel and tenanted by Henry Wells. Generally these larger farms employed three men each and two had a boy. Lunces (84 acres) and South Colwell (80 acres) employed three and four men respectively.

The remaining farms in the parish were smaller - nine having between 40 and 61 acres, mostly with two men but three of them also employed a boy. There were seven farms of 16 to 32 acres, two of which employed one man and the others worked by the farmer's family but without hired labour. This made a total of 19 farmers and three farm bailiffs, with the

Plate 27. Strood Farm, 1994. The pond in the foreground probably dates from the early days of the 'Stanmer hamlet' at Strood.

spare farm houses occupied by agricultural labourers. The land which had belonged to these houses had been absorbed into larger holdings, as, for example, Manns farm which had absorbed Hole and North Hole. There was still only one woman farmer in 1851 and she, Hannah Whiting, was also the publican of the Cock Inn.

Wivelsfield farmers in 1841-51 were still producing hops, as they had done in earlier centuries.[6] The main area of hop gardens which was by the Fox and Hounds Inn was known as Scrases Hop Gardens, but there were also hop fields on five farms, More House, Cleavewater, Hursthouse, Townings and North Hole. The small building, now a house, behind Cleavewater Farm, was originally an oast house, built in the square rather than the round tradition which is prevalent in Kent and the east of East Sussex.[7]

iii. Tradesmen and craftsmen

A similar range of trades was being practised in Wivelsfield in 1841 as in the two previous centuries (Chapter 5). In 1851 the numbers of men employed in each trade are detailed. By that date seven carpenters, four sawyers, four bricklayers and a thatcher, namely 6.6% of the working population were employed in the building trades, much the same numbers as in 1841. There were also three blacksmiths, three wheelwrights, three glovers and a fellmonger (a dealer in skins). In those days the blacksmith also made nuts, bolts, screws, hinges and other ironwork used in buildings. A major trading loss to the parish was the closing of the Tanyard. Though still referred to by that name in 1841 it was not functioning and the house was occupied by an agricultural labourer and his family.

Trades not in evidence earlier but possibly carried on before the 1840s, were harness-making and rope-making. Two women gave their occupations as dressmakers, perhaps taught their craft from those we met in Chapter 7 making clothes for the inmates of the workhouse. A local tailor, Ebenezer Knight, living at Dumbrells, was responsible for men's clothing in the village. Four shoemakers, including Thomas Ockenden who, with his thirteen-year-old nephew as apprentice and a female 'shoebinder', made shoes to measure. It is interesting to note that William Gammon, a deaf man, remained a journeyman shoemaker (that is, paid by the day) with Thomas Ockenden from 1841 to 1861.

William Kenward, the harness-maker, (who employed two men and three boys including an apprentice) and his wife, ran a grocer's shop in their home. This was Tapestry Cottage, Church Lane, next door to Thomas Ockenden's, into whose house they moved in 1862 taking the shop with them. William ultimately became the oldest postmaster in England, aged 86. (See Chapter 9 and plate 26.) He died in 1910.

An earlier shop at the other end of the village was at "Wheelwrights" where in 1841 William Knight was a grocer. By 1851 Charles Avery, a miller and grocer, was established in "Shop House," newly built   on the opposite side of the road. This building, later extended in front, as shown by the panel dated 1878 is now the Post Office. Charles had married Mary Ann, daughter of William Gravett, the pastor of Otehall Chapel and retired potter of Ditchling (Chapter 8). Charles employed two assistants, but where was his mill?[8]

Plate 28. Dumbrells Cottages, 1994.

Several of the timber-framed houses in the parish were rebuilt in the early-19th century when, even for the smaller houses, a brick and tile construction became widespread.[9] Two of these were Dumbrells, in the twitten between Green Road and Eastern Road, and Stream House, originally named Sayers, in Green Road. Both houses had been built in about 1600 and were copyhold of Ditchling Manor, each paying a rent of 8d. per annum for a cottage and about an acre of land. In the mid 1700s Edward Townsett lived in the former and his brother William, in the latter, was the tenant of Abraham Sayer. The Townsett brothers were weavers and in 1745 Edward's name appears on bills for weaving cloth made of tire and delivered to Marten Richard Webb of Fanners. When Dumbrells fell into decay it was rebuilt by John and Ebenezer Knight father and son, tailors by trade.

Stream House was rebuilt by John Picknall in the early 1800s. He also built Moat House on land belonging to Pepperhall. Stream Cottage and some outbuildings at Fanners have brickwork in rat-trap bond, which was an economical use of bricks at that time. In 1851 a butcher, John Avery, used the west room of his house, Stream Cottage, for his shop, which had a separate entrance and a cellar. He was also a farmer

employing two men and a boy,
including an eighteen-year-old
apprentice. It is noteworthy that
each shopkeeper employed a young
girl as a domestic servant. In 1959
when Stream Cottage, by then
Stream House, was divided into two
dwellings, the eastern end was
named Avery House after the
present owner had discovered an
iron fire-back there bearing the
name 'Avery'.

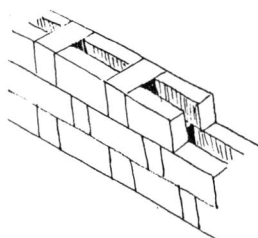

xxxvii. Rat-trap bond at Stream House, Green Road *circa* 1820.

A new trading opportunity, the market garden, had appeared in the
parish by the 1840s. Those shown on the Tithe Map were along what is
now the A272. One of half an acre at the north end of Slugwash Lane,
was referred to as 'late Ockendens', after a former owner. The eldest
Thomas Ockenden who died in 1822, was a gardener according to the
will of his son, the second Thomas Ockenden, a shoemaker of Church
Lane, whose son Thomas Ockenden (the third) appears on the 1841,
'51 and '61 censuses. There were two more market gardens covering
two acres of Lyoth Common which were run by the Jeffrey family.
The houses in which they lived had formerly been the Parish Poor
Houses. The fourth market garden, of half an acre, was at Birch Green
and was run in 1841 by John Eade. By 1851, at the age of 67 he was a
nurseryman at Mount Pleasant (now North Haven, Fox Hill) where he
employed one man.

The location of these businesses on the main east—west road in the
north of the parish should provide a clue to the destination of the
market garden produce. They were not ideally placed to serve the
newly-growing town of Burgess Hill and the heath at Haywards Heath
was not yet enclosed, so there had been little new development in that
area. The goods were probably destined for the London or the Brighton
markets, by way of Haywards Heath Station and the new railway line.

iv. The labouring classes

The farmers were Wivelsfield's main employers and it is therefore no
surprise to find that agricultural labourers were the mainstay of the
local workforce in the mid-19th century. From the 1851 Census the total
number of men and boys employed by the farmers was 62 (56 + 6)
adding, say 15 more for the three large farms run by farm bailiffs, who
were not directly employing labourers. This still does not account for
all the 120 agricultural labourers listed under Wivelsfield, which
included three shepherds, three cowherds and 18 wagoners. The latter,

with their mates, could have been doing general carrying as well as farm work, but where and how were the others employed or not employed? Two of the older labourers had entered themselves as paupers. Some perhaps worked seasonally outside the Weald.

There were several very large families but the older children had often left home before the youngest was born. Moors Cottage in Slugwash Lane, had earlier been described as a 'hovel',[10] or animal shed. By 1851 it had been converted to a three-room dwelling, the home of James Jenner, aged 37, his wife Ann, two sons of 16 and 13 working as farm labourers, two younger sons and a two year old ward. Skinners, an old timber-framed house at the east end of the Green, had been divided into two dwellings. In one William Whiting and his wife had five children under 12 years old and a 40-year-old lodger who was a farm labourer. The other half was occupied by Emily Mills, widow and charwoman, whose 18 year old son was a labourer and there were four younger children.

Oak Cottages, in Eastern Road, had been built before 1600 as one three-bay, timber-framed house. (Chapter 5) By 1841 it had been divided into three dwellings for farm labourers, each having two rooms downstairs and two rooms up. There were at least two wells but only one privy shared by all the inhabitants. In 1851, the owner Mary Jane Jenner and her sister Elizabeth, had moved from Bankside Farm into one of the end dwellings. In the centre part lived Henry Welfare, aged 45, with his wife, two labourer sons of 21 and 19, a 17 year old daughter, three girls at school and two infants, a total of ten people. At the other end was William Welfare, 55 years (his brother?), with his wife, a 15-year-old son, two daughters and a lodger, six people in all. The son and the lodger were farm labourers.

The impact of the London to Brighton Railway on local population figures in Burgess Hill in the 1840's has been well documented.[11] Wivelsfield, whose western parish boundary runs roughly parallel with, and only a short distance from the railway, was also affected. In 1841 the population of the parish was increased by 55 railway labourers, the wives of eight of them and twelve children. Some of them lodged with farm labourers at Theobalds, at Church Lane and on Lunces Common. At Puddledock the tenant Arthur Parsons, a farm labourer, had his wife and five children as well as five lodgers, all railway labourers, occupying one small cottage. By the Fox Inn, two houses were taken over by these labourers with their wives and children.

These locations were within walking distance of the section of the railway which was currently being constructed. The line as far as Haywards Heath, had been completed by the time of the 1841 Census but south of this, between Haywards Heath and Valebridge, work was still in progress. The huge workforce, varying between 500 and 1,000 navvies found accommodation as and where they could. Some were in temporary huts near the line and others spilled over into nearby villages. Due to landslips and the instability of the new embankments over the Adur valley the work was desperately behind schedule and went on day and night.[12] The influx of temporary inhabitants caused over-crowding in houses which lacked sanitation, water and were without any means of lighting other than candles and oil-lamps.

At Jefferys Green, sharing his home with two railway labourers and their wives, lived a carpenter Joseph Farncombe (the eldest son of Joseph Farncombe of Fanners), his wife Mary and their two sons Joseph and Michael. There was no trace of the family in local records after 1841, the reason being that in 1842 they had emigrated to Upper Canada. By 1856 he was a member of the Wallace Township Council and in 1861 his status had improved to that of a landowner. [13] By 1851 all but two of the 55 transient workers had left Wivelsfield, presumably to continue the track towards Brighton. The only two remaining had been born locally and stayed to return to agricultural work as a shepherd and a farm labourer.

v. The arrival of the Middle Classes

Wivelsfield prior to the 19th century was a community of families whose personal wealth was, to a great extent, linked to the agricultural wealth of the parish. By 1851 this had started to change. Whereas 53% of the working population were still employed in agriculture, and a further 7 percent were agricultural employers, there was now a new element. Seven persons, 4.1% of the population, were engaged in a professional occupation or were in receipt of pensions.

Of the seven professional people, only Henry Travers Owen, a civil servant, would have been likely to have worked far from his home. He had worked for the British Government in the East Indies, where most of his children were born. Aged 51 in 1851, he was retired and living at home. In the 1840s he had built the large house called Franklyns on high ground in the north of the parish at Birch Green (now Beechmont in the Princess Royal Hospital grounds). It had large rooms with high ceilings and delicate plaster mouldings. The elegant staircase is still in place. There were also stables and two cottages for the families of the groom and gardener, both men from local villages. The indoor staff consisted of a Russian-born governess for his four younger children, his two eldest daughters aged 22 and 18 appear to have had no occupation. The cook came from Barmouth in Wales and two sisters from Gloucester were the house and parlour maids. By the 1861 census the whole family had departed, meanwhile the Sussex County Asylum had been built on adjoining land. Was this the reason for the departure of the Travers Owen family?

Coldharbour House, built on a ridge south of the Green and first mentioned in 1851, was owned by a solicitor, who was away from home on the night of the Census, leaving his house servants in charge. However we know from the Land Tax Returns he was Mr. Faithfull. His occupation is indicated by his son's entry on the 1861 Census as Albert Faithfull, solicitor's son. In more recent times Coldharbour House was divided into several residences, one of which was destroyed by fire in the 1970s but the fine brick-built stables remain, now occupied as private houses.

Plate 29. Franklyns House: the main staircase, 1991

Three men not engaged in gainful occupation were Chelsea Pensioners. Until 1955 such people fell into two categories - In-pensioners and Out-pensioners. The former lived in the Royal Hospital in lieu of receiving a pension while the latter received their pensions at home. Henry Bristow, son of James Bristow the thatcher, although only 26 was in receipt of such a pension and thus had probably been invalided out of the services. Two further 'annuitants' deriving their income from investments were Joseph Jenner, aged 72, a lodger at Lyoth Common and George Lenton, aged 43, in Merryfields on the present A272. At Birch Green, John Ayers Wicheloe, aged 64, also derived his income from investments in property.

The rise of local education began to make its mark on the community, a theme to be explored more fully in Chapter 12. Mary Smith of "School House", now Hamlyns, may have been a retired school mistress. Aged 66 in 1851 she had a private income and lived with her two schoolmistress daughters. Charlotte Hart, wife of a musician pensioner, was a 'schoolmistress' educating her children at home in 1851. The remaining two professionals were Stephen Bean, formerly a shoemaker and Parish Clerk, (Chapters 5, 7) and his wife Mary Ann. Both aged 73 in 1851, they were running the National School in

Plate 30. Church Lane, *circa* 1900.

Plate 31. Green Road, *circa* 1905: showiug Green Park Farm (right) and the village post office & stores etc. in the distance. The grassy strip between the farm and the road was once part of the old village green.

CHAPTER 11

BUILDING FOR THE FUTURE: WIVELSFIELD 1881-1910

"Architecture would lead us to all the arts, as it did with earlier men: but if we despise it and take no note of how we are housed, the other arts will have a hard time of it indeed."

William Morris, *The Beauty of Life*, 1880

The preceding chapter looked at Wivelsfield in 1841 and 1851. By 1881 there had been changes in the pattern of peoples lives. In earlier years possession of land was significant in determining a person's status but by 1910 it was noticeable that the wealth of those styling themselves 'gentlemen' was not from farming but from what today might be regarded as invisible exports. Among these were trade in manufactured goods, insurance and banking. Families of all classes were moving into the village from further away and some people from distant places were, by marriage, becoming Wivelsfield residents.

The sources of information used for 1841 and 1851 were the Census Returns and the Tithe survey. For 1881 the Census was again used, while for 1910 Lloyd George's 'Domesday Book' proved invaluable. Commissioned in 1910, this was a land survey of every property in the country. In it were recorded details of landowners and tenants, together with acreages and rateable values. Further contemporary evidence was provided by a series of Kelly's Directories and some personal recollections.[1]

Though Wivelsfield grew only moderately overall from 1851 to 1910, its new architecture at all levels was interesting and varied and has made a lasting contribution to the visual heritage of the area at large.

years an old villager, Mr.Tom Cook, then aged 94 years, recalled going to Church each Sunday and always sitting in the seats on the right.

By 1881 the total population of the parish, excluding the inmates of the Asylum, had risen to 1024, compared with 608 in 1851. Of these 432 were in employment (314 male and 118 female) and 30% of this number were still engaged in agriculture, as compared with the 60% of 1851. However, the numbers in domestic service had risen greatly from its level of 13% of overall working population in 1851. Female servants, gardeners, grooms & coachmen working for the middle classes had pushed the percentage to 36% by 1881. Only two of these gardeners had been local farm labourers in the earlier census, the majority being newcomers. The numbers of those employed in public and professional occupations had also risen, some of whom worked for the Asylum.

By 1881 the new asylum dominated the northern skyline in Wivelsfield. Yet, in the parish as a whole, the old threads remained interwoven with the new. Let us now look in more detail at the people themselves.

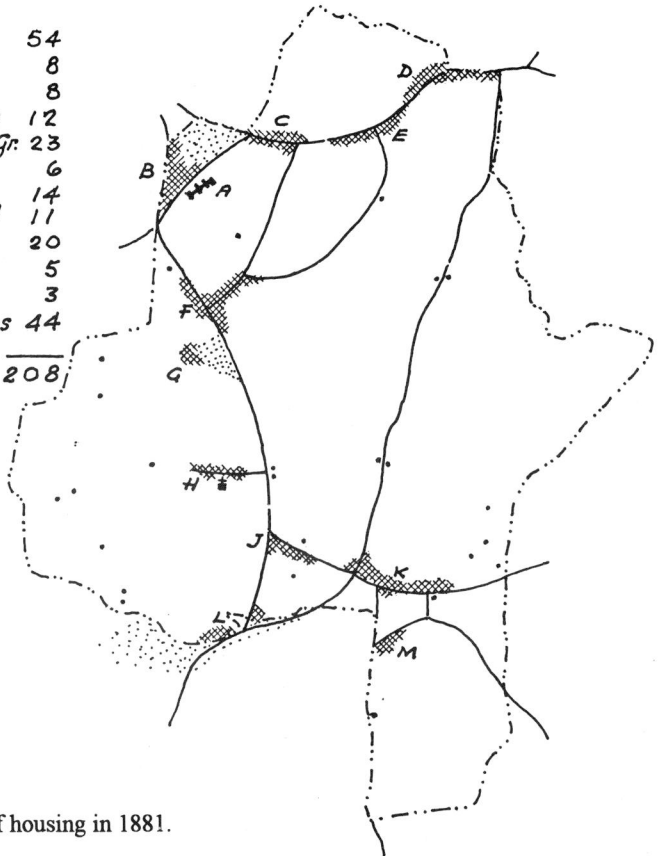

A Asylum
B Kents Rd. area   54
C Birch Green   8
D Lyoth Common   8
E South of A 272   12
F Fox & Jeffreys Gr. 23
G Lunces Com.   6
H Church Lane   14
J Otehall Chapel   11
K The Green   20
L Lockstrood   5
M Coldharbour   3
Scattered farms   44
& Cottages   ____
Total   208

housing

common

Figure 12. Areas of housing in 1881.

ii. The Landowners of the Parish

Previous chapters have shown that in the period 1840-1851 the Tanner family had become the principal landowners in Wivelsfield, holding between them around 640 acres. Their family home was More House but their property also included Pepper Hall, North Colwell, Strood, Lockstrood, Townings, Birth, South Slugwash, Hundred Acres, Hole, Bulls of Fanns, Moat House and Great Otehall as well as cottages in Church Lane. They were also in receipt of the Tithes. This extensive holding was shared between William Tanner and his two sisters Jane Tanner and Martha, the wife of Rev. George Dixon. The family were largely responsible for funding the Victorian extension to the Parish Church.

William Tanner died in 1870 without a son to succeed him and Jane Tanner died early in 1881 so that, when the 1881 Census was taken, their remaining holdings were in the hands of executors. Martha Dixon, nee Tanner, still held Colwell House, South Slugwash, Townings and Rookhurst. William's son-in-law William Farncombe, husband of Philadelphia Tanner, had managed the estate from 1854 to 1880, living in More House. Following his death in 1882, the house and its 340 acres were tenanted by Charles Longley, a timber merchant and member of the family who founded 'Longleys' the building firm. The ownership of the estate then passed to William and Philadeliphia's son William of Wake Colne in Essex, who added Tanner to his surname and became William Tanner Farncombe Tanner.

The farms of North Colwell and Lockstrood together with Hundred Acre Wood, were inherited by Philadelphia Farncombe's sister Jane Tanner (the 2nd) who lived at Patcham. Great Otehall was in the hands of executors in 1881, as William Tanner's sister Jane (the 1st), had died aged 90 in Brighton, where she had been living with her niece Jane (the 2nd). The aunt was brought back to Wivelsfield Churchyard to be buried and in her memory a stained glass window was placed in the north wall of the Chancel.

Sampson Copestake, the brick and tile entrepreneur of the Keymer Tile Works, owned Little Otehall and was also the tenant of Great Otehall where he employed a farm bailiff. Great Otehall was bought back into the Godman family by a distant connection, Major General Richard Temple Godman, gent, of Highden in Goring, West Sussex.[9] He extended the house but his wife refused to live there, so it remained in the occupation of a farm bailiff. By 1901 Major Godman had also acquired Little Bankside and, on the death of Lord Monk Bretton (Sir John Dodson's son), the Theobalds estate. By adding Little Otehall, Great Bankside and Blackmores he created a holding of about 450 acres by 1910.

Apart from the Tanner family and Lord Monk Bretton, the other large land owner in Wivelsfield was John Marten Cripps of East Chiltington. His son Rush Marten Cripps, inherited and after his death in 1885, South Colwell, North Slugwash and Mores Farm were sold to Combridge, a butcher of Hove. From him Major General Sir Wykeham Leigh-Pemberton KCB., JP., Aide de Camp to Queen Victoria, bought all three in 1891. In 1892 Pemberton built a new house, Abbots Leigh, on high ground, facing south. Now known as Abbots Leigh Place, it was built in half-timbered and gabled style to a design of the architect Frederick C. Lees. The interior is notable for its panelling, gallery piers, balustrades and fireplaces with William Morris tiles inset.[9] This together with the surrounding 435 acres was the start of the Abbots Leigh Estate. It was sold to Charles Hales in 1919 who increased his holdings to 1,000 acres, buying anything in Wivelsfield that came on the market.[10]

Fanners had been bought by Thomas Jones Bellamy in 1853 for £1,100. He had the old farmhouse pulled down and erected a simple, square building with whitewashed stucco walls under the wide eaves and gables of a slate-covered roof. (The matching north wing was added by the present owner in the 1960s). His widow was able to capitalise on the venture by selling the property, now named 'The Ferns', in 1859 for £4,000. The purchaser was Lt. Col. Rose Holden-Rose, a newcomer from Ireland. He later acquired The Berth, Hole and Strood from the Tanners. At the age of 71 in 1881 he was starting to build his own empire based on Fanners.[11]

By the time of his death in 1898 Lt. Col. Rose Holden-Rose's estate amounted to about 360 acres. After his death his daughter Mary kept only Fanners, the Wheelwright's Shop and eight cottages along Green Road (about 30 acres in all). Arthur Rydon of Awbrooks, Lindfield purchased Ham and Wilderness adjacent to his own land, but the bulk of the farmland went to Frank Bradley, that is the Berth, Manns, Shoulders and part of Strood. He also bought Townings from Martha Dixon's daughter Mrs. Neame, to bring his total acreage to around 320. By 1910 he had pulled down the old Berth Farm cottage in Slugwash Lane and built 'The Hall' in Edwardian style, facing south on the ridge.

The various owners of Coldharbour, on the ridge south of The Green also added land to their estate, employing a farm bailiff to run it and keeping the sporting rights themselves. Coldharbour was eventually acquired by Sir Charles B. Renshaw, who gave land and money to build the Reading Room in Green Road, in 1912. Another Renshaw, Thomas C. Renshaw of Sandrocks Haywards Heath, had as early as 1860, bought Clearwaters Farm in the west of the parish from the last of the Dancy family, who had held it for over 300 years. Renshaw added Rogers, Puddledock and Scrases Farms over the years, all of which were adjacent to his original land north and west of the parish boundary. He let the farmland out to small farmers. South of Clearwaters, Lunces farm was owned and farmed by William Bacon, who added Griggs, making his holding up to 100 acres. He had built the pair of lodge cottages in Church Lane by 1871 and the lodge and a pair of farm cottages on the edge of Lunces Common by 1881. William Bacon also rented South Colwell and Lower Ham from Rush Marten Cripps for a short period.

Much of the farmland bought up by the foregoing landowners was still farmed by tenant farmers in 1881. There were in fact 15 tenant farmers only two less than in 1851 but there were more farm bailiffs, a total of six. Only one farm under 30 acres and four more of up to 100 acres had been amalgamated with others, whereas two of the larger estates (More House and Manns) had been split up. George Hills, the tenant farmer of Cleavewater with Franklands in the 1860's, had by 1871 bought and farmed 90 acres of the land, to be followed by his son James Hills. After his and his brother's deaths, Dr. Marcus Pembury of Mount Pleasant (Fox Hill) bought 56 of the acres and employed a farm bailiff. The northern part, called Franklands on the Land Taxes Returns, was bought in 1885 by Alexander Honeyman, a Wandsworth builder. It was perhaps he who speculatively built the large houses on the south side of the A272.

Ownership of land and property has always been regarded as a wise investment. It has allowed entry into higher social circles. When the first William Tanner inherited More House and Townings in 1780s he was 'a carpenter of Ditchling', who had married an heiress Sarah Hampshire. As a tradesman he would not have been far removed socially from the farm labourers who occupied the cottages on his estate. By 1838 his son Richard Tanner who inherited More House, had also acquired Lockstrood, Pepper Hall, the Berth and Naldred and several smaller timber-framed houses had been bought. Among these were Late Chatfields and Turners in Church Lane, now known as Tapestry and Glebe Cottages and 'late Fosters' on the Green. By 1849 the great estate was complete and the family were 'gentry'. Their empire had swallowed up that earlier gentlemanly estate, Otehall, whose descent had failed in the direct male line (Chapter 3). The wheel then began to turn full circle. The failure of a direct succession in the Tanner family enabled the Godmans to re-establish themselves in their old estates by repurchasing Great Otehall from the executors of Jane Tanner (1st) who died in 1880. [12]

iii. The middle-class life style

Alongside the old rural gentry there were new purchasers arriving in Wivelsfield. These were the sons of professional families whose future in the army, the civil service or other suitable career had been secured by their fathers. Lt. Col. Rose Holden-Rose of Fanners and Rear Admiral Pakenham of Franklyns were of this class. Similarly lawyers Thomas and Walter Renshaw of Sandrocks and William Cotterill and John Saxby of Coldharbour, would initially have been subsidised by their families. Entry in those days was by wealth and privilege. The Weald, by then crossed by several railway lines, yet still scenic, wooded and unspoilt, had become a natural choice for the wealthy. A little to the west, St John's Common, Burgess Hill had attracted a vibrant new middle class, while Haywards Heath, a more-recently enclosed common, was beginning to do the same.[13] Wivelsfield, in easy reach both of London and of county town and coast, offered them business opportunities, a social life with their peers, and later a tranquil retirement.

Plate 32. The Birch Hotel, Haywards Heath: originally built as a private house for Dr. Jowers *circa* 1874 (Kellys Directories).

The northern part of Wivelsfield, with its high ridges and its easy access to Haywards Heath station was favoured for new houses. Several commodious establishments were built along the Lewes Road, now the A272, some with cottages to house their gardeners, coachmen and grooms. Franklyns, which had been built just before the Asylum, was bought by Rear Admiral Pakenham, (retired). Liaisons were forged with the established local gentry. The Rev. George Dixon married Martha Tanner and together they built Colwell House, a square, whitewashed building with sash windows and a low pitched slate roof. Nearly opposite this Lyoth House, a Regency style building, was bought in 1881 by Charles Poley Descou a stockbroker, aged 59 and born in Huntingdon. He and his wife Elizabeth employed two general servants to care for them. There were two coachmen living nearby and as neither Mrs. Dixon nor Mr. Descou had a coachman recorded in the 1881 Census, it is likely that these two men worked for them. Cambridge House, also on the A 272 but no longer standing, was the home of the Rev. T. Crallan M.A., Chaplain to the Asylum.

At that time there were not many consumer luxuries and moneyed people satisfied their desire for better living by engaging a number of 'living in' servants. This meant that the lady of the house and her daughters had little to occupy them besides charitable works, music making and various arts and crafts. Although there was by the 1880's a Board School, elementary education was intended for the working class and thus middle class citizens engaged private tutors or governesses for their children. Evidence of this is found both at Franklyns and at nearby Haute Terre. The latter, now demolished, was the home of the Rev. J.H. Rush who was the son-in-law of Rev. and Mrs. Dixon. He described himself in 1881 as "clerk in holy orders without care of souls". These two families also had a nursemaid each for the younger children. Britain's relationship with Germany in the 1880's was cordial, the two Royal families having intermarried and Admiral Pakenham engaged four German staff (a governess, nursemaid and both housemaids). Staff by this time came from much further afield than before and one may conjecture that, with the improved literacy, they were now able to respond to advertisements for staff which appeared in the many newspapers once the working classes could read.

Hurstwood House, which had been built in about 1870, stands on the site of the Tanyard at the bottom of Colwell Lane (Chapter 5). The occupier in 1881 was Edwin A. Hickley, who 69 years before had been born in Worcestershire. He had spent some time in Sydney Australia, where his daughter Eva was born in 1856. Mr. Hickley was the proprietor of a tin mine in Cornwall where he employed 20-30 miners. His two domestic servants, a cook and a housemaid had both been born in London. In the same vicinity George Prosser-Thomas, a civil engineer, lived in Tavistock House, now demolished, which lay opposite the Fox & Hounds public house. Aged 59 in 1881, he had been born in Middlesex. His 20 year old son William who was a Government employee in the Forest Dept. of India, ultimately married the daughter of John Saxby of Coldharbour in the south east of the parish. At Tavistock House there were two locally born domestic servants, while at Coldharbour Mr. Saxby had an Irish cook, a housemaid from Middlesex, a coachman from Wadhurst and a groom from Hampshire.

ii. One School for all

The 1870 Education Act enabled schools to be set up in localities where there had previously been no provision. Boards of managers were to be elected by the ratepayers and were empowered to levy rates for the purpose. Wivelsfield responded by holding a meeting on 28th February 1872 to *"...consider what steps shall be taken for providing the required school accommodation for the children of the parish"*. For some reason the meeting was adjourned but later the Rev. J.S.Foster, Mr. James Hanning and Mr. G.W.Dixon. son of the late Rev. George Dixon were appointed for *"...ascertaining what subscriptions can be obtained for the building of a school under managers"*. The Education Department was pressing for a suitable building.

On 2nd April a meeting was called to get Parish consent for *"...utilising the present school house so that it may meet the requirement of the Education Department..."*. However, the motion tabled was that *"... the Old Workhouse in the Parish should be fitted up and permanently used as a school house and that the chairman be requested to apply to the Local Government* [presumably the Guardians of the Poor] *for their consent to permit this house to be held by a school committee as a school house without rent"*. Sometime before the 31st October 1874 a Final Notice was received from the Education Department. This produced the following decision, on a motion proposed by Charles Knight and seconded by Hon. T.A Pakenham, *"...that a Committee of Managers be appointed to carry out the requirements of an Act of Parliament relating to the Education of children of the poor of this Parish that a committee shall consist of five members comprising the Chairman, The Rev. J.S.Foster, two members of the Church of England and two non-conformists"*. Under the provisions of the 1870 Act a voluntary Parish rate was to be levied, for education of the children of the poor of the Parish.

Things began to move more quickly, for on the fourteenth of November 1874 Mr. R.Pannett, a builder, was asked *"...to produce a plan and estimate for a school house 60ft x 18ft x 10ft, high to the spring of the roof and also for converting the present school house into a suitable residence for a schoolmaster and mistress to include removal of the two old cottages and erection of necessary conveniences"*. Mr Pannett's family had owned Fanners, but by this time he was living in Haywards Heath. He had formerly been involved in building the Asylum.

Mr Pannett produced his plans and then the Vestry had to decide whether the school should be a voluntary one or one run by a Board.

They chose the latter. By the 28th February 1875 the School Board had been nominated. Its members were Rev. J.S.Foster, James Hanning, William Farncombe, Henry Martin and Edward Randall. One of the two non-conformists must have been Edward Randall who had married the daughter of minister William Gravett; Henry Martin was perhaps the other. The Guardians of the Poor gave their consent in July 1875, "...*to convey all that freehold messuage, or tenement, yard, garden, and outbuildings and premises now and lately used as a schoolhouse but which were formerly the workhouse of the Parish and are now commonly known as the Old Workhouse, with appertenances to the School Board for the said parish for the purposes of the Elementary Education Act of 1870*".[14]

It is not known to what extent the new school achieved its aims of integrating the Chapel children and the Church children of Wivelsfield. Charles Knight, member of the Bethel congregation, was still "..*master of a private school*" in 1881. After his death in 1884 the chapel perhaps continued to be served in this way by John Holman who was described as a private school master in 1891. By 1895, however, Holman ceased to teach independently and he became a manager of the Board School in 1897, expressing a voice on that Board for the non-conformist point of view.

iii. Management of the Board School 1894-1903

The Board School opened in 1876. Its early records have not survived and only a few details can be gleaned, from Kellys' Directories. C. Weston of Lewes was Clerk to the Board and William Kenward who lived first at Tapestry Cottage and then at Verger's Cottage, both in Church Lane, was appointed Attendance Officer. He was often known as "The School Board Man" and his duties, as directed by the Board, were to follow up absentee children. If attendance did not improve a summons would be served on the parents after a warning had been given. The school was designed to cater for 120 children but the average attendance was 80. In 1878 John Roberts and his wife Agnes were still master and mistress but by 1887 Thomas Treloar had been appointed a master and Mrs Agnes Roberts remained as Mistress.[15]

From 1894 full details of Board meetings are available and these were held monthly at the school, usually on Saturday mornings.[16] At that time the committee was under the chairmanship of Lt. Col. J.R. Holden Rose who lived at Fanners and owned a considerable amount of property in Wivelsfield. Mr. George Prosser Thomas of Tavistock House, on Fox Hill,[17] the Vicar Rev. H. Thomas and Mr. M. H. Woods, tenant of Great Otehall, were other members of the Board, school walls, scrub the floors, that the ashpit should be emptied and the school walls whitewashed. For the 1896 examination "...*the school cleaner to sweep the school walls, scrub floors, clean windows, whitewash school closet and empty cesspool*". He must have dreaded the inspection as much as the teachers and pupils did.

Religious instruction was a matter of great concern to a school Board whose members represented the free as well as the established Church. In 1895, when Mr. George Prosser Thomas resigned from the Board owing to increasing age and infirmity, Mr. Pullinger, of Ote Hall Chapel, requested that Mr Thomas' place on the Board should be taken by one of the trade or working men of the Parish. He also asked that the Board should meet at a more convenient time either 10 A.M. or in the evening. In January 1896, Mr. John Holman, of Mount Pleasant (now North Haven), Fox Hill, Assistant Overseer, was unanimously elected to fill the vacancy. Evidently, both he and Mr. Pullinger were non-conformists and were not happy with some aspects of the religious instruction, assembly hymns, and prayers. Mr. Pullinger also moved that the Press be invited to the Board's monthly meetings.

Alfred Edward Hooper became headmaster in 1897, following the departure of the Mattas.[18] As part of his duties he was asked to produce a scripture syllabus for one year and a list of passages read in school each month. Mr. Pullinger also asked that the teaching of the Apostles' Creed be discontinued. Mr. Hooper replied that he did not read a scripture passage every morning, as some lessons were re-capitulation and therefore he could not give the Board a day to day list. Mr. Pullinger, at the next meeting, withdrew his motion on the Apostles' Creed and offered six prizes for those who did well in the annual scripture examination. Another proposal made by him was adopted and still continues, namely that members of the Board should take turns to visit the school, one member per month. At that time the visit was to be during Religious Instruction and once a week during ordinary school work.

Around the same time a proposal to have a lady manager was defeated. This did not happen until after the 1903 Education Act gave control of the schools to Local Education Authorities. An issue raised by Board member Mr. Holman was by what right the managers of the Church Sunday school had the use of the Board's schoolroom on Sundays. The outcome was "...*That a charge of a shilling per week be made to the Church Sunday School for the use of the Board's schoolroom on Sundays*".

In 1898 Mr. Pullinger was again dissatisfied with the Religious Instruction in the curriculum. He moved that "...*The services of the Diocesan Inspector be discontinued after the next examination and that children should be examined by Mr T. Wells of Lindfield.*" Mr. Holman seconded the motion, while Mr. Woods, evidently of the established church, proposed an amendment, *"...That the Diocesan Inspector continue."* The amendment won the day with only Mr Pullinger and Mr Holman against it. Evidence of some friction from time to time at Board meetings is shown when Mr. Pullinger moved from the district and resigned. His letter of resignation contained the following comment, that, *"....during the many years that he had been associated with the Board, although he had had occasionally to differ as to the policy of the Board"*, he acknowledged the kindness and courtesy he had generally received".

The minutes of the Board end in 1903 when it was abolished. The records of the School Managers, who succeeded them, have apparently not survived. A.E. Hooper continued as headmaster until 1924.

iv. The Staff and the Curriculum

Religious differences had delayed State control of education, the Non-conformists and the Church of England each fearing the other's bias. The Church of England took the lead in Sussex in establishing a training college, Bishop Otter College, in Chichester. This was for male teachers only. A Diocesan Training College for the 'Mistresses of National Schools' was built in Brighton in 1853-4 with accommodation for 40 female students. Bishop Otter College closed in 1868 but re-opened in 1873 as a women's college. [19]

In the 1870s and earlier a pupil-teacher system was used whereby the more able pupils helped the teacher during school hours and received extra lessons after school to keep them ahead of the class. Later, if they proved successful they could go on to one of the few teacher training colleges. In the 1890s this was still going on. While Mr. and Mrs. Matta were at Wivelsfield School there had been a pupil teacher named G.J. Randall. Mr. Randall's salary paid quarterly, was £15 per annum. He resigned in March 1895 to accept a post with Burgess Hill School Board. There was also a monitress, probably about 15 years old, Mabel Spice, and she resigned at the same time as Mr. Randall. When she was 17 she returned to the school. Pupil teachers, like uncertificated teachers, had to go to Brighton to take examinations. There was one such exam. on October 17th 1896 and they appear to have been held annually.

At the time when Mr. Randall and Mabel Spice left, a new teacher was urgently needed. Adverts were put in the 'School Mistress', 'Mid Sussex Gazette', 'West Sussex Gazette' and 'Sussex Daily News' offering a salary of £35 per annum. The advertising cost 11 shillings. There was only one applicant, Miss Eliza Emma Hollamby of Helpringham, Heckington, Lincs. who had been teaching for ten years.

She had been called for interview by telegraph, confirmed by letter and was appointed 26th March 1895 to commence her duties on 2nd April 1895. A month's notice on either side was agreed. Her expenses were £1 15s. plus 6s 0d. for a horse and trap to fetch her from and return her to, Haywards Heath Station.

Plate 33. Mr Matta, schoolmaster in the 1890's, with Mrs Matta. Photo kindly lent by Miss I. Bartlett.

Miss Hollamby proved to be a good teacher but she and the Mattas did not work happily together. She resented Mr. Matta inspecting the children's work. Mr. Matta wrote a long explanatory letter to the Board who sent a copy to Miss Hollamby and asked her to "...come before the Board". She felt that with ten years experience she knew how to teach but was told that Mr. Matta had responsibility for the school. This she accepted with reluctance.

Later she was in trouble again, as she told the children not to bring their lunch when a half-day holiday had been planned. Unfortunately,

Mr. Matta had not intended to tell the children until after morning school. Miss Hollamby's pre-warning caused both infants (her class) and the older children, in many cases, to take the whole day off. Once again Miss Hollamby was asked to attend a meeting of the Board. She then sold to the children, handkerchiefs which they had hemmed. These had cost 1s. 3d per dozen and she had charged only a penny each. Again she was reported to the Board by Mr. and Mrs. Matta. Finally in September 1896, the Board asked for her resignation. She asked for a testimonial and received one "...*her duties were performed efficiently and her character was satisfactory*".

Mr Matta then needed another member of staff. The Board proposed to get a young man but Mr Matta was of the opinion that this could not be done for £40 per annum, certainly not an ex-Pupil Teacher; the minimum which would be expected would be £52-£55. An "article 68" teacher would expect £35 or a female ex-Pupil Teacher for the infants could be had for £40 a year. Mr. Matta then suggested that if his wife took over the infants and Standard 1 with the help of a monitor and he himself took over on the upper school single-handed, they could manage, provided that the Board offered some addition to his and his wife's salary. Alice Henty, a monitress $11^1/_2$ years old, was suggested. Her father Mr Henty, agreed and she was placed with the infants on trial. She was described as a tall, intelligent girl and her parents wished her to be a teacher, "..*if she could keep up her duties at home*". She was paid 2s. 0d. per week. No addition was made to the Mattas' salaries. They were not satisfied and complained that extra was due to them. Finally Mr. Matta was given an extra 8s. 0d. per week.

Each year around Christmas time the Rev. I. P. Davies, who was the Diocesan Inspector of Schools for Religious Knowledge, came to examine the children in this subject. There were also annual drawing examinations by the Inspectorate and a general inspection of the school each year. At this the older children might be considered fit to leave school if by the age of 12 they had reached a sufficiently high standard. It was recorded in 1896 that by ruling of the Education Department, a child's certificate would be accepted as evidence of age.

At that period there was great concern that Religious Instruction should include lessons on Temperance. This was the re-action against cheap gin which accounted for drunkenness, particularly among the poor and labouring classes. Viscount Templeman had written to School Boards for their support of his plan to put before Parliament that the Education Acts should rule that all school reading books should incorporate chapters on "The Evils of Drink" and that teachers should be required to give the children 15 hours minimum per annum in the subject and examinations on these chapters should be held. The Board's opinion on the desirability of this teaching was favourable (temperance was not to mean abstinence) and gave their support.

Attendance of 75% at least was required and progress in work. The first prizes to be awarded in the day school had cost £2 for the total number. The incentive improved the attendance at the evening school and in April there was yet another lantern lecture entitled "The Transvaal".

Reading, writing, composition, geography, arithmetic, mensuration and shorthand continued, the classes being held on several evenings each week. Each subject attracted a variable grant of 1s. 6d. per student. In June 1900 this made a total of £4 7s. 0d. A fixed grant of £4 9s. 0d. was also given. When Mr. Garland, an Inspector, visited the school he reported, "...the good conduct and behaviour of the school" were the best that he had ever witnessed. He made a suggestion that "...swinging lamps would be desirable". These would have been oil lamps and no doubt safer than those standing on tables or desks. When term ended prizes totalling £2 8s. 6d. were awarded.

xliii. Magic lantern, 1890's.

There was co-operation between the two schools and a few day school pupils were invited to join in a lantern lecture on "Butter and Cheese Making". This was followed a fortnight later, by a written examination in agriculture but numbers by then had dropped to eight on roll. The Inspectorate reported that for 1900-1901 "...the evening school continues to be carefully taught by Mr Hooper" but there was no special grant for drawing. The payment received was £4 19s. 6d.

By 1901 the numbers in the Adult School had dropped to nine and the Board School managers took the decision to close it as soon as possible without affecting the Government Grant. Tom Cook (Chapter 13) remembers an evening school at Newside and Sunnywood, where Charles Knight's school had formerly been held. In 1911 the day school Log book noted that there was a village library in the school for which a charge of one old penny per month was made but only 9 children out of 45 were said to use it regularly. In 1912 a Reading Room was given to the village by Sir Charles Byne Renshaw and is still fondly remembered as we shall hear in the following chapter. It is known that Mr. Hooper became its Secretary and continued there with his valuable work in giving local people of all ages access to learning.

vi. School Days, 1903-1918

That Mr. Hooper was a conscientious headmaster for his day pupils as well as for his adult students can be judged from the school log book from 1903 onwards.[22]

It is interesting that even at that date there was integration and correlation between subjects taught. Reading was taken from history, geography and nature study books. Nature study and object lessons included what we today would consider as ' healthy living' (food, fresh air, etc.). Most nature-study subjects would have been familiar to country children but a few unknown ones such as 'the orange' and 'coal' were introduced. Drawing was integrated with geometry and cones and prisms were drawn. The use of ruler and set-square were included in the scheme, which was comprehensive. There was little time for self-expression except in design.

Elementary Science.
30 lessons on Nature Study, Hygiene, General Knowledge Questions, & Current events.

Mixed Depart. Class Two. Stand: III & II.

English.

(a). Recitation :- "Admirals All" and other pieces contained in the "Laureate" Poetry Book. (Standards I, II, & III taken together).

(b). Reading :- (1). Literary :- "Sonnenschein". Pts III-IV "Science & Nature Study" Reader.
(2). Historical :- "Chambers" Stand : III
(3). Geographical :- "Holborn" Stand: II & III.

(c). Composition :- Schofields & Sims "English". Pts : II & III

(d). Dictation :- Easy passages from Nature Study Reader.

(e). Transcription :- Nelson's "Royal Star" Copy Books.

xliv. Alfred Hooper's copper-plate handwritng.

History was taken from readers while geography included political geography but tended to concentrate on Europe, the British Isles and the Colonies. Needlework covered all the processes which the girls would have needed when the time came to clothe their own children. They learnt darning, patching and making garments by sewing and knitting. The syllabus remained virtually the same year after year with the children moving up a class to reach the next stage. The recitations, learnt by heart, were poems by contemporary poets and were still being taught in the 1920s.

Grammar was taught systematically. Parts of speech, nouns and verbs first, progressing to pronouns, adjectives and adverbs, parsing and analysis, subject and predicate. 'Drill' was perceived as an important aspect of health education and consisted of, on wet days, exercises indoors to music and when fine in the playground without music. The children left the school at the latest at 14 years and if they were bright could pass an exam. to leave and go to work at 12 years. It was a curriculum very different in emphasis and direction from that of today.

Attendance was consistently poor in winter months. Time and again the school had to be closed for epidemics of chicken-pox, whooping-cough, measles, mumps and influenza. This was a wise precaution as there were no immunisations except for small-pox. When the weather was bad the roads turned to mud and this also lowered attendance, as the children had to walk to school. Arriving wet through with little hope of getting dry clothes and having to go home for the mid-day meal meant that parents kept the children indoors to keep them warm. Out of 108 children on roll on 27th January 1904, only 39 attended. The staff too succumbed to illness quite frequently, particularly Mr. Hooper with his neuralgia. In January 1903 both he and his wife being off sick, the school closed for a week.

Staffing caused problems as replacements took a long time to arrive after a teacher had resigned. Monitors were pressed into service to fill the gap. On October 6th 1903, Miss E. Day left and no replacement was appointed until July 1904. From December 15 to January 22nd the Christmas holidays were lengthened owing to an outbreak of measles. In June 1904, the little monitress, Miss Henty also left. The Inspector reported that "....work was hindered by lack of qualified staff." Miss Edith Gardner joined the staff in June 1905 and in the same year it is recorded that Elizabeth Hicks, a pupil teacher, went off to attend the Pupil Teachers' Centre in Haywards Heath, every day except Wednesdays. Miss King left in February 1906. In October 1907, Ethel Hemsley became a monitress.

Miss Stillaway was obviously a valued long term member of staff, but in 1912 she married Charles Baldock and they were presented with a music stool and an autograph album by staff and pupils. As Mrs. Baldock, she returned quite often for short spells of supply work, teaching needlework. After she had had a son absences, due to his illness, appear from time to time. Mrs. Baldock was not replaced until 22nd July 1913. She came and went on supply until 1927 when Miss Harman came to teach at the school. Mrs. Hooper remained until October 1920 and Mr Hooper until April 1924.[23]

School outings were, according to modern standards, not very exciting, but local people offered the children entertainment of various forms. In the summers of 1904 and 1905, Mr. and Mrs. Hennessy of Coldharbour, invited them together with the staff to their home. In 1919 both pupils and teachers went to meet Dr. Montessori when she visited Botches in Green Road where babies who were war victims were receiving re-habilitation. In 1907, Mr. Hooper formed a cricket team which played against neighbouring schools in the East Sussex group, including Haywards Heath and Ardingly. Of the national events, one is outstanding for the headmaster's heartfelt comment, "...*Fri. 16th June 1911. School closed in the afternoon for one weeks holiday on account of the Coronation of the King. 'God Save the King'!*"

Plate 34. A class at Wivelsfield School in the 1930's.

Empire Day was celebrated with great patriotism. The entry for 1909 reads "...*Timetable not observed, songs, recitations and ceremonial instruction, half day holiday*". Empire Day was 24th May, Queen Victoria's Birthday, and in 1908, after registers had been marked at 9 a.m. and prayers said, there was a lesson on 'The Empire'. The flag was saluted, the National Anthem sung and by 9.50 school was over for the day. Twenty scholars and staff went off to see the sights of London, visiting the Houses of Parliament, Westminster Abbey, St. Paul's Cathedral and the Tower of London. One wonders how they reached the station, was it by carrier's cart or did they have a waggonette? By 1911 children were reported as being in trouble for throwing stones at a passing motor-car.

Trafalgar Day too, was recognised as important, in spite of the battle having been fought one hundred years previously. Again the flag was hoisted, (October 1912) and lessons about the battle were given. It is remarkable that there is no entry in the Log Book in 1914 to say that England was at war. However, after the Church Room was built in 1916 a kitchen was opened for soup for the children. By 1917, a shortage of books and apparatus was noted. In the autumn of 1918 the children went blackberrying twice weekly. Fruit stones and nutshells were collected in 1918 to help in making gas masks.

Wivelsfield's school Log book in the first two decades of this century thus reflects the aspirations and limitations of society at that time. It is doubtless typical, as a school, of countless others across the country. The girls' future duties, it was assumed, would be in the home and their education was tailored to these ends. The boys, by contrast, might be called upon to serve their country and the Trafalgar Day and similar celebrations helped create the right attitude. It is no wonder that when World War I came in 1914, the patriotism of the young men led them to volunteer in their thousands. Wivelsfield already had one war hero, P. Macklin, a former pupil who had died in the Boer War. A plaque had been erected in the school in his memory in 1902.

The war, despite all its miseries, was to open new doors for women who eventually, as full voting citizens, were to press forward into the professions and to relegate needlework to the back end of the curriculum.

But for the time being the agenda ran along on traditional lines. To celebrate the end of the war a new flagstaff was erected in the school. A half day's holiday given on July 4th 1919 to recognise the 'Signing of Peace'. The children had a tea party and sports and the King gave a week's holiday.

CHAPTER 13

THE VILLAGE IN LIVING MEMORY

"I cannot but remember such things were,
that were most precious to me"

Macbeth Act IV

In Spring term 1991 our tutor 'deserted' us for three months in order to take up a temporary archivist's post at East Sussex Record Office. Rather than waste our now free Monday afternoons we invited small groups of long-standing residents of the village to join us and we plied them with tea and cakes. A series of questions was prepared to stimulate discussion and to prompt the recall of events which had taken place during living memory. Our tutor resumed classes for the Summer Term, after which the 'oral history' sessions continued in the summer recess, either at "Frolic" or "Bostandjik", Green Road.

The warp and weft of the residents' tale is inter-woven with further documentary information, much of it kindly lent by its owners.[1] A tape recording made by Rhonda Baldock of Tom Cook and articles from Sussex Life by Vida Herbison were also valuable. The guests who contributed memories were Joan Penfold, Joy and Horace Thorpe, Ivan and Ena Smith, Agnes and Olive Millam, the late Doug Fry and Freda his wife, Ellen Hilborn, Ron Fryers, Nan Rendell, Vera Roberts, Dot Millam, Vera Brewster, Hilda Rogers, Sybil Bartlett, Mona White, Lily Banks and Joan Finzel. Reg Brinkley's contribution will be found in the following chapter. Thanks are due to everyone who contributed in any way. Apologies are offered to those whose stories have been condensed or omitted but it is hoped they can be published at a later date. These memories have been reproduced in good faith by the Wivelsfield History Study Group whose members cannot, individually or collectively, be held responsible for any errors that may have occurred in the telling.

The 'living memory' contained here relates, in the main, not to the outlying parts of the parish but to Church Lane, part of Ditchling Road, Green Road, part of North Common Road, part of Hundred Acre Lane, South Road, Downsview Drive, Allwood Crescent, and Birch Way. It is the story of the heart of the parish.

i. As remembered by the late Tom Cook

Most of the people who have contributed to this chapter received part, or even all of their education at the village school in Church Lane. The earliest reminiscences which we have are on a recording made by Tom Cook who lived most of his life at Diamond Cottages, Green Road. Born in Church Lane, he was taught "the 3 Rs" by 'Old 'Ooper', Alfred Hooper whom we have met in Chapter 12.

Having left school in about 1893 at 10 years old Tom went to work at More House Farm as a carter's boy. There were three teams of horses and later one of Tom's jobs was to plough the fields where Baldings Cottages stand today. He remembered that the coachman and the gardener employed at Lunces Hall lived in the pair of cottages at the entrance to 'The Avenue'. There was no doctor in Wivelsfield, the nearest being in Haywards Heath or Ditchling. Tom used to walk from his home in Church Lane to Ditchling, four miles each way, to get a prescription, and received a ha'penny for going. This, he said, was quite a lot compared with any pocket money which he might be given. He also told of a primitive box mangle at Moat House which neighbours were allowed to use.

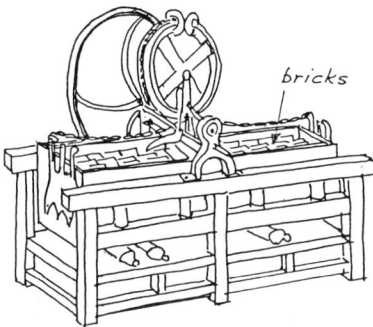

bricks

xlv. A box mangle. Sheets were wrapped round rollers

Tom enlisted, under age, for the Boer War and he also served in World War I. After his de-mob in 1919 Tom returned to Wivelsfield and lived with his wife and children at number 1 Diamond Cottages, then owned by their employer Thomas Baldock for whom Tom drove a horse-drawn coal cart. The coal was stored behind a retaining wall on the site of the present warehouse behind Barnard and Brough's Garage. Percy Everest worked with Tom Cook delivering the coal. These two men, like most workers here at that period, spoke with a broad Sussex 'burr' which today we should find almost unintelligible. Sadly, this all but disappeared with the arrival of the 'wireless' in the 1920s followed later by T.V.

When Tom Cook died in the late 1970s he was 95, the oldest inhabitant of Wivelsfield.

ii. In the Great War, 1914-1918

The Parish Room in Church Lane was given in 1916 by Mary Holden-Rose, and it immediately became the home of the newly-formed Women's Institute.[2]

At the outbreak of war the W.I. went into action. Mrs. Godman of Little Otehall was responsible, with help from Mrs. Louie Woods, her tenant at Great Otehall and the vicar, Mr. Wood for inaugurating the Institute. She persuaded a Russian aristocrat, Princess Kropotkin, who was living in Brighton., to become President, which gave the new group prestige. More than 70 ladies joined and together held 'Fur and Feather' shows and 'Make-do and Mend' competitions. They learned how to use a hay-box to save fuel when cooking and how a bread mixer could save time, freeing women to work on the farm. They entertained wounded soldiers and, long before school dinners were available, provided soup for the children who were on war-time rations. In 1922 the W.I. was disbanded and Louie Woods and others set up the Women's Social Club in its stead, a society which still flourishes in the village today.

How many people realise that when the Great War ended in 1918, a house in Wivelsfield became part of Chailey Heritage, the now nationally famous school and hospital for disabled children? Grace Kimmins, who had founded the Heritage Craft School in 1903, found that many babies were emotionally and/or physically shattered by air raids. Mrs. Rees-Mogg gave her house Botches, in Green Road, as a home for these young children. They left when a unit was built for them at the Heritage. When Madam Maria Montessori personally inspected Botches to advise on how best to help the babies, the Head Teacher of Wivelsfield School, staff and some of the pupils were invited to meet her.

The war ended and memorials to the dead appeared all over the country. In Wivelsfield there is one in the churchyard, one in the north aisle of the church and another in Green Road opposite Jenners, a stone cross on a plinth. They commemorate the 21 people from the parish who gave their lives. The cross in Green Road carries the following inscription:

> *" Not once or twice in our rough island story,*
> *The path of duty was the way to glory."*

iii. Housing and employment after the War

St. John's Water Co., though formed in 1870, could not supply any water at all for Wivelsfield and surrounding villages until 1903. The school well had become contaminated in 1897-8 and children died of diphtheria, but still no water came.[3] Even a large house like Roselands, in North Common Road, built in about 1902, had to make do with a well and pump. When the men returned home after the War housing was scarce and mains water was still not generally available. Not until 1926 did the first Council-built houses appear. These were 'Baldings Cottages' in Green road, built without mains sanitation, electricity or gas. A bucket privy, oil lamps and candles had to suffice.

Working people did not buy their homes, but rented. When landlord Thomas Baldock put in a new fireplace in Diamond Cottages he raised the rent by 2s. 0d. per week. The inside bedroom walls of Baldings Cottages were simply asbestos sheets which the children knocked through, not to be replaced by better material until about 1981. Mrs. Banks who captained the Ladies' Whist Team, still lives in Baldings cottages.

Plate 35. Baldings Cottages, *circa* 1926. Kindly lent by Wivelsfield Parish Council.

There were a few new job opportunities after the War but each large residence still employed an army of servants. Mr. Foster, a banker, lived at Coldharbour and had a butler, a head gardener, six under-gardeners, a farm worker, a chauffeur for the Rolls Royce and, of course, indoor staff. His wife and daughter were founder members of the W.I. and used to entertain their fellow members by singing and playing various musical instruments.   The Fosters gave to the village the land on which the council built houses in the 1930s, now known as Fair Place.

Whitebreads (Green Park Farm), once home to farm workers at Coldharbour, belonged in the 1930s to Colin White.   After the First World War he married Mary Adams, who had been a land girl at Great Otehall.   Free from the milk-marketing restrictions of today, Colin drove his pony cart from house to house filling jugs left on doorsteps. The land he owned was used for the pre-fab Airey houses, built after the war in Eastern Road and of necessity since demolished.

A lorry-driver's wage in 1936 was £3 10s. per week and a charwoman 6d. per hour. Agricultural labourers received 30s. weekly but might be given a piece of pork now and then by their employer. There were several dressmakers in the village but most working-class wives made clothes for their family, including their husbands' shirts.

iv. Commerce and trade

The village has enjoyed a flourishing commercial life throughout the century which it still retains, unlike some unfortunate parishes in the Weald which have now lost their only shop and Post Office. Tradespeople from Haywards Heath called at village homes for orders in the '20s and '30s, telephones being a rare luxury. Liptons and the International Stores were the grocers patronised.   A butcher, baker, paraffin man and a dog's-meat man brought their wares round the village in carts.

There were various shops, two with post offices, one in Verger's Cottage, Church Lane and one at the Green, opposite Botches.   Mrs. 'Deaf' Everest had a shop in her house in South Road; while in Ditchling Road, opposite the Royal Oak, there was a shop in 'The Limes', owned by Mr. Emery, father-in-law of Thomas Baldock. It was just in Ditchling parish, but used by Wivelsfield people. It is remembered that he used to watch what was going on in the shop through a spy-hole in the floor of the room above ! Opposite the new development 'Tanners Field' there was a general stores.

Wivelsfield Green Post Office and Shop After World War II the owners of the shop and Wivelsfield Green Post Office were Joy and Horace Thorpe, Canon Hughes' daughter and son-in-law.The name Wivelsfield   Post Office was already in use in Church Lane. Village postal addresses and the telephone exchange became 'Wivelsfield Green', the latter initially using single numbers only. Horace Thorpe's parents came to the village in the 1930s and bought the shop freehold. In the early 1900s the shop had included a butchery department run by a Mr. Cornwells.

Tea deliveries came in large chests and cheese in crates, two to the crate. The tea had to be weighed into quarter pounds and then packaged and the cheese 'skinned', that is the cloth in which it had been made had to be removed. Then with a cheese-wire, each customer's requirement was cut off and weighed to the ounce. Any slight overweight was given to the customer. Dried fruit, delivered in bulk, sugar and rice in sacks and biscuits in tins, were all weighed and wrapped before sale. Bacon was sliced to the required thickness for each customer. Prices in the 1930s never varied and therefore Joy and Horace and many who shopped at that time, can still remember the cost of each commodity. When buses came to the village some people may have patronised the larger stores but on the whole, the shop and post office remained the centre of the community and was used by everyone.

A doctor held a weekly surgery in a room at the Post Office. Come rain, come shine, the patients queued outside in the Thorpe's garden. Wilfred Broadley, a local chemist, would collect prescriptions left at the shop, dispense them at his premises in Ditchling and return them to Wivelsfield. Not until 1981 and the coming of the new Village Hall could local people wait under cover to see the doctor.

Robert Millam, blacksmith and Reg Porter, wheelwright   Robert Millam, the village blacksmith (see Plate 37) and Reg Porter, the wheelwright, needed a good supply of water for one of their joint enterprises. The wooden cart-wheel being ready for the iron rim, Mr. Millam made it red hot. To avoid charring the wood the Millam children had to stand by with buckets of water and, when told, poured it with great gusto onto the rim. The Millams lived in 'The Forge', formerly called 'Goldsmiths', but now 'Blacksmith's' at the Green. Originally it was one room up and one room down and the inside walls were wattle and daub. The hair of Red Sussex cattle was used to bind the infilling and for many years Agnes Millam kept some of this as a curiosity. In the 'outshot', or scullery, at the rear there was a very big copper, filled with well water, in which all the laundry had to be boiled and then washed by hand. The unplastered scullery ceiling is remembered as 'mainly cobwebs'. An open entry, without a door, led from the scullery to a second scullery and in winter a curtain was hung across the opening to keep in what little warmth there was. The floor was uneven, simply bricks laid on the earth. An old unglazed sandstone sink on which the Millams sharpened their knives, stood on the right. When the family had a fish meal, the knives were dug into the garden soil to remove the fishy taste and smell. The floors were covered with linoleum and in winter, water left in jugs or bowls would soon become thick ice.

Robert Millam took the forge in 1927. His daughter won a scholarship to go on from the village school to a grammar school in Brighton, but she could not accept it because the family had no means of transport to get her there. Philosophically she recalls that it made no difference, as there would have been no suitable job in the village for her afterwards. Another village girl, Mrs. Hilborn's daughter, was able to accept her place at Hove County School, having received financial help with the school uniform.

Thomas Baldock   Thomas Baldock was born in Wivelsfield, son of John and Philadelphia and great-nephew of Thomas the former pastor of the Bethel chapel. He owned all the land and the property on it from Common Cottage, Ditchling Road (except Otehall Chapel), right along Green Road to the twitten leading to Dumbrells Cottages. Well before the Great War he had established himself as a coal merchant and a butcher. He owned the slaughter house behind his home, Stream House. Meat from the slaughter-house was sold from the west end of Stream House which was the butcher's shop. Thomas Baldock and his wife Flora lived in the other part of the house, under which there is a cellar where bacon was salted in tanks. The slaughter-house in 1967 was said to be the most up-to-date in the country, but it has now closed.

Amos Hemsley, the bricklayer responsible for the brickwork of Woodland View and Stream Villas, lived with his family at no. 3 Diamond Cottages now the home of his grand-daughter, Vera Roberts, her son and her grandson. In no. 2 Stream Villas lived Doug Fry. He was a car mechanic who was drafted to work for Thomas Baldock at the time of World War II. Thomas owned an old red Vauxhall car which he used not only on roads but also for work in the fields. One day it broke down and Doug mended it - with his wife's hairpin! Thomas Baldock was never told how it was done.

Thomas Baldock built Baldock's Garage for his son, another Tom, and gave land for the three houses south of it to his three sons. A member of the Bethel chapel, he went to his last resting place in the Bethel graveyard in 1957 and his wife Flora followed him in 1958. His youngest son Dick took over the garage, while Charlie built 'Wyndals', where he came to live when he married in the 1930s.

Harold Bartlett   Around 1910 another employer in the village was Harold Bartlett, a builder. He was born in 1876, son of Thomas and Eliza Bartlett of

Whitebreads. He married Phyllis Chart and took her to live at Baldings in Slugwash Lane. Four of Harold's brothers and sisters had died in a diphtheria epidemic in 1898 and he lost his only son from meningitis. Sadly, there remains no male heir to this family who came to Wivelsfield before 1881. Harold Bartlett built Field House in Green Rd., since enlarged, but did not like it. The chimney, with its interesting brickwork and its strange trap-door is worth a second glance.

Harold's yard was at the junction of Green Road and Eastern Road. Around 1950 a local joiner, Ren Mills, took over the firm from Harold and enlarged the workshop while Sired's of Brighton later added office accommodation. Finally, Brian Beer developed it into 'Otehall Switches', a small electronics factory. Both Baldock's Garage and Bartlett's yard had become munitions factories during World War II and Mr. Beer and his wife had managed them both.

Harold Bartlett had owned all the land on the east side of Eastern Road and in 1938 he offered it to Herbert Hilborn for £90. Herbert was about to get married and could only afford the plot on which he built his own home, the Lilacs, and the garden plot beside it. As a boy, Herbert Hilborn was apprenticed as trainee carpenter to Thomas White, builder, of Haywards Heath. The lad's pay was at 4s. a week the first year, 8s. a week the second year, the third year 3d. and the fourth year 4d. per hour. That was in 1921 when there was no other way to learn a trade.

Harold Bartlett and Thomas Baldock must have been Parish officials as they are remembered as having been responsible for setting the rates. In the early days of cars both wanted one but neither could afford it. They solved the problem by purchasing one between them and using it on alternate days. There were no driving tests before the 1930s. Harold built the four houses in Green Road to the east of the Playing Field. Harold's employees included Joe Botting of Baldings Cottages, Bill Rogers, a plumber, of 4 Baldings Cottages, Bill Warnett, a joiner, Bob Clements and Ren Mills, carpenter and joiner. They worked not only in the village but further afield sometimes having to live away from home from monday until friday. They built all the houses from Greenfields to Lapworth in Eastern Road, and some of the houses at the northern end of Fox Hill. Ren Mills later built 'Renville' for himself.

The junction of Green Road and Eastern Road is still known to long term village inhabitants as 'Bartlett's Corner'. All the local coach drivers knew where one meant by this term. Likewise, the corner opposite Thomas' yard became 'Snell's Corner', as Snell, the baker, had his shop and bakery in what is now Country Curl. 'The Green' is, of course, a much older local name referring to the old Green around the Forge, now Thomas' yard.

Allwoods Nurseries   Allwoods employed most of the young girls in the village who did not want to go into service after World War I. Their work was the cultivation of carnations and the name of the village became world famous when one successful variety was named 'Sweet Wivelsfield'.[4] Monty Allwood and his wife Doris, one time president of the Women's Social Club, lived at The Old Cottage, North Common Road. His nephew Robert had Horseshoe Cottage, Green Road, built when he married Sheila Moore of 'Boerth Park' in the 1950s. Monty always had a stand at Chelsea Flower Show which initially either he or his brother George attended, accompanied by several of the workforce. One of these was Ron Fryers. When Monty died his widow Doris had a memorial window put in the north wall of the Parish Church. It shows St. Francis, surrounded by birds and flowers, with the inscription "Montague Charles Allwood 1880-1958. He loved this place." His widow Doris died in 1969.[5]

Plate 36. Allwoods Nursery cart. Photo kindly lent by Eileen Hallett of Burgess Hill.

v. The Slate Club at the Cock Inn

Before the Second World War sick leave meant no pay and prolonged absence often meant 'the sack'. To mitigate financial distress Slate Clubs were formed, often organised from public houses. Wivelsfield Slate Club was run from the Cock Inn and from 1924 Edward Birch was secretary. There was a chairman, a 'sick-steward', and a committee of three men and two women. Thomas Baldock and Harold Bartlett were elected as auditors.

On the death of a member the next of kin would receive 1s. from each member towards funeral expenses. The rules insisted, however, on certificates of proof of marriage and death for each claim. Mrs. Agate received £4 14s. towards her husband's funeral expenses in 1928. At that time a memorial wreath cost about 7s. 6d. Any member failing to pay was fined 6d.

Members paid in a subscription of a few pence each month and if they fell sick they received a small weekly payment subject to strict conditions. For example, anyone on sick pay had to be indoors by 6pm. Defaulters were reported to the Sick Steward. When accounts were balanced at Christmas anything left was shared between all the members. In 1924, 76 members received £1 0s. 10$^1/_2$d. at the share out. In 1925 £1 4s. 4d. was the share out and for half a year's work the secretary and stewards were paid, between them, £3 7s. 6d. Applications for membership were rigorously screened.

With 90 or more members in 1928 rules later had to be tightened as too much sick-pay was being claimed. The maximum entitlement in any year was £3 10s. 0d. and once this had been drawn out no more could be claimed until the next year. Those who moved from the village could not be re-elected and *"...no member who is in arrears will have any claim on the club for sick-pay whether contributions are paid personally or otherwise"*. In 1932 it was decided not to invest club money with the Post Office but with the Brewers. In 1934 it was decreed that *"...no member will in future, be allowed to cycle when receiving sick-pay"*. Later this was permitted if covered by a doctor's certificate. The villagers must have been spying on the culprits and reporting them to the sick-steward! Evidently the Christmas spirit prevailed in 1934, for on December 17th it was proposed to deduct 1s. from each member at the end of the year, *"...the same to be spent over the bar"*. The landlord of the Cock was not entirely altruistic in allowing the use of his premises for the Slate Club.

By 1938 there were only 38 members, but it picked up again after the War and in 1951 there were 73. By then, however, the new National Health Scheme had made the old slate clubs redundant and the last entry for the Wivelsfield club was in 1955.

vi. Leisure time

The Reading Room   Standing next to Field House in Green Road is the former Reading Room, a building whose earliest role was touched on in the previous chapter. It was given to the village in 1912 by Sir Charles Byne Renshaw of Coldharbour who at the time also provided the newly-formed scout troop with their uniforms.

The Reading Room hosted most village clubs and some weddings until the Village Hall was opened in 1981. The Little Theatre, Whist Club, Billiards Players, Baby Clinic, Chiropodist, Red Cross and even the Playgroup shivered in the Reading Room in winter.[6] It was a cold place, having only a tortoise-stove and there are memories of sitting there, wrapped in blankets, for winter meetings. During World War II it became a First Aid Post and a ceiling was put in to try to conserve some of the heat.

xlvi. The Reading Room, 1912.

Mrs. Parks of Hamlyn's Cottage, Mrs. Dark the elder of 'East Lynn' and 'Doss' Wadey each in turn cared lovingly for the Reading Room. Doss, daughter of Ethel Cornford (nee Everest), was great-grand daughter of old Amos Jenner after whom the house 'Jenners' in Green Road is said be named.

Jerry Masters was Letting Secretary for many years and no-one - even regular users - was allowed to hold a key, which meant that he or his family had to be available whenever access was needed. Bill Rogers, who was the colour bearer of the local British Legion, hired the room in 1946 for his wedding reception. The charge was ten shillings, a laughable sum by modern standards.

The sale of the Reading Room in 1980 raised £20,000 towards the new Village Hall, opened in April 1981. It was fitting that Winifred

Mein, grand-daughter of Sir Charles Renshaw, officiated at the opening ceremony and that the small hall is named 'The Renshaw Room' while the committee room is "The Reading Room". The old Reading Room was mourned by many who had enjoyed their leisure hours in it, not least Doss Wadey who never became reconciled to the new Village Hall.

The Donkey Derby & the Playing Field The field in which the Village Hall now stands is properly known as the 'Playing Field'. In the distant past it would have been part of the 'Green' but in the '20s it was farmland worked by Colin White. Thanks to Jim Dinnage (who owned Dinnages Garage in Haywards Heath) it was bought for the village in 1949, never to be built on, but to remain a sports field. As one of the fund-raising events towards the purchase Harold Bartlett was elected 'Mayor of Wivelsfield', whereby each vote cast raised cash. Publicity was helped along by Mrs. Luckett of Church Lane who had reached her 100th year. Harold Bartlett posed for the press photo while presenting her with the King's telegram. Prior to 1949 the sports clubs used a field in Slugwash Lane and another field north of More House, on the B2ll2. Before the first World War General Sir Wykeham Leigh Pemberton used to host a cricket team in the 30-acre park at Abbotsleigh and W.G. Grace captained the opposing team.[7]

Plate 37. R. Millam shoeing donkeys for the Donkey Derby, 1947. Photo kindly lent by Miss S. Bartlett.

Jim Dinnage rescued over-worked donkeys, saved them from slaughter and then set up a donkey sanctuary, where St. Peter's and St. James' Hospice is situated. Thus the local name for the hospice is 'The Donkey Home. The first Donkey Derby was held in 1952 and is said to have attracted 30,000 people. The roads were blocked for miles around and Jim had to send out to all the surrounding pubs to buy up soft drinks for the thirsty crowds. The Derbies raised money for good causes and when Chailey Heritage was presented with an orthopaedic bath from the profits, all the volunteer workers received personal invitations to the ceremony.[8]

Jim died in 1963 and £4,000 was collected by his friends to erect a pavilion in his memory. Designed by Stitchbury of Lewes, it was built by Ren Mills.

The traditional Sussex game of stoolball is played on the Playing Field. Doss Wadey was a member of the team until she was over 60. After her death the team put a seat outside the Pavilion in her memory. There is also a seat in memory of Doris Freeman, who ran a riding school at Roselea, South Road before, during and after World War II. Others have since been commemorated in this way for services to the village.

On Sundays When Doss Wadey left school in 1931, she went into service at the Vicarage. Out of her meagre wage she was told to put 6d. each Sunday into the collection. She and the other domestic staff had to leave the service early to return to the Vicarage to prepare lunch. Life was hard for village girls in those days.

At the Bethel Chapel deacons were in charge after 1924 and one of them, Samuel Leaney, gave faithful service for 40 years until 1965. He is remembered by Bill Baldock who, as a child, came under Mr. Leaney's eagle eye during the services when the boy imagined that he was out of sight in the gallery. At the Otehall Chapel between the wars the Twose family of Mann's Farm were a familiar sight as the parents shepherded their eleven girls and a boy in crocodile formation to the services.

The Wivelsfield Ringers Several of Allwood's employees were bell ringers at the Parish Church. The ringers organised beetle drives, dances and a fete to raise £1,000 to buy the bell which commemorates the coronation of Queen Elizabeth II in 1953. Two bell ringers were Mr Walker, who worked at The Forge and Mr Turner of Baldings. Among the women were Agnes Millam, Dilys Smith, Jenny Pierce and Edna Everest. At Christmas there was carol singing around the village to raise money. Mrs. Walsh, a gracious lady living nearby at 'Chippinge', always delighted them by wearing evening dress to receive them. The ringers included two boys named Collins, who managed to buy a second-hand set of hand-bells which were then re-cast at Whitechapel. Later they spotted a set of bells once used in large houses to summon servants up-stairs. These were also re-cast to give the semi-tones between the original set. Bernard Harfield, who worked with the wheelwright, made a coffin-shaped box which still keeps them safe and sound. They are still used on special occasions.

Getting around   Until the early 1950s, bicycles costing at the most £5 were a popular means of getting around. With little traffic except horse-drawn vehicles, they were relatively safe. The roads were almost impossible to cross when most of the staff at Allwoods Nursery took to two wheels; firstly to get to work, then to nip home for a mid-morning cup of tea and back to work in about 15 minutes, until lunch time. Back and forth they went until they went home again at 5p.m. The 'knocking off' bells at Allwoods were a sign for villagers to keep indoors until the rush had subsided.

Reg Porter the wheelwright was also the village undertaker. He had a hearse and a limousine which doubled as wedding transport. Both vehicles were kept in a shed sited where 'Ahlen' now stands, at the junction of Green and South Roads. The first bus service to run was the no. 29, in 1929. It was housed by M. Brant, haulage contractor and foreman at Allwoods Nurseries, who owned Wivelsfield Green Garage. There was a no. 23 bus to Brighton - fare 2s. 0d. and Wivelsfield to Crawley, 2s. 2d. It picked up at Otehall Chapel. From there to Haywards Heath the fare was 3d. or less. In about 1928 shares were floated to form a "South Downs Bus Co."

Other vehicles on the roads in the 1920s were the chara-bancs. Holding 24 or so passengers, they had open tops with folding roofs, which in cold or wet weather could be used to keep out the worst of the rain. These were hired for outings such as school treats and sometimes the children were taken for a picnic to Clayton Hill, near Jack and Jill. At other times they simply walked to the Vicarage for tea and games in the garden. Dr. Watts gave Saturday film shows at his house, Botches, for 1d. a head, which included lemonade and a bun. No-one interviewed recalled visiting London for national celebrations, not even the coronations of 1902, 1911, 1937 or 1953. However, in 1935 the King's Silver Jubilee had been celebrated on Mr. Godman Irving's 'fourteen-acre field. All the children were dressed patriotically in red, white and blue.

Plate 38.   Fred and Harriet Everest's Golden Wedding, 1937:-

Stanley Frank 1907	Eric 1911	William Edward m	Ernest Frederick m	Ethel Mary 1892 m	Reginald George 1903	Norman Harold 1900	Percy Charles 1899
		Mary Eliza White (Mrs 'Deaf' Everest)	Charlotte Ellen Nichols	Joseph Cornford			
Kathleen Hetty 1905 m William Graham	Rose Edith 1887 m Percy Farmer	Fred 1862 d1937 at Manns	----- m ----- 1887	Harriet Esther Jenner 1868-1938 (daughter of Amos Jenner & Emma Osborne)		Lily Emma	Daisy Olive 1908

Most people had heard of the Festival of Britain held in 1951, but low incomes precluded visiting it. People in better circumstances did, from time to time, visit the Theatre Royal in Brighton and some had accounts at William Hills in Hove or Hanningtons in Brighton. For drinkers there were two local inns, the Cock and the Fox, while the Royal Oak at the north end of Ditchling Common, was also used by the villagers. At Haywards Heath the 'New Inn', now known as the Ugly Duckling, was built within the boundaries of the parish.

These fields they rented out to Ernest Hicks who came to Multan Farm in 1936, from Bedelands, which he had rented since 1930. Multan had first been bought by a retired Major who named it in memory of his army days. He planted daffodils by the present house and roses by the present cowshed. A man lived in a hut (present farm yard) and travelled to work at Grimsdick's, a greengrocer and nurseryman in Haywards Heath. When Ernest and his wife Trudy arrived they lived and stored their possessions in this hut until they could afford to have a bungalow built in 1937. Disaster struck one autumn when a spark, from a bonfire of hedge-cuttings, blew onto a small haystack which caught fire and in turn ignited the hut and all their belongings.

Making a living   It was not easy to make a living selling milk before the days of the Milk Board. A buyer had to be found and the best price possible negotiated.

Some milk, butter, cream and eggs were sold to the local shops. Ernest had to be at Miss Cook's dairy in Junction Road, Burgess Hill, by 7.15 a.m. every morning having collected milk from Theobalds and Folly Farms en route. Surplus eggs and cream (9d. a carton for "Devon" cream) were sent to Haywards Heath market. During the war, when fuel was scarce, Trudy took over a peat delivery round to raise extra money; a strenuous and dirty job which entailed unloading the peat from rail shipments to Newick or Burgess Hill and then delivering them as far away as Henfield.

Plate 40. Trudy Hicks at Multan Farm. Photo kindly lent by Trudy Hicks.

When the Hickses first moved to Multan the only access to their two fields, at the north west of the Estate, was by the old bridleway. They bought the top part of Mr. Wiles' field to make the present entrance, plus 12 acres of field, half of which belonged to Mr. Wiles and the rest to his son. Mr. Wiles was an amateur photographer from Brighton who lived next door at Five Acres on the site of Tile Barn. When he had first moved here he had realised his assets by selling off the tiles from the old Tile Barn. Some of these went to repair Ditchling Church roof. Apart from Theobalds and Antye Farms, Tile Barn had been the only building on the Valebridge estate before 1920. For it and the four and a half acre field in which it stood, Mr. and Mrs. Tophill had paid £252 10s. in 1920. Two years later Mr. and Mrs. Brockhurst had taken out a mortgage to buy the property, then renamed Highams, but after two years they sold to Mr. Wiles.

On the other side of what had been Tile Barn pond lived Mr. and Mrs. Searles, a railway worker, who had built his small bungalow with the help of his father and his wife, who mixed the concrete. Mrs. Searles remained at Lake Dene until her death in the late 1950s when the property was bought by Mr. Cunningham, a builder from Surrey. He kept the cottage, together with its pond, as a weekend retreat but only for the statutory three years until he was allowed to sell at a profit without its being taxed. The field he sold, in 1960, to Kenneth Hicks, who built up Diadem Poultry Farm, the only remaining chicken farm on the Valebridge Estate.

To the east of them was Wychwood, built by Mr. Maddocks and named after the place he had left in the Cotswolds. He was an artistic man who decorated the panels on his internal house doors with painted flowers and foliage. In 1926 Wychwood was bought by the Thompsons who left London when Mr. Thompson was advised to move to the country for the sake of his health. The poultry farm did not prosper but Mrs. Thompson continued to commute to her dress shop in London and remained the breadwinner until her retirement in 1973, at the age of 75.

To their north, at Ryevale, lived Charlie Vizer. He may have bought his strip of field from Mr Maddocks. Down by the stream was his brick built house in the other half of which lived his pigs. Charlie's new wife was not too enthusiastic about this arrangement and he started another building halfway up the field. This was abandoned and his third and final bungalow built in the present position but the pigs continued to share the kitchen when they were "...under the weather". Vizer supplemented his income from the pigs by growing daffodils and vegetables and doing various jobs such as working for the Gell-Wooleys or, when they left, in the Burgess Hill brickyards.

Between Lisnagreugh (Brooklodge) and Copse End, where Miss Peggler lived, was the Plantation Piece. Here, in the 1920s, a young fellow had tried to make a living growing strawberries but he failed and the land was annexed to Lisnagreugh. Miss Peggler sold to the Race family who retired to Copse End and built two long sheds in which to keep poultry. Another poultry farmer, White, set up opposite Theobalds at Oakfield (his bungalow sited at Leah's). In half the slip field (Sedge Meadow/ south Goose Neck) lived Parks, the man who built the first bungalows up Valebridge Road; selling them for £500 each. Pooley built the houses along Janes Lane as well as Zenda and Futility in Theobalds Road.

The smallholders who set up home on the Valebridge Estate plot referred to Worlds End in Burgess Hill as 'the village'. It had the nearest shops and 'Wivelsfield Station' on the main London/Brighton railway. The only road access to and from their properties was via Worlds End, as it still is today. However, Wivelsfield was their parish and, it was in Wivelsfield that they went to church . Like the residents of the Charlwood Gardens area in Burgess Hill today, their children were sent to Wivelsfield school. Though it was, and is, a long way round by road, the footpaths were direct. The ancient tracks down the valley, across the stream and up to Church Lane served the Valebridge smallholders as they had served many generations before them.

iii. The demise of the Commons and Greens

"Ye commons left free in the rude rags of nature,
Ye brown heaths beclothed in furze as ye be,
My wild eye in rapture adores every feature,
Ye are dear as this heart in my bosom to me."

John Clare (b. 1793), The Village Minstrel

We left the story of the commons and greens in 1840 when enclosure and encroachment had turned all the common meadows and much of the common pasture into farm land. Yet in 1840 common pasture still covered 146 acres of the land of the parish. Now, due to continuing encroachments and enclosures all has gone except the 4.3 hectares, a little over 11 acres, of Lunces Common.

In the north of the parish, Lyoth Common was at first taken over by market gardens and Charlesworth's Nursery, famous for its orchids, but now it lies buried under acres of urban development. On account of the boundary being redrawn it is no longer in Wivelsfield Parish or even in the same part of the county. Otehall Common, once an outpost of Wivelsfield, is also now part of Haywards Heath in West Sussex, immersed under housing in the Kent's Road area, Wivelsfield Road and the expanse of St. Francis Hospital (now part of Princess Royal Hospital).

Development has also engulfed our village Greens. The Birch Hotel, Colwood Hospital and the surrounding houses now cover Birch Green. A wider than usual grass verge at the junction of Hurstwood Lane and Fox Hill might be considered to be the only vestige of Jefferys Green to survive. Wivelsfield Green is submerged beneath a form of ribbon development so at variance with the older properties which still lie behind it, edging the perimeter of the old Green; houses such as Baldings, Jenners, Verandah, Manns and Skinners. The modern estate of Fair Place has been built, as the name implies, on part of the site of Wivelsfield Fair. In the past all three greens were at crossroads and, although now the roads form busy T-junctions, the probable line of the old cross road in each case can be traced along adjacent footpaths.

It has been written that Lunces Common, our remaining piece of ancient common land, was enclosed in 1889 against gipsies but here the word 'enclosed' is used in a different context. A 'Presentment as to Vagrants encamped on Lunce Green and permission to erect a fence and warn off Trespassers' was issued around the turn of the century. Four commoners were named, Walter Renshaw, James Freeman, Henry Martin and Henry Butcher. In 1904 John West (Reeve of Ditchling Manor) wrote to Walter Renshaw asking for 3s. 0d. being three years 'sufferance rent' due to the Lord of the Manor of Ditchling to cover the administrative costs of the fencing. These measures were taken to preserve the pasturage and other rights of the commoners, which were presumably still being exercised.

Plate 41. Lunces Common, 1994. Cottages at the common's western edge, 1994.

Gipsies, though perhaps always perceived by householders with suspicion, were nonetheless an accepted part of the rural scene while there was sufficient waste land to accommodate them. In this area in the 1880s a vast tract of open common, Haywards Heath, had recently been enclosed. This included that part of the heath that belonged to Otehall manor, in Wivelsfield parish.[5] Not only had the gipsies lost their anchorage but commoners had presumably lost their pasturage rights. It was stated in an undated letter of around 1923 from C.H.B. Franklin of Lunces Hall (in Otehall manor) to Mr. Neville of Rogers Farm that Mr. Bacon, a previous owner of Lunces Hall "...made a chalk road from the [Lunces] Common to Lunces Hall."[6] He presumably wanted a direct access towards the growing town of Haywards Heath, for Lunces Hall itself had no rights of common on Lunces Common.

The preservation of a common depends upon its registration under the Commons Registration Act of 1965. Fortunately, Lunces was so preserved. It may seem a contradiction, but all common land has always been, and still is, owned by someone. What is more, it is not and never has been the property of the general public. The ownership of Lunces Common was sold out of the Abergavenny Estate in 1952 to Mr. W.E.K. Lincoln who, in 1965, duly registered his interest as owner under the Commons Registration Act. Under the same Act the original commoners' rights for the taking of gorse, furze bushes, underwood and peat over the whole area of the Common were registered for the Old Cottage. Other commoners' rights existed for Rogers Farm, Clearwaters and part of Cleavewater, all held of the Manor of Ditchling, but sadly these rights were not registered with the County Council before January 1970 and therefore, have been extinguished.

The initial registration was made by Dr. K.E. Pembrey of Eastern House, Hurstpierpoint. Perhaps he had happy childhood memories of Lunces Common, for forty years previously a Pembrey family had lived nearby on Fox Hill.[7] The common had certainly played its part in community life for Gus Bellchambers recalls camping there as a youngster with the Wivelsfield Scout troop. Lunces Common continued to be grazed until the early 1960s but since that time much of it has been used as arable land growing the traditional variety of corn crops, beans and recently linseed. All the trees are protected by a Preservation Order, bluebells grow in the woodland, rabbits are plentiful and foxes frequently seen. Perhaps in time the fritillaries and orchids, once so prolific, will return.

CHAPTER 15

A POSTSCRIPT

History, like language is a living thing. Daily both move slowly onwards. Science brings new words to our language, such as television, telecom , computer & fax, and the concepts represented, consistently change the pattern of our lives.

$$* * *$$

One hundred & fifty years ago , at the time of the 1841 Census, not only Wivelsfield, but most of Great Britain, lived in rural communities, where each person was dependant on his neighbours and his own efforts, to provide the necessities of life. Rich, middling and poor lived side by side in well-defined class system. The rigidity of the system was tempered by good neighbourliness. The rich helped those less fortunate than themselves. The workers in general in their turn respected and cared for their employers' daily needs.

Few people nowadays experience the feeling of living in a close community. Science has made communication much easier and travel to the ends of the earth has become a matter of days rather than of many months. The 'plane & the car have made it possible for one to travel hundreds of miles every day to earn one's daily bread. From Wivelsfield, it can be as easy for those with money and a car to get to Manchester as it is for those who rely on public transport to reach Brighton, particularly on Sundays, when the bus service does not operate. We are only two or three generations from being country people who depended on the land for our livelihood and most of us have not yet come to terms with being town dwellers. By our longing for a rural life we are destroying the very conditions which we hope to enjoy; the peace of the countryside, green fields and the woods re-echoing with bird song. As recently as the 1960s the nightingale could be guaranteed to sing in many parts of the village but housing developments such as Kents Road, Downsview Drive, Birch Way, and Farncombe Close have destroyed the habitat of much of our wildlife.

Of the four general stores which used to serve the village, only the shop and Post Office at the Green remains. Supermarkets in Burgess Hill and Haywards Heath, being able to purchase more cheaply by buying in bulk, threaten even this last one which is forced to sell more expensively than the average villager can afford. An Appraisal taken in 1990 showed that far from being an agricultural community as in the 19th century, the majority of Wivelsfield residents are commuters engaged in white collar occupations and working as far afield as Brighton, Crawley, Gatwick and London.[1]

New regulations are forcing farmers to diversify and to a small extent this is providing some light industry in the village. It is noticeable, however, that the owners of the larger and older established estates by tradition try to keep their holdings intact. By contrast, those owning land which was bought as small parcels of the waste or common land, such as that at "The Green" end of the village, have hastened to cash in on their speculations. They have sold to developers. The results have been housing estates of which Downsview Drive and Allwood Crescent, standing on land once occupied by Montagu Allwood's Nurseries, are typical examples. An outstanding example of a family caring for their heritage is that of the Godmans of Great Ote Hall, who during the last century have repurchased the estate, which was lost through the death of several heirs in succession. Recently both Sir Bryant Godman Irving and his wife have died but it is planned that their family shall continue to maintain the estate.

Modern inventions have enabled people to enjoy more leisure time activities; domestic service, which until the First World War was one of the few forms of employment open to country women, is no longer acceptable to most girls and young men. An illustration of the changing pattern is that of the old vicarage in Church Lane, where, even as recently as the 1940s domestic staff were employed. When in 1987 it was sold to a private purchaser, it was occupied by a servantless household who struggled alone with the daily chores. It was replaced by a much smaller labour-saving residence on a smaller plot of land which became the home and garden of the Vicar and his family.

Before the Second World War when the only communal meeting places were the Parish Room, the Reading Room and the public houses, there were village clubs; but these were mostly of a different type from those of the 1990s. Whist and billiards were played in the Reading Room and sports clubs had been formed; football and cricket around the 1890s or so, stoolball rather later. The present Women's Social Club was formed by those belonging to the Women's Institute when it was closed down in 1921. The 70 members transferred to the new club because it was organised locally without management from a national committee. Being an afternoon club numbers have continued to fall since women became engaged in full time employment.

A sudden surge of new clubs began after the Village Hall was opened in April 1981. There had been Brownies and Guides from 1928 with Rene Bartlett as Guide Captain and Jean White her lieutenant, but more recently the local company lapsed for want of guiders and has since joined with Plumpton. The Theatre Club transferred from the Reading Room and is still going strong. Its former leading light, Derek Cox, is commemorated with a seat in the Playing field.[2] New clubs included Badminton, (a special sprung maple floor was built into the hall for this sport), Bowls, Flower Club, Gardening Club and Bonsai. A new Historical Society has now sprung out of the interest generated by the research for this book. An annual Festival of Carols is organised at which each club is invited to sing a carol of its choice. Most clubs are represented each year and the audience which fills the hall to capacity, enjoys community carols between these items.

Wivelsfield Village Hall.   1992
                                                            M. Goodare

xlvii. The Village Hall.

The Young Farmers, the Playgroup and the (recently closed) Infant Welfare Clinic transferred from the Reading Room to the new Village Hall and a new group was formed for mothers and toddlers. Formerly the Little Theatre had somehow managed to erect a stage and scenery in the limited space in the Reading Room and to fit in an audience of about 70 people. Now, in the new Hall, they have a fixed stage plus an apron-stage, their own theatre lighting and storage in the east loft for some of their equipment. Many older Wivelsfield couples had held their wedding reception in the Reading Room but nowadays they use the new Hall. This hall is helping to revive the community spirit in a village whose character has been much altered by the spread of building and the change in work habits since the Second World War.

Improved mechanisation has supplanted the work of the village blacksmith, by producing machine made iron-work such as screws, hinges, bolts, nuts and wrought-iron gates, leaving the one smithy at Walstead to cater for all the needs of the surrounding villages. Since 1967 Wivelsfield has had no blacksmith although Wayne Upton, who operates the forge at Walstead, is a Wivelsfield man.

A part of the village which has suffered minimal change is the area around the Church and the School. This is likely to be preserved for the foreseeable future, having been designated a conservation area. The School, built in the 1870s, still operates in the original building. It none the less provides an education sought after by the parents of local children, including those who travel across part of West Sussex by taxi to reach the school from Charlwood Gardens, an 'out post' of Wivelsfield parish, within the urban area of Burgess Hill. Certainly, for the past fifty years or so, ideas for a new school have been floated and the discussion still continues. Now and again a new 'pre-fab' building is installed and in between whiles a developer will offer to donate a school in the hope of being granted planning permission to swallow up a few more rural acres. Only time will tell how and when a new building will be acquired.

In the 1860s the Church was an important focus in centre of village life and the building had to be enlarged to accommodate a congregation of around 200 souls. Today the electoral roll of the Parish Church numbers around 214, but this figure is now a small percentage of the overall population. Thus the Victorian church extension, substantially funded by the Tanner family, has proved a sufficient investment for today's needs. However, although no further seating is necessary in the Church itself, a 'Church Room' has recently been erected adjoining the vestry. 20th-century builders are adding to the fabric of the church and to history of the future.

During excavations for the foundations of the new Church Room a tomb holding four lead coffins was unearthed. The stone, which had been used face downwards to pave a path, showed that four people, two adults and two children, had been interred between 1816 & 1860. What would this family, the Lawsons of Brighton, think if they could see Wivelsfield today? They would certainly miss the muddy roads without pavements, they would surely marvel at the comforts within our homes, they would probably be petrified by the volume of traffic, but most of all they would miss the burr of the Sussex speech and recoil from the unbelievable volume of noise and the pace of day to day living.

If they were to stroll down the church path and out into the fields of the Otehall Estate they would find a landscape that lies unchanged by the passage of time. The hedgescape, unaltered since 1641 and the near horizon filled with wealden oaks are etched against the bare line of the Downs beyond. This is a view which not only the Lawsons but Thomas Godman who built Great Otehall would recognise as his own. The past is woven with a strong thread into the fabric of Wivelsfield, giving it a quality and texture that does not fail to attract those who come to visit or to stay.

xlviii. The churchyard gate and beyond.

GLOSSARY

Advowson	the right to appoint clergy to a living
Ashlar	stonework, square-cut and laid in regular courses
Bay	section of a building divided by posts, roof trusses, etc.
Cartulary	a monastery's register book, containing lists or copies of deeds of title to the land it holds
Copyhold	Legal title to land held by the custom of the manor; the tenant's title deed being a copy of the entry in the manor court roll or court book
Conventicle	a secret meeting place of religious dissenters
Crown post	short timber post, standing on a tie beam and supporting a crown purlin or collar
Dais beam	a moulded cross beam in the partition of an open hall house; in front of which the head of household sat, denoting the upper end of the hall
Enclosure	re. common land used by a group or a neighbourhood of 'commoners': the dividing up of that land into privately-held parcels
Finial	end of moulding, often decorated with a carved head
Gentleman	a person whose investments (in land, stocks, sinecures etc.) provided his means of support
Heriot	death duty payable to the lord of the manor; originally paid in kind, eg. best beast, later the money equivalent
Healing	roof or overhead covering
Hundred	subdivision of a district, originally based on the notion of 100 participating families; responsible for civil order until 16th cent.
Husbandman	a small farmer, usually a copyholder, dependent on his peasant holding for his livelihood
Indenture	a deed written in duplicate on one sheet and cut in a jagged line across a set of marks; each party kept a portion and authenticity was proved by matching the cut edges and marks.
Inventory	a list and valuation of possessions. Cottage inventories were usually for probate purposes
Manor	Estate containing a lord and his tenants, each with their own land to farm and responsibilities to each other. Prior to c. 1600 the manor was the smallest unit of rural admin., below the Hundred (q.v.)
Mathematical tiles	tiles manufactured and hung on outer walls to look like bricks
Messuage	originally 'the homestead plot' including all its buildings, yards etc. Later the sense was generally limited to the dwelling house on that plot.
Moulding	an ornamental strip carved from wood or stone

CHAPTER 1

1. Personal communication, David Rudling, South Eastern Archaeological Services, Turner Dumbrell Workshops, Ditchling. His report on the findings (Ditchling to Wivelsfield Pipeline, 1993) will be forthcoming.

2. TQ 197331; found by L. Gaston of Burgess Hill.

3. TQ 344201; found by Mr. Bert Charman. This and the Roman pottery were found on land not released for agriculture until the medieval period or later (demesne woodland of Ditchling Manor).

4. Ms. rentals can be consulted at ESRO for the manors of Hurstpierpoint, Clayton, Ditchling, South Malling, Lindfield (formerly Stanmer), Middleton, Streat and Balneath, for which the relevant lists and indexes at ESRO should be consulted. Published rentals of the 16th or early 17th centuries exist for Houndean, Plumpton Boscage and Withdean Cayliffe in SRS xxxiv and SNQ ii. For title deeds consult 'Wivelsfield' in the card index at ESRO and then the appropriate lists.

5. M. Gelling, *Place-names in the landscape*, (Dent, 1984), 235-245.

6. See M. Gelling, *Signposts to the past* (1978), pp.143-4. The topographical case for the early origins of 'the Berth' are strong. However, it was *not* a named Domesday manor as has been previously assumed, e.g. in J. Morris (ed.) *Domesday Book: Sussex* (1976) Phillimore (re. Domesday text 13.3). His map showing this manor in Wivelsfield (ref. Streat Hundred No.1) is wrong. His was based on an earlier assumption and the mistake has since been copied by other Domesday scholars. Wivelsfield's 'Berth' was a copyhold of Plumpton Boscage manor. I tentatively suggest that Domesday 'Berts' may

have been an outlier of part of Perching ('Berchinges' {12,28}) which appears to have been split up by the creation of Bramber Rape. See also note 25 below.

7. SNQ xi, 62-64; my own field work leads me to differ from Margary's assumed route south of Wivelsfield Green. I believe the track is Eastern Road, and not as Margary suggests; and that it either went via Lockstrood and the modern B2112 or it went south into West Wood at TQ 199344 and along the modern bridle path due south to become Spatham Lane; then to cross the Downs as Margary suggested.

8. E. Ekwall, *The Concise Dictionary of English Place Names*, (OUP), 1960. It has also been suggested that Walstead, also near the track, a little to the north, may mean 'Welsh people's place', although Coates (note 9 below) does not include it in his list.

9. The pioneer work in this field is by Dr. Richard Coates, lecturer in linguistsics at Sussex University. See his *The Linguistic History of Early Sussex*, (Sx. Univ., CCE), 1983, which has a useful bibliography.

10. ESRO AMS 5735 (map) and AMS 4255 (written survey of same date).

11. For text of the whole charter see W. G. Birch, *Cartularium Saxonicum* Vol.1, No.197; text and commentary E. Barker, *Sussex Anglo-Saxon Charters*, Part 1, in SAC lxxxvi, 42-101; commentary, M. Holgate, *The Canons Manor of South Malling* in SAC lxx, 183-195.

12. BL Add. MSS. 33182-3.

13. ESRO AMS A2327/1/1/1 and following.

14. This subject is currently being researched by Rev. Tony Way of Lindfield.

15. Map and schedule, ESRO AMS 2327/1/5/15,16.

16. See commentaries as in note 11 above. The present author has also done some (unpublished) field work on the Anglo-Saxon bounds of Stanmer as part of her work on *Stanmer, a restructured Settlement* in SAC cxxvii, 189-210.

17. P. H. Sawyer, *Anglo-Saxon Charters*, (Royal Hist. Soc., 1968), No.50.

18. My thanks to Dr. Richard Coates for his assistance with the Old English text. My interpretive approach is holistic, believing that the land itself has survived as a back-up text against which to measure a flawed and faulty document. My work is, of course, open to further scrutiny. I am happier to have started the ball rolling than to have the final say.

19. O.S. 6 inch series, sheet 39, 1873-4.

20. The old name survives at Scaynes Hill.

21. I have yet to publish this research. The strips in the common meadows in Wivelsfield in the 16th century were called 'lands' (Chapter 6) *Maebe* could be an error for *maed* - meadow.

22. Re. the change from a 'folk' or regional system to manorial organisation in the Kent Weald, see K. P. Witney, *The Jutish Forest* (Athlone Press, 1976); and in the Surrey Weald see J. Blair, *Early Medieval Surrey* (Alan Sutton), 1991.

23. SRS xiv, No.475 and ESRO SAS/FA 928 show that Otehall manor held land in Plumpton.

24. See "The case for Ditchling as a Regional Centre" in H. Warne, *Ditchling Parish Survey* (East Sussex Archaeological Project) 1984. Due to inertia this work has not yet been published by the County Archaeologist and I have therefore deposited a typescript in the library of the Sussex Archaeological Society.

25. Evidenced by their rentals (see also note 4 above).

26. Locatable chiefly by ESRO AMS 696, the parish Tithe map, ESRO TD/E 23 and rentals of Ditchling Manor in ESRO ABE (passim) and SRS xxxiv.

27. See Barony of Lewes accounts in SRS xliv; and SAC cxxiii, 127-143 in which it is shown that the Fishery was of Stottesforde *and* Wivelsfield, not Stottesforde *in* Wivelsfield as the Barony accounts state.

28. I assume the fishery went from TQ 308204 and followed the river north east to Cleavewater at approx. TQ 332217. The quantity of mussels has declined drastically in recent years, perhaps due to pollution.

29. G. Ward, *A suggested identification of Berts*, in SNQ, Vol.V, No.4 (1934), p.111-2. And see note 6 above.

30. BL Add.Ms. 33182, f.12

31. SAC xxxv, 29, 46. Note, however, that the surname Inthehurst has been wrongly transcribed as Nithahurst.

32. SRS x, 52; BL Add.Ch.24685; ESRO AMS 696.

33. BL Add.Ms.33182, passim compared with rental c. 1800 on ff. 178-181.

34. SAC xxxv, 29; BL Add. Ch. 24685.

35. SAC xxxv, 46.

36. ESRO SAS/OR 2.

37. J. Geraint Jenkins, *Traditional Country Craftsmen* (Routledge) 1979, 206-7.

38. BL Add. Ms. 33182, passim.

39. BL Add. Ms. 33182, f.4.

CHAPTER 2

1. A. Meredith, *Conservation Foundation*, Information Sheet. Allen Meredith, with the support of the Conservation Foundation, 1 Kensington Gore, London, has become an expert on yew trees.

2. John Blair states "It is, above all, to late Saxon thegns that the building of local churches should be ascribed," *Early Medieval Surrey: landholding, church and settlement* (1991), 115. The arguments re. church foundation in Chapter 5 of this book are of general relevance to Wealden Sussex; and see P. Brandon, *The Sussex Landscape* (1974), pp. 81-83.

3. SAC xxii, 53.

4. SRS xxxviii, 20-22; SNQ I, 49; VCH Sussex, vii, p. 123. Where Wivelsfield is not mentioned by name its tithe details are included with Ditchling and this continued to be the case (see for instance Calandar of **Inquisitions Nonae**, 1341). In 1095, where the tithes of Withdean are mentioned, a contributary share from Lunces and Otehall should be assumed.

5. As above, and see VCH Sussex, vii, 123.

6. SNQ ii, 253.

7. See John Blair (above), pp. 154-5 for similar cases in Surrey.

8. For example in c. 1250 in ESRO SAS/HA 392; in 1343 in ACM 529 (see below, note 14); and in 1379 in BL Add. Ms. 33182, f. 12.

9. For discussion and plan of early church architecture see Rev. H. J. Rush in SAC xxii, 50-56 (1870); VHC Sussex, vii, 123; T. W. Horsfield *History of Sussex*, Vol.1, 229; *Short Guide to the Parish ChurchI*, (Charles Clark, undated); abridged version available at the church.

10. SRS x, 53.

11. SAC xxxviii, 3.

12. Aspects of general Church history cited in this chapter are based upon: J. H. Betty, *Church and Parish*, (1987); G. G. Coulton, *Ten Medieval Studies* (1959); A. J. Fielder, *The Village Church*, in *This England*, summer 1980, p. 71; L. E. Jones, *Old English Churches* (1973); E. Plowden, *Elizabethan England* (1982); W. E. Tate, *The Parish Chest* (1983).

13. AC M529; re. the Keymer chapel see SAC cxxiii, 132-134.

14. ESRO SAS/ABE 1.

15. ESRO PAR 514/1/1/1.

16. SRS xlv, 410.

17. This is generally accepted as a musician, although it is sometimes referred to simply as a 'grotesque', (see VCH Sussex, vii, 123).

18. W. D. Macray, *Sussex Deeds at Magdalen College, Oxford*, Vol.2, No.67 (in which the editor has erroneously rendered 'Wivelsfield' as 'Winelsfeld').

19. SRS xxxvi, 84.

20. See W. E. Tate (note 13 above), pp. 43-83 on registers. Wivelsfield's are kept at ESRO, ref. PAR 514/1.

21. ESRO, Wills A 1, 47; A 1,56. John at More was resumably the same person as the John More who was farming the profits of Ditchling Rectory with Wivelsfield in 1535. See 'A Living or an Income,' below.

22. ESRO Will, A 2,24.

23. Bishop's Visitation; cited in BL Add. Ms. 39, 350, fo.75.

24. ESRO Will A3, 271.

25. SRS lxv, 410.

26. This and subsequent information on the incumbents see SAC xxxvi, 55 etc.

27. ESRO A 27, 171.

28. SAC lxix, 62.

29. BL Add. Ms. 33182, f.188. This deserted chapel site awaits a proper topographical investigation.

30. BL Add. Ms. 33182, f.17.

31. WSRO Ep. IV/10/15.

32. SAC xxxvi, 87-88.

33. SAC xlix, 48.

34. SAC xlix, 56-57.

35. SAC xxxvi as above, 64-65; Samuel Smith, John Falkner and widow Pilbin were also probably from the Stanmer/South Malling hamlet.

36. ESRO SAS/ABE 2, f.92r.

37. G. P. Elphick, *Sussex Bells and Belfries* (1970), pp.55, 415.

38. ESRO Will A 1, 47.

39. For this and the following Archdeaconry Court cases see SAC xlix, 56-64 passim.

40. Cited in G. G. Coulton (see note 12 above), p.236.

41. SAC xxxvi, 63.

42. See SRS xi, 174 and following for details of a dispute which seems to have begun in 1381. In 1419 John Horsham received a stipend of 6s, 8d. a year for his services as chaplain at Wivelsfield (SRS xxxvi, 140).

43. VCH Sussex, vii, 108, 123.

44. SAC xlvi, 51.

45. PRO E 134/35-6 Eliz.. Mich.32; this case is detailed in SAC xxxvi, 90-94.

46. SAC xxxvi, 96.

47. For example, in 1603 John Jenner, licensed curate of Wivelsfield, received a stipend of £10 a year from Richard Pope of Chailey, farmer of the 'rectory of Wivelsfield' (BL Add. Ms. 39350. fo.77).

48. VCH Sussex, vii, 123-4; yet, (see note 47) this right could be leased out to another.

49. This correspondence was first published in SAC iv, and in SAC xxxvi, 54-55. It has been republished here in order to make it available to people in Wivelsfield.

CHAPTER 3

1. The descent of families and their properties and personal information not otherwise acknowledged in this chapter derives from Captain F. W. T. Attree, *Wivelsfield* in SAC xxxv, 1-60 and SAC xxxvi, 19-74. These articles contain pedigrees of the more prominent families.

2. The discussion in this chapter is based upon: M. Campbell, *The English Yeoman* (1967); William Cobbett, *Rural Rides* (1830), *Cottage Economy* (1822); G. E. & K. R. Fussell, The English Countryman /Countrywoman (1955/53); D. Hartley *The Land of England* (1979); C. E. Mingay, *The Gentry: rise and fall of a ruling class* (1976); H. Newby, *Green and Pleasant Land?* (1979).

3. SRS xliv, passim.

4. SRS x, 53, 180.

5. SAC xv, 136.

6. SAC xviii, 29.

7. ESRO SAS/ABE 18R/1, ff.8v-9r.

8. SRS xxxiv, 8.

9. Shiela Blair's fuller study of woodland and farm ecomony in Wivelsfield will be published separately at a later date.

10. ESRO AMS 4150.

11. WSRO Add. Ms. 17269.

12. ESRO AMS 3504, 5735, 6145.

13. ESRO Will A 7, 202.

14. ESRO Will A 30, 254.

15. The Lewes Rape manors were universal in this. (See SRS xxxiv). The alternative (?more general) custom required the widow to vacate the premises if she remarried.

16. ESRO AMS 4242, 4235, 4236.

17. ESRO Will A, 47.

18. See the Richbell monument in Wivelsfield church belfry.

19. ESRO AMS 4150.

20. ESRO Wills A 1, 47; A 28, 77.

21. SNQ ii, 188. The outlier was held at red rose rent and thus came to be known as 'Roseland' and is in Plumpton parish.

22. ESRO Wills A 2, 24; A 7, 202; A 20, 57; A 28, 139.

23. SAC xxxv, 29-32; Captain Attree's subsequent account of the devolution of Lunces contains some errors and omissions.

24. ESRO Wills A 2, 24; A 5, 468.

25. ESRO Will A 28, 139.

26. ESRO AMS 4333. Shiela Blair's further work on the intermixed histories of the Lunces and Theobalds' estates in the 18th and 19th cents. will be published at a later date.

27. ESRO Will A 46, 199.

28. ESRO BRD 4/2.

29. The name 'ar Ree' is evidenced in 1327 by Walter ate Ree (SRS x, 180) who can be assiciated with Ryelands Farm in Balcombe. Thanks are due to Joan Dutton of Balcombe for this information.

30. See SAC xxxv, 32-44 for devolution and abstracts of early estate deeds; original deeds are now held at ESRO, ref. ESRO AMS 4195-4350.

31. AC M 529.

32. 'Woodwards' in 1544 was owned by Richard Attree of Theobalds and was probably the large field 'The Woodwards' shown in 1641 (ESRO AMS 3504) as on the extreme west of the Otehall estate (adjacent to Theobalds).

33. See SRS xxxiv, 42: manor of Ditchling rental 'certain lands called Folders in Dichlinge and Wivelsfilde at rent... 11s. 7d.'

34. ESRO Will A 4, 372. The fulling mill lands were at Hassocks ('Shepherds Walk' area), shown on ESRO AMS 4952.

35. See, for example ESRO AMS 4130; WSRO Misc. Papers 37.

36. The architectural information and dating in this book is by Margaret Goodare, by personal observation, unless otherwise credited. Other, anecdotal information is generally based on Captain Attree's article in SAC xxxv.

37. ESRO AMS 4250.

38. ESRO SAS/ABE 1, pp.26, 29.

39. ESRO SAS/ABE 1, pp.33, 93, 99, 121, 129, 139, 150; SAS/EG 418-419; ESRO AMS 4250/5. These refs. show that James Godman was Thomas' youngest son, a point on which Attree's pedigree is not clear. These properties passed to Ralph Dyne then George Dyne on whose death his brother Thomas inherited and added a cottage called Knaves Crooke.

40. ESRO AMS 4150.

41. ESRO AMS 5735.

42. SRS x, 180, 293; SAC xxxv, 46 (twice); ESRO AMS 4249.

43. M. Bassett, *The Hentys: an Australian Colonial Tapestry* (London, 1954). Families of the name Henty still lived in nearby

Worlds End, Burgess Hill, in the 1960's.

44. ESRO AMS 4242.

45. ESRO AMS 4230/2-8; AMS 4245, 4248.

46. ESRO AMS 4228/4, 4229/1-4.

47. ESRO AMS 4235-4240, 4256, 5735; DAN 1126. fo.229A. A more detailed study of farming and self-sufficiency on the estate has been prepared (see note 9).

48. ESRO AMS 4228/1-2.

49. ESRO Will A 1, 58.

50. ESRO AMS 4228/4.

51. For the court books of Keymer Manor see ESRO SAS/Acc 966 and following.

52. ESRO SAS/ABE 1, ff.121v, 208r; SRS xxxiv, 36.

53. ESRO SAS/ABE 1, f.251v.

54. ESRO AMS 5735.

55. ESRO SAS/EG 420-1; AMS 4250/6.

56. ESRO SAS/EG 424.

57. SAC xxxv, 56-7; the interior of Theoblads has not yet been seen by Wievelsfield History Study Group.

58. SRS x, 180; but also see remarks re, origins of Clearwaters Farm in Chapter 4 below.

59. VCH Sussex vii, 121.

60. SAC 1, (Vol.50) 61-107.

61. ESRO AMS 4113.

62. Perhaps a further iron-making connection, Bowyers having been ironmasters at Cuckfield.

63. ESRO Microfilm XA 5/2.

64. WSRO Sergison Papers.

65. SRS x, 52. The name often means 'baker', but more broadly 'provider'. A William ate Venne/Fenne, taxpayer in 1327 and 1332, may also be linked to the property (SRS x, 180, 294). In the 1379 Poll Tax there was a Ralph Fornere in the parish (SAC xxxv, 46).

66. See ESRO SAS/ABE 18 R/1, f.11v in which Richard Michelborne was farmer of Shortfrith in 1594 ar 20s. rent a year. Earlier accounts have not survived but it should be assumed that the land had been farmed since at least the close of the medieval period.

67. ESRO AMS 696.

68. ESRO AMS 6111; SRS xxxiv, 44. The rent in 1484 was to be 10s. 9d. plus a variable liability of 4d. or more for scutage.

69. ESRO SAS/HB 468; SAS/OR 2-3.

70. The editor has puzzled long over this early history of Fanners and hopes that someone may take on further, more conclusive research.

71. SAC xxxv, 47. Captain Attree's 'assumption in the same place that the surname Easterfield indicates an origin from Henfield is exteremely doubtful. It is more likely toponymic from an east or easterly field, which could have been anywhere.

72. ESRO AMS 6108; Will A 14, 63. The inscription does not, as Attree suggests, mean 'Thomas Lucas of Wivelsfield' . Christian-name initials were customarily wrapped round surname initials in date stones.

73. ESRO SAS/ABE 3, p.403; AMS 6108. The family gave their name to the Lucastes Road area of Haywards Heath which was formerly in Cuckfield parish.

74. ESRO AMS 1756.

75. SRS x, 53.

76. SAC xxxv, 29.

77. SAC xxxv, 52.

78. ESRO Will A 8, 463.

79. ESRO Will A 28, 77.

80. As above.

81. SAC liv, 120-124.

82. C. T. Stanford, *Suusex in the Civil War and the Interregnum 1642-1660* (1910). For further background to the county gentry in the period see A. Fltcher, *Sussex 1600-1660: a County Community in Peace and War*, (Longman 1975).

83. PCC Will, 279 Bogg, 1769.

84. SRS lxxvii; AMS 6145.

85. WSRO Add. Ms. 17262; ESRO ADA 1. Webb had bettered himself by land purchases in Ditchling and St. John's Common (Burgess Hill).

86. ESRO AMS 6108; see also AMS 1753-1786, bills and accounts for the Webb period at Fanners.

87. This and the subsequent information on the Shirley family see SAC xix, 66-69.

88. A more detailed study has been prepared (see note 9).

89. For further information re. the Hamsey connection see Langridge family Mss. (ESRO LAN).

90. Betty Osborn, *The Bacchus Story* (Bacchus Marsh and District Historical Society, 1973).

91. ESRO LT/WIV, 1828. His overall estate in 1819 can be judged from estate maps ESRO AMS 4952. Biographical notes, see DNB.

92. ESRO AMS 6112/5.

CHAPTER 4

1. Dating from observation. Pepperhall and Shoulders have not been visited. For a general introduction to timber-framed buildings see R. Harris, *Discovering Timber-framed Buildings* (Shire Publications, 1981).

2. Dating based on documentary evidence.

3. It was given a rateable value in 1637, (ESRO QR/E 38 f.2) but this may not necessarily imply a dwelling house. However, the parish tithe map shows there was an earlier house on a different site than the dilapidated Victorian building on the A 272 today.

4. SRS xxxiv, 75-92.

5. See, for example, ESRO SAS/ABE/1, passim.

6. It was described in 1624 (SRS xxxiv, 44) as a copyhold which had become a freehold. It was still copyhold in 1596-7.

7. ESRO Will A 10, 10.

8. SRS xxxiv, 48.

9. ESRO TD/E 23 (Parish tithe map).

10. ESRO Will A 16, 8.

11. The records of Keymer manor, (ESRO SAS/ABE 1) show that the Nutleys lived at Holmbush Farm.

12. ESRO Will A 14, 229

13. Ditchling Manor records ESRO SAS ABE/19, f.390; ABE/20, f.19. These and other early references from the Ditchling Court Books were supplied by Dr. Violet MacDermot whose help is hereby gratefully acknowledged.

14. ESRO SAS/ABE 20, ff.463-573.

15. SRS xxxiv, 48-49 gives the situation in 1624. The developed holdings can be seen on the parish Tithe map and the Ordnance Survey 6 inch sheet 39 (1879) and subsequent editions.

16. ESRO SAS/ABE 6, ff.29, 158.

17. ESRO SAS/ABE 9, f.62.

18. ESRO AMS/6112/5/4.

19. ESRO W/INV 1338B.

20. ESRO AMS/5789/57, 59.

21. ESRO PAR/514/1/1/1; SAS/ABE 1, f.280; SRS xxxiv, 42.

22. Personal recollections, see Chapter 13 below.

23. WSRO Sergison Papers No.132.

24. ESRO AMS/4119, 4128.

25. ESRO SAS/FA 902.

26. ESRO W/INV 459.

27. ESRO AMS 1767.

28. ESRO SAS/ABE 18, ff.115, 124, 134; LT 1780-1808; parish tithe map TD/E 23.

29. BL Add. Ms. 33182, ff.141, 145, 179; ESRO A/2327/1/5/1, ff.94-5.

30. SAC liv, 3.

31. ESRO A/2327/1/5/2, ff.2, 5; and see Chapter 6, The Bishoprick.

32. ESRO XA 5/2 (microfilm of Hearth Tax; original in PRO).

33. ESRO A/2327/1/5/ 15, 16.

34. BL Add. Ms. 33182, ff.151, 160.

35. ESRO A 2327/1/5/1, f.95; - 1/5/2, f.2.

36. ESRO W/INV 1537.

37. SRS x, 179; SAC xxxv, 44.

38. ESRO SAS/N 264a.

39. ESRO LT 1788.

40. ESRO AMS 4952/1/17, 18.

41. ESRO QR/E 38, f.136.

42. ESRO AMS 1767; SRS lxxvii; LT 1818.

43. ESRO W/INV 2091.

44. ESRO AMS 1767; he may have been the former tenant of South Colwell.

45. ESRO W/INV 2209.

46. ESRO Will A 53, 97; AMS 1767.

47. ESRO W/INV 1044, 2369.

48. ESRO W/INV 2237. The location of his farm is not known.

49. The surname is recorded in the area from the 14th century onwards in BL Add. Ms. 33182.

50. ESRO LT 1818; A/2327/1/5 15, 16.

51. See O. S. 25 inch, sheet 39/3, 1910; modern grid ref. TQ357 209.

52. ESRO W/INV 3237.

53. For obsolete words see Glossary after Chapter 15; also P. Hall *A Dictionary of the Sussex Dialect* (Bexhill, 1957).

54. See ESRO LT, 1818.

CHAPTER 5

1. ESRO Will U1/63.

2. See rental descriptions in 1624 in SRS xxxiv.

3. ESRO Will A 10/41.

4. See Chapter iv in J. Thirsk (ed.), *The Agrarian History of England and Wales, 1500-1640* (C.U.P. 1967).

5. ESRO A/2327/1/5/3, p.7.

6. ESRO PAR 514/1/1/1.

7. See note 11.

8. This analysis is based upon research by Heather Warne into the local brick and tile trade for *Heart of Burgess Hill: the history of its Brick and Tile Trades 1578-1855* (forthcoming).

9. ESRO AMS 1775.

10. Ibid.

11. The details given in this chapter of possessions and cottage interiors are from probate inventories: *Lewes Archdeaconry* ESRO W/INV 1864 Thomas Caine; 2841 John Coleman; 1832 Edward Fairhill; 3179 John Knight; 1558 Richard Mills; 2891 Richard Mills; 2966

John Parsons; 3010 John Renville; 2406 Thomas Renfield; 459 John Turner. *South Malling Deanery* ESRO SM 4 Samuel Smith. Descent of ownership and evolution of cottage plots are, except where otherwise noted, based on ESRO: the 1637 valuation, QR/E38, f.2; the 1766 valuation, Shiffner Ms. 2028/17; the 1785 Land Tax, SRS lxxvii; Land Tax 1788, 1798, 1808, 1818, 1828, LT/WIV; Parish Tithe survey TD/E23, 1838-1844.

12. ESRO AMS 4212, 4216.

13. ESRO AMS 4115.

14. ESRO AMS 3504.

15. ESRO AMS 4146.

16. ESRO AMS 4148.

17. ESRO SAS FA/898-905.

18. BL Add. Ms. 33182, ff.181 and 151.

19. ESRO AMS 6110; and cf. TD/E 23.

20. ESRO SAS/ABE 6, f.38; ABE 7, f.218; ABE 18, f.609.

21. Worthing Reference Library Microfilm: Sussex Advertiser.

22. J. Geraint Jenkins, *Traditional Country Craftsmen* (Routledge 1978); J. Seymour, *The Forgotten Arts* (National Trust, 1978). See also M. Holt, "Tanning in Sussex" in *Danehill Parish Historical Society Magazine*, 2, No.2, pp.13-18.

23. Wivelsfield History Study Group, Index of Occupations (card index).

24. WSRO Sergison Ms. 128.

25. VCH Sussex, Vol.iv, 259.

26. SRS lxxiv, 22; SAC xxxvi, 52; and see Lockstrood in Chapter 4 above.

27. SAC 50, pp.61-107.

28. WSRO Sergison Ms. 139.

29. ESRO DYK 1121 (Barony of Lewes roll: Streat Hundred).

30. ESRO Will A 10, 45.

31. WSRO Sergison Ms. 149, 153.

32. See Chapter 4, South Colwell. Another tanner, John Davy, was mentioned in 1698 (ESRO SAS/B 337).

33. ESRO W/INV 1407.

34. SRS xxviii; ESRO QR/E 476.

35. Donald F. Burgess, *No Continuing City*, (Redhill, 1989).

36. ESRO Q 1/EW 2.

37. ESRO AMS 4284.

38. ESRO BRD/4/2.

39. Census, 1841-1871; ESRO TD/E 23.

40. Cal. Sussex Assize temp. Eliz.I, No.1203.

41. See note 23.

42. ESRO AMS 1774.

43. ESRO AMS 1754

44. SRS lxviii, 261.

45. Wivelsfield History Study Group thank Agnes Millam for permission to use this document.

46. SRS xxviii, 7.

47. Cal. Sussex Assize, temp. James I, No.280. The location of this house is unknown.

48. ESRO Will SM/F 36.

49. ESRO Will A 71, 158.

50. ESRO A 2327/1/5/2, f.9; Will SM/E 126.

51. For background to this class see M. Beswick, *Brickmaking in Sussex* (Middleton Press, 1993) Hurst's kiln was probably on Haywards Heath (see Chapter 6).

52. SRS lxviii; and see WHSG Index of Occupations.

53. ESRO AMS 4320-4338; see also H. Warne forthcoming (note 8 above).

54. SAC xxxvi, 25; and parish registers, ESRO PAR 514.

55. ESRO ABE 19, fos.135, 202, 342; PAR 514/30/1; PAR 514/31/1.

56. ESRO Will A 76, 456.

CHAPTER 6

1. ESRO A 2327/1/5/15, 16. TQ 355212; and see Chapter 1.

2. ESRO TD/E 23.

3. M. R. Mitford, *Our Village* (1824). Republished in paperback by Penguin, 1987, O.U.P., 1987.

4. See Ardingly Tithe Survey, WSRO TD/E 32.

5. G. R. Jones, "Multiple Estates and Early Settlement" in P. H. Sawyer (ed.) *Medieval Settlement* (1976); J. Blair, *Early Medieval Surrey* (1991), believes that Wealden hamlets could be the earlier 'cells' from which later 'multiple estates' were concocted; G. Maitland, SNQ xiii, 4-11 (1950), in discussing the Stanmer Charter of AD 765, concludes that the Wealden settlements within the overall estate predate the Saxons; although he attributes settlement to the 'Jutes' and overlooks the case for an indigenous British population. For regional case-work in land settlement, Saxon and earlier see D. Hooke (ed.) *Anglo-Saxon Settlements* (1986).

6. See, for instance, P. Jerrome, *Cloakbag and Common Purse: enclosure and copyhold in 16th century Petworth* (Petworth, 1979).

7. SAC cxxvii, 189-210.

8. SRS xxxiv, 49.

9. BL 33182, passim; ESRO A/2327/1/5/1, passim.

10. Rev. A. Young, "General View of the Agriculture of Sussex, 1813"; *The British Travellor*, Vol.iv (1819)

- in which the fair was said to be on the 29 July. John Bleach (personal communication) informs that no 17th century references to the fair have been found but that it was recorded between 1780 and 1858 and had lapsed by 1888. In 1808 and 1858 it was held on the 29 June, but in all other years it was on the 29 July.

11. ESRO A 2327/1/5/15, 16.

12. WHSG has made a start, and there is scope for further work, on the evolution of the Green from *circa* 1800 to the present day.

13. ESRO SAS/B 57: mentions Jefferyes Green in 1673; Richard Budgen's map of Sussex, 1724 ('Cliffords'); O.S. 1st. ed. 6 inch 1874, sheet 26; modern O.S. scale 1:25000, TQ 22/32.

14. ESRO AMS 4113.

15. ESRO AMS 4129.

16. BL Add. Ch. 24689, 24690.

17. SAC xxxv, 33; ESRO AMS 4129. It may be of relevance that the surname Gifford is of Norman French origin. One Gautier Gifford came over with the Conquerer, William of Warenne, etc.

18. WSRO Sergison Ms. 527.

19. Otehall Manor enclosure: ESRO QDD/6/E 9.

20. ESRO AMS 3504. 'Carr' turns up sparodically in Sussex to describe wet meadows and is not apparently of English derivation. 'Wish' also means wet meadow and the word may therefore be a tautology.

21. ESRO SAS/OR 2, 3; AMS 6112/5/1.

22. Not only this track but both the 'Hassocks' and the 'Lewes' Roman roads converge in river meadows at the Sussex, Surrey and Kent borders near the Dry Hill encampment which must have also

been a key area of Wealden meadowland.

23. See SRS xxxiv.

24. ESRO AMS 6112/5/1; AMS 6108/1.

25. SRS x, 180.

26. Information kindly given by David Anderson of Burgess Hill who grew up in a rural area of Scotland.

27. ESRO AMS 4952/1/17; AMS 2327/1/5/15.

28. ESRO AMS 6112/2.

29. ESRO DAN 1126, fo.213v. The pit is still there, best looked for in winter. It was perhaps used as a source of marl.

30. It was so called in ESRO AMS 2739, A 2327/1/5/1, passim, DAN 1126 as above, and elsewhere.

31. P. Brandon, *The Common lands and wastes of Sussex* (London Univ. PhD. thesis, 1963). This is essential reading for anyone wishing to pursue the subject of Sussex commons; copy available in Sussex Archaeological Society library, Barbican House, Lewes.

32. Touched on by H. Warne in SAC cxxiii, 137-8.

33. SAC xxxvi, 52. For background to this sort of unrest see J. Thirsk (ed.), *The Agrarian History of England and Wales*, Vol.IV, 1500-1640 (C.U.P. 1967); R. B. Manning, *Village Revolts*, (O.U.P. 1988).

34. ESRO AMS 2725-2740.

35. ESRO A 2327/1/5/1, fo.286.

36. ESRO DAN 1126, fo.213v.

37. BL Add. Ms. 33182, fo.24.

38. Ibid, fos.24, 177.

39. BL Egerton Ms. 1967, fos.73-76.

40. Star Chamber Proc., Jas I, 1104/9, cited in Brandon (see note 29 above).

41. ESRO SAS/ACC 966. Signatures were collected but the scheme went no further.

42. ESRO QR/EW/35/14.

43. ESRO A 2327/1/5/1, fo.135 and following.

44. Compare ESRO A 2327/1/5/15, 16 (date 1830) with Ordnance Survey 6 inch, sheet 39 (1874) and modern maps.

45. ESRO SAS/ABE 2, fo.208; ABE 6, fo.3.

46. ESRO AMS 1755.

47. ESRO AMS 1754-5; 6107-6111.

48. ESRO A 2327/5/2; QR/E 38. fo.2.

49. ESRO AMS 2327/1/5/15; O.S. 1st. ed. 6 inch map (1874) sheet 39. This striking field-scape, unusual for this part of the Weald, led the editor some years ago to search the early Court books of South Malling Lindfield manor for evidence of a former common and an enclosure; the Court books eventually obliged.

50. ESRO SAS/C 664.

51. ESRO TD/E 23 (Parish tithe map).

52. Census Returns, 1841, 1851; ESRO AMS 6112/5.

53. ESRO Will A 10, 41; contemporary term for his occ. is 'stone healer'.

54. WSRO Sergison Papers 27.

55. SAC xxxv, p.29.

56. ESRO AMS 4125.

57. ESRO AMS 4129.

58. WSRO MP 37.

59. As in note 56.

60. SRS xxix, No.659.

61. WSRO Sergison Ms. 527.

62. SRS xxxviii, 8.

63. ESRO ABE 1, f.258.

64. ESRO AMS 4113.

65. WSRO Sergison Ms. 527.

66. ESRO BRD 4/2.

67. No.3a on the Definitive map.

68. ESRO ABE 1, f.258; and see Mid Sussex Times 21.8.87.

69. Devolution of Wivelsfield properties held of Ditchling Manor has been traced by Dr. McDermott of Ditchling and by Margaret Goodare of WHSG from ESRO SAS/ABE series of Manorial records.

70. ESRO QDP/E 88; Ordnance Survey 25 inch, sheet 39/3, 1874.

71. T. W. Horsfield, *History of Sussex*, Vol.1 (1835), p.227.

CHAPTER 7

1. P. Slack, *The English Poor Law 1531-1782* (1990), pp.17-21.

2. Ibid, pp.22-29.

3. Ibid, pp.29-34; see also J. D. Marshall *The Old Poor Law 1795-1834* (1985), pp.23-30; D. A. Baugh, "The Cost of Poor Relief in South-East England 1790-1834", in *Economic History Review*, 2nd Series, XXVIII (1975), pp.50-68.

4. SAC xxxvi, 43; ESRO MF XA 26/13, 5 & 207; MF XA 26/14, 8; Par 514/24/1.

5. SAC cxvi, 51; ESRO QR/E 36; QR/E 38.

6. ESRO SAS/ABE 3, ff.91, 130; ABE 5, ff.50, 72; ABE 7, ff.77, 81, 88.

7. ESRO AMS 6112-5; PRO MH 12/12800-1.

8. ESRO Par 514/31/1.

9. Ibid.

10. See P. Slack (note 1).

11. ESRO: Abstracts of Returns relative to the Expense and Maintenance of the Poor (43 Geo IIIA 1803).

12. WSRO Par 416/10/1.

13. SRS liv, 51.

14. WSRO Par 21/32/2.

15. WSRO Par 21/11/2.

16. WSRO Par 416/32/1/66.

17. WSRO Par 416/32/2/45.

18. PRO MH 12/12829.

19. See W. E. Tait, *The Parish Chest* (1946, 3rd reprint Phillimore, 1983).

20. J. D. Marshall (as note 3), pp.13-14.

21. ESRO Par 308/30/1-3.

22. PRO MH 12/12829.

23. 43 Geo III A.

24. Abstract of Returns 1803.

25. ESRO Par 514/31/1.

26. H. Matthews, *Burgess Hill* (1979), p.78.

27. WSRO Par 21/33/1.

28. J. Richardson, *The Local Historian's Encyclopedia* (1985), p.46.

29. E. J. Hobsbawm & G. Rude, *Captain Swing*, Appendix III (1969), pp.4, 7, 9, 20.

30. PRO MH 12/12800-1.

CHAPTER 8

1. For further reading consult J. Farrant (ed.), *Sussex in the 16th and 17th Centuries, A Bibliography* (Univ. of Sussex C.C.E., Occasional Paper No.2): in which the various works of N. Caplan are particularly relevant, e.g. "Sources for the history of Sussex Religious

Dissent, 1600-1860", SAS *Newsletter* 24, 147-8.

2. For further work on ejected ministers consult A. G. Matthews, *Calamy Revised...an account of the Ministers and others ejected and silenced, 1660-1662*, (1934).

3. Hurst was described as the son of John Hurst of Cuckfield and grandson of the John Hurst who died in 1614 and who owned Tapestry Cottage in Church Lane, Wivelsfield. Thomas Hurst made various sales out of the Hurst House estate from 1659 onwards and in 1675 he sold off the house itself (see SRS xxix, Nos.647-659).

4. N. Caplan, *An outline of the Origins and development of Noncomformity in Sussex: 1603-1803* (unpublished typescript: copies in BL, Dr. Williamson's Library and SAS Library).

5. SAC li, 1-13.

6. SAC xlv, 142-8.

7. Edward Tanner was a predecessor of Anthony Tanner (the Tanyard) and William Tanner (More House) of Wivelsfield.

8. ESRO ADA 174, f.36v.

9. SAC lxvii, 208.

10. ESRO NV 2/2/2. See also 'The non-conformist connection', pp.79-81, in M. Beswick *Brickmaking in Sussex: a History and Gazeteer* (Middleton Press, 1993); and see note 14 below.

11. WHSG research notes (from sources at ESRO).

12. SRS lxxviii, 157.

13. SAC lxvii, 209. John Marten Cripps, the later Wivelsfield landowner, was great great grandson of Michael Marten and Anne, nee Webb and was to inherit several 'Marten' estates.

14. ESRO NV 2/2/1; H. C. Cheale jun., *History of Ditchling* (Lewes, 1901)

states that Marten Richard Webb of Fanners is buried at Ditchling Church, while John Dancy (d. 1800) and Josiah Dancy (d. 1802) have memorial stones in Ditchling Chapel yard.

15. See: *"Bethel": Strict Baptist Chapel, Wivelsfield 1789-1980. A short history* (1980) published by Rev. Reg S. Payne former pastor of the Bethel Chapel, available from the chapel. WHSG warmly thanks him for all his help and hopes to publish more of the information he has given at a later date. For a general background to rural chapels see J. Hibbs, *The Country Chapel* (1988).

16. ESRO AMS 1767.

17. Further details re. local families, from Chapel's gravestones have been prepared by Olive Morely and Margaret Goodare, to be published later.

18. *The Evangelical Register*, July 1825.

19. For the history of the Connexion see G. W. Kirby, *The Elect Lady* (pub. by the Connexion, 1972); B. Little, *Selina, Countess of Huntingdon* (Huntingdon Centre, 1989); *The life and times of Selina Countess of Huntingdon*, Vol.I (pub. by W. Painter, London, 1840).

20. See note 11 above. In 1766 the tenant of Great Otehall was one Richard Ashdowne (ESRO AMS 1767). 'Ashdowne' in 1714 was probably the farm tenant at Otehall. Olive and Oliver are almost certainly variants of the same name.

21. C. Brent, *Georgian Lewes, 1714-1830* (Lewes, 1993).

22. Transcripts at ESRO of the Countess's correspondence include some details re. preaching at Wivelsfield *circa* 1767-1790 (ESRO NH3/1/4; NH3/1/13; NH3/1/15).

23. ESRO NH 2/1; ESRO SAS/EG 373, 373A; he died in 1841 and Robert Taylor Hunt inherited; re. Keymer, see card indexes prepared by and in possession of Heather Warne on Burgess Hill properties, taken from the records of Keymer Manor, ESRO SAS/ACC 945-82.

24. ESRO ABE 44 (map of the manor of Ditchling, 1819); SAS/EG 400-417, SAV/1325-7.

25. ESRO TD/E 103 (Ditchling Tithe map); Foster's will, A 74, 775; F. M. Avery, *Development of Burgess Hill and its Potteries, 1828-1978* (Typescript deposited in Burgess Hill Library).

26. SAC xxxvi, 61. Subsequent info. re. incumbents in this chapter, where not otherwise acknowledged, is from the same source (passim).

27. ESRO PAR 514/6/1. For background to the Q. Anne's Bounty see J. R. H. Moorman, *A History of the Church in England* (1961).

28. Reasons for providing west galleries are discussed in V. Gammon, *Popular Music in Rural Society: Sussex 1815-1914* (D. Phil. thesis, Univ. Sussex, 1985), chapter 1. Available in SAS library.

29. Ibid.

30. ESRO Will A 46, 199.

31. D. F. Burgess, *No Continuing City*, (Redhill, 1989).

32. See note 11 above.

33. SAC cxx, 193-203.

34. ESRO QCR/I/II/E1.

35. A. Stephens, *Suusex Data, Sussex Studies*, No.10 (Univ. Sussex, 1988).

36. Personal communication from Pat Avery of Haywards Heath. Yokehurst was built in 1821.

37. SRS lxxv, 76.

38. *The Evangelical Register*, July 1825.

CHAPTER 9

1. F. M. Stenton, "Anglo-Saxon England" in *Oxford History of England*, Vol.II, pp.583-4, (1963).

2. H. E. Malden in SNQ i, pp.7-10; R. A. Pelham in SNQ iv, 129-131.

3. See Chapter 8 in R. Welldon Finn, *Domesday Book: a Guide* (1973).

4. For example ESRO SAS OR 3; ESRO AMS 696, 4114; and see AC M 529 in which a letter from John earl of Warenne is dated at Cuckfield in 1344.

5. J. Morris (ed.), *Domesday Book 2, Sussex*, (1976), No.12, 1 (26a).

6. SAC xxxvi, 183.

7. A. Everitt, (1967) in J. A. Chartres (ed.), *Agricultural Markets and Trade 1500-1700*, (1990) p.24.

8. *The British Traveller*, Vol.IV, 366 (1819). See also Chapter 6, note 10. John Bleach informs that in the years when Wivelsfield's fair was on 29 June, Chailey's was on 29 July.

9. SAC cxxxiii, 131, 134.

10. Source as in note 8 above.

11. S. and B. Webb, *The Parish and the County* (1906), pp.7-8.

12 14 & 15 Hen VIII c.6 (1523), 26 Hen VIII c.7 (1534), 2 & 3 Pp. & Mary c.8 (1555), 5 Eliz I c.13 (1562-3).

13. SAC xv, 142.

14. See, for example SAC lviii, 6-20.

15. SRS xxxiv, p.132.

16. J. H. Cooper, *History of Cuckfield* (1912), p.179.

17. Calendars of Assize Records, Sussex, Eliz. I and Jas. I.

18. ESRO/QI/EW2-EW6.

19. SRS lxviii, 35, 44-46, 52-53, 59.

20. WSRO Par 416/10/1.

21. ESRO/AMS 5150.

22. WSRO Par 416/10/1.

23. ESRO/ A7-202.

24. SRS xxix, nos.626-7.

25. SRS lxviii, 261-2, 302.

26. Letter to George Montagu 26th August 1749.

27. J. Burton, *Journey in Surrey and Sussex* (1751); Mm. Postlethwayt, (1774) *Universal Dictionery of Trade and Commerce* (1774).

28. SAC xix, 69.

29. W. E. Tate, *The Parish Chest* (1983) pp.243-6.

30. J. A. Chartres, *Road Carrying in England in the Seventeenth Century*, EcHR 2nd series (1977), XXX, p.77; J. Crofts, *Packhorse Wagon and Post* (1967), p.13.

31. SAC cix, 21-2.

32. Sussex Weekly Advertiser, 14 September 1761.

33. J. R. Armstrong, *A History of Sussex* (1984), pp.132-5; I. V. Margary, *The Development of Turnpike Roads in Sussex* (1950), in SNQ, xiii, 51; ESRO QDD/E4.

34. ESRO QDD/EW/1.

35. J. Copeland, *Roads and their Traffic, 1750-1850* (1968), p.37.

36. ESRO Will A 74, 700.

37. D. F. Burgess (ed.) *No Continuing City, The Diary and Letters of John Burgess* (1989).

38. 53 Geo. III, c.208.

39. ESRO QDP/E 88.

40. ESRO AMS/4272.

41. Rev. A. Young, *General View of the Agriculture of Sussex* (1813), p.416.

42. J. Copeland (1986), as in note 35 above.

43. 1 Geo. IV, c.95.

44. ESRO QDT/EW/1.

45. ESRO QDT/2/EW1.

46. J. Copeland (1986), as in note 35, p.54.

47. ESRO QDD/EW5.

48. Wivelsfield Vestry Minute Book, 1857-1894 (held locally and consulted by kind permission of the Churchwardens).

49. Post Office Archives, Mount Pleasant, London.

50. Kellys Directories 1867, 1887; B. Short (ed.) *A very improving Neighbourhood: Burgess Hill 1840-1914* (1984) and Census (Keymer Parish), 1871, 1881. 'Wivelsfield Station' was not opened until 1888.

51. Trad. song "Pretty Sarah", recorded by Shirley Collins (1970's).

52. F. Thompson, *Candleford Green* (1943).

53. Census 1881; Kellys Directory, 1867.

54. Information from members of the Bartlett family re. their grandparents at Whitebreads farm.

55. Kellys Directories, 1909, 1915, 1922, 1938.

CHAPTER 10

1. Tithe Survey: ESRO TD/E 23; Census Returns 1841-1891: microfilm copies are available at ESRO.

2. Further background on the early 19th century is provided by the Land Tax series, ESRO LLT/WIV.

3. For further background on the Census, see E. Higgs, *Making sense*

of the Census (HMSO, 1989); D. Mills and C. Pearce, "People and places in the Victorian Census", *Historical Geog. Research series,* 23, (1989).

4. Kellys Directory, Sussex, 1855.

5. The details given in this chapter are limited. Further work on the 1841 and 1851 would reward those wanting more information. The 1861 and 1871 returns have not yet been studied by Wivelsfield History Study Group.

6. 'Hop gardens' were shown at Great Otehall in 1641, Theobalds in 1659 and More House in 1792, (ESRO AMS 3504, 5735, 6145). Further research in local agriculture is being undertaken by Study Group member Sheila Blair.

7. For recent research on the Sussex Hops industry see G. Jones *Oasthouses in Sussex and Kent* (1992); and G. Jones and others in SAC cxxvi, 195-224.

8. Original research by M. Goodare shows that the mill was south of Green Road, O.S. Grid ref. TQ 349 145. Burgess Hill historian Fred Avery informs that Charles Avery was noted as owner of St. John's Common windmill (located just west of Mill Road, Burgess Hill) in 1858.

9. These buildings are dated by architectural observations.

10. ESRO AMS 6112/2.

11. B. Short (ed.), *A Very Improving Neighbourhood: Burgess Hill 1840-1914* (1984), p.31.

12. Ibid.

13. Information supplied to Wivelsfield History Study Group by Maureen Singh, nee Farncombe, a descendent, now living in Sheffield, Yorks.

CHAPTER 11

1. This chapter was mainly based on the following sources:- Census, Sussex 1881 (ESRO microfilm); Lloyd George's survey 1910 (ESRO IRV/1/126); late Land Tax (ESRO LLT/WIV); Kellys Directories (available in the larger reference libraries). See also SAC cxxv, 199-224 re. the 1910 survey. This study is based on the copy of that survey at ESRO but the accompanying field books, etc., at the PRO conatin material for further research.

2. There is much scope for future work on the history of the parish 1851-1881, using the 1861 and 1871 censuses (etc.).

3. WSRO QDD/6/E/11, 1862.

4. ESRO QAL/2/7/E1.

5. Censuses and ESRO 6108. See also W. K. Ford and C. Gabe, *The Metropolis of Mid Sussex* (Charles Clarke, 1981).

6. ESRO PAR 514/4/1.

7. WSRO Ep.II/27, 256; OR, ESRO PAR 514/4/2, 3. A more detailed account of this restoration of the church has been prepared by Barbara Hall and will be published bt WHSG at a future date. Janet Pennington, archivist at Lancing College, informs that the college was also built of Scaynes Hill stone. The quarry was east of Scaynes Hill on the A 272.

8. A copy of this photo is held by WHSG.

9. Descended from the Godmans of Park Hatch, Godalming, Surrey. See *Who was Who* 1897-1916; Burkes *Landed Gentry* (18th ed.), Vol.1, pp.307-9. Charles B. Godman of Woldringfold, Horsham (d.1941) published a family genealogy in which a connection with the Wivelsfield Godmans was shown.

10. WHSG is grateful to the present owner Howard Johnson Poensgen for this and other information he has given concerning the house and estate. The development and history of this large estate is touched on in Chapter 14 but is generally outside the scope of this book. It is hoped that a future researcher will take it up.

11. ESRO AMS 6108, 6112; and see Chapter 14 below.

12. Devolution based on Land Taxes, ESRO LLT (19th cent.).

13. B. Short (ed.), *A Very Improving Neighbourhood: Burgess Hill 1840-1914* (Sussex University 1984); and W. K. Ford and C. Gabe as above.

14. See Chapter 12.

15 Montagu C. Allwood, *The Third and Fourth Generations* (Allwood, 1940).

16. Lilian E. Rogers, *Yesterday and Today*, (private publication, 1981).

17. See: H. Barrett and J. Phillips, *Suburban Lifestyle: the British Home 1840-1960* (Macdonald Orbis, 1987); and "Victorian and Edwardian Houses" in A. Quiney, *Period Houses* (London, 1989).

18. Known until recently as St. Francis' Hospital, the new General Hospital for Mid Sussex, the 'Princess Royal' has now been built in its grounds. Although affectionately still referred to as 'St. Francis' by most locals, the old asylum is officially the 'Princess Royal West Wing'. Under the recent Mental Health Act changes a private buyer is to be sought for the old 'St. Francis'.

CHAPTER 12

1. See VHC, Vol.ii, pp.397-440 for the history of grammar schools in Sussex. The Wills of the local yeomen and other moderate landowners in the 17th century frequently contain provision for their children's education. In 1718 the parson at Wivelsfield was the schoolmaster at Cuckfield school (SRS lxxviii, 11).

2. W. Cobbett, *Cottage Economy*, p.7 (O.U.P. 1979, first printed 1822). Cobbett opposed the 1833 Act in Parliament.

3. SAC xxxvi, 41-2; for educational provision in Sussex in the 17th and 18th centuries see E. Doff, "Spare the Rod," Part 1, in *Sussex History*, Vol.1, No.7.

4. The name derives from the cottage and three acres in Slugwash Lane, purchased in 1760 for the purpose. See also ESRO PAR 514/24/1-3.

5. For a general background see H.C. Barnard, *A History of English Education from 1760* (1968); a list of licensed village schools in Sussex 1579-1800 is given by J. E. Wadey in SNQ xiv, Nos.15 & 16, (1957), 270-277; a detailed account of a Wealden Sussex village school exists in S. Wright, *Payment by Results: Uckfield Parochial School 1863-1895* (Uckfield and District Preservation Soc., 1991).

6. Census, Sussex 1851.

7. Re. Ditchling's schools 1814-1834 see E. Doff, "Spare the Rod", Part II, *Sussex History*, Vol.I, No.9, pp.23-4.

8. Piggott's Directory, Sussex, 1858.

9. Census, Sussex 1861.

10. Census, Sussex 1871.

11. The identical positions of the old workhouse and the school can be judged from the Parish Tithe Survey of 1838-44 and the 1st ed. (25 inch) Ordnance map, 1874, sheet 39/3.

12. Parish Records, consulted by kind permission of the Churchwardens.

13. 1868 is the date on the outside of the building.

14. Since the 1st printing, the School House has been proved to be a considerably altered timber-framed house. In illustration xxvii the Workhouse is shown as an L-shaped building. This included what is now the School House.

15. Kellys Directories, Sussex, 1878, 1887. Re. attendance, see note 17 below.

16. ESRO C/E 111/72.

17. The house has since been demolished. Thomas' grave may be seen just SW of the south door of Wivelsfield church.

18. A full account of the problems between Mr. Matta and the Board and the deatils of his departure has been prepared by Olive Morley, for publication at a later date.

19. G. McGregor, *Bishop Otter College and Policy for Teacher Education 1839-1980* (Chichester, 1981); T. Brighton and H. Warne, *A Portrait of Bishop Otter College, Chichester 1839-1990* (Chichester, 1992).

20. Full accounts of the water supply problem, various repair problems and some case histories of absenteeism have been prepared by Olive Morely and will be published separately by WHSG.

21. Personal communication from Mr. Derek Walter, Mr. Hooper's great nephew. A photo of Mr. Hooper has recently been acquired by WHSG.

22. This account is based on the School Log Book currently on loan to the author.

23. It was thought that Mr Hooper and his wife were first appointed in 1897 but the 1891 Census Return revealed that he and his first wife were living in the School House. This could account for there being no record of an interview in 1897 when he returned with his second wife to become Schoolmaster and Mistress. Of the first Mrs. Hooper Tom Cook (Chapter 13) recalled....
"'E carried 'er out to a cart and I never saw 'er again. She must a' died."

CHAPTER 13

1. School Management Committee Minutes 1897-1903 (see Chapter 12). We thank the following persons for permission to use documents in their keeping: Miss Tipple, Headmistress, Wivelsfield School (School registers 1901-40); Ron Fryers (Minutes of the Cock Inn Slate Club); Agnes and Olive Millam (Account book of Robert Millam, last working blacksmith in the village). Other recently published oral history includes: *West Sussex within Living Memory* (W. Sx. Federation of W.I's. Newbury 1993). This has some information on Wivelsfield and two wonderful photographs supplied by Rene Bartlett, who has recently moved from Wivelsfield to nearby Scaynes Hill in West Sussex.

2. ESRO (W.I. records).

3. The water problems at the village school will be published later by WHSG.

4. M. C. Allwood, *The Third and Fourth Generation* (Allwood 1940).

5. Montagu Allwood was actually born in 1879. WHSG thanks Robert Allwood for this information and for corrections to our original draft. Additional material he has supplied will, hopefully, be used in a future publication.

6. The Playgroup was started by Anne Martin in her home in Downsview Drive.

7. Information supplied by Howard Johnson Poensgen, present owner of Abbots Leigh Place.

8. See *Mid Sussex Times*, 14.3.1980 for a brief account of the Derbies. It

is believed that a booklet of the Derbies was written by Mrs. Dinnage for private circulation, but WHSG does not know whether any have survived.

9. The names and place of origin of each evacuee is entered in the school records.

CHAPTER 14

1. See Obituary and articles, *The Times*, 19 Aug., 28 Oct., 27 Nov. 1954; *Who was Who* 1951-60; ESRO ADA file 1009C; and H. J. Dyos and D. H. Aldcroft, *British Transport* (Liecester, 1967), p.367. Our thanks to John Farrant for supplying these references.

2. The core estate, South and North Colwell, Slugwash and Rockhurst farms and Moores Cottages, was purchased by Charles Hales in 1919. The title to these, as well as to the additions purchased 1924-1937, may be traced in ESRO AMS 6112.

3. The documentary sources used in this account are WSRO SP 2106, SP 2208.

4. Kellys Directories, Sussex 1909.

5. ESRO QDD/6/E9 (Otehall enclosure, 1861); ESRO QDD/6/E 11 (Haywards Heath enclosure, 1862).

6. William Bacon lived at Lunces Hall from at least 1887-19911 (Kellys Directories).

7. Dr. Marcus Pembrey lived at 'Mount Pleasant, Scrases Hill' from at least 1909-1927 (Kellys Directories, Sussex).

CHAPTER 15

1. Wivelsfield Village Appraisal: Report, 1990. Wivelsfield Parish Council.

2. Also commemorated on the same seat is the name of Dave Morris who was particularly remembered for his work with the Football Club.